The Car Design Yearbook **5**

Stephen Newbury

The Car Design Yearbook 5

the definitive annual guide to all new
concept and production cars worldwide

MERRELL
LONDON · NEW YORK

Contents

Trends, Highlights, Predictions

Trends, Highlights, Predictions

In the relatively short five years that the *Car Design Yearbook* series has been in existence we have covered upward of six hundred new models—so it is now starting to be possible to look back and gain some perspective on the evolution of car design over that time. In fact, our objective back in 2002 when the very first *Car Design Yearbook* was compiled was exactly that: to produce a series of books that would chart the progression of car design over the years.

So in this, the fifth yearbook, we will not only examine the trends and the highlights of the past twelve months and make predictions for the future; but we will also look back over the last five years to pick out some of the key developments in design and technology—many of which take place without most people even realizing.

First, taking a closer look over the past year, most of the carmakers seem to be focusing on launching contemporary replacements for existing models: the competitiveness of the industry is preventing companies from taking chances with radical new models. Trends that have become commonplace include body styles with better integrated, more flowing surfaces, headlamps that follow these surfaces, and blackened upper pillars that create what look like large areas of glazing. SUVs and trucks now have a tendency to be more carlike in their design: the Toyota Hilux and the Chrysler Aspen are just two examples to sport more sophisticated front-end designs. For many new cars the popular move toward rear lamps featuring LED technology is sure to extend

further; new LED headlamps being developed by Hella in conjunction with Volkswagen are expected to reach production in 2008. The small size of the LEDs coupled with their powerful light emission, low energy requirement, and long lifespan support the view that this technology is the real future of automotive lighting. The conventional incandescent bulb could be heading for extinction.

The increased use of glass in modern car design is to be welcomed. It is well known in architectural circles that brighter spaces increase people's feelings of happiness: this is equally valid for the car. Glass roofs have been featuring on some models for more than five years, and more and more cars now have them. Manufacturers are also investigating other ways

to incorporate glass. For example, the Mercedes-Benz F600 Hygenius concept uses darkly tinted glass to dramatic effect, making the upper canopy appear mostly glass. Development of more sophisticated crash technologies should lead to more interesting use of glass upper architectures in the future. For example, it would be good for a company to champion getting rid of the A-pillar, that irritating obstacle to good vision that is, however, needed for crash strength: Saab has already made an interesting first step with its Aero X concept, where the one-piece side windows, windshield and roof open upward like the canopy of a fighter jet.

The Nissan Urge and the Citroën C-AirPlay both use glass in a new way. Both these models incorporate a glass viewing panel along the base of the door, thus giving the driver a view of the road as well as enhancing the sense of speed felt by the occupants.

Manufacturers seem to be focusing very little on radical new energy-efficient cars that are smaller than those we know today. Instead, the effort seems to be going into designing cars of the same size but incorporating more fuel-efficient engines. As the next generation of young people reaches car-driving age, it is a shame that there will not be a better selection of small and exciting cars for the environmentally aware and cost conscious younger buyer. There are some exceptions, of course: the Mini continues to sell extremely well and a new generation is set for 2007. Later, this will expand to include an estate, due by the end of 2008. Long gone, of course,

aro the days when small cars needed to bc boring little A-to-B boxes on wheels: modern small cars can be exciting and well-equipped. A particular role model could be the imaginative Toyota Endo concept, with its high-tech interior and distinctive two-tone exterior with wrap-around upper body. High-spec interiors arc now becoming available for small cars as more options open up to thc dosigners in terms of in-car equipment and the use of differently textured finishes and materials.

Production cars powered by gas, alcohol or hybrid engines have increased significantly, though admittedly from a very low base, over the past five years. Although the option of hybrid power is ctill a rarity in the vast majority of new cars, the psychological effect of such high-

profile hybrids as the Toyota Prius is not to be underestimated. Toyota and Honda still lead the way in hybrid technology, but most of the major European and North American automakers have been forced to include some form of hybrid in their future plans.

By looking back over the last five years at the number of concept cars that included alternative drivetrains in their specification, we can see a clear increase in the adoption of new technologies. Sadly, the take-up into production cars is still slow; yet this does at least show some attempt by manufacturers to raise public awareness and to ready the consumer for future power systems. The percentage of concept cars shown with hybrid systems, electric motors or gas-fueled engines is shown in the graph overleaf.

Opposite
The unconventional Mercedes-Benz F600 Hygenius has an upper structure that creates new relationships between glass and body.

Top
The Citroën C-AirPlay is a funky new experimental concept that played well with motor show crowds.

Above
Nissan's Urge was, for many, the pure sports-car concept of the 2006 Detroit show.

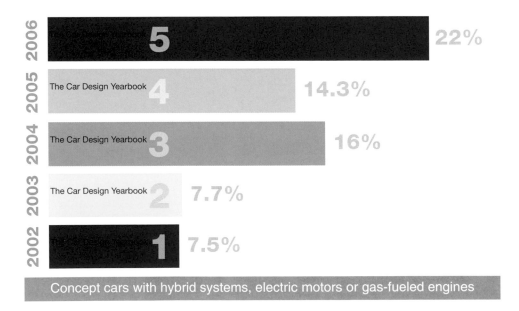

2006	**5** The Car Design Yearbook	22%
2005	**4** The Car Design Yearbook	14.3%
2004	**3** The Car Design Yearbook	16%
2003	**2** The Car Design Yearbook	7.7%
2002	**1** The Car Design Yearbook	7.5%

Concept cars with hybrid systems, electric motors or gas-fueled engines

In another development, designers can be seen trying hard to recapture in concept cars the spirit of what makes great cars great, and to connect with the emotions of consumers, giving them what they want (even if they don't yet realize what it is they are missing). In mixing heritage with contemporary design, the creators of the new Jaguar XK Coupé and Convertible have succeeded in capturing that elusive spirit which makes a truly beautiful car; many other brands fail to come nearly as close.

As population demographics shift, the market for cars changes, as it does for all products. With more people choosing to work from home, cars are less about simply being a tool to get to and from work and are being used more and more for leisure time. The past year

has seen the launch of many new convertibles—
a prime expression of the car as fun-machine
—while cars with large glass roofs are growing
in popularity. The Volkswagen Eos is a good
example of a convertible car that is designed
with fun and leisure in mind.

A particular milestone event was witnessed
in 2005: the launch of the Bugatti Veyron, with
its sixteen cylinders, four turbochargers and
incredible 1001 horsepower. Following years in
development and a number of huge engineering
challenges, the Veyron finally emerged as the
world's fastest production car: it is capable of
well over 400 km/h (250 mph), eclipsing the
McLaren F1 by a substantial margin. The
development costs incurred in overcoming the
enormous obstacles—including developing a

driveline strong enough to handle the 1250 Nm
of torque—mean that Bugatti will never make
a profit from this car, especially as only about
300 of them will be produced. Even a selling
price of £800,000 ($1,200,000) apiece cannot
come anywhere near to covering the rumored
£5,000,000 that each car will cost to build.
And because of the prohibitive costs of
developing models of such extreme complexity
and engineering integrity, this type of car may
never be built again. Yet, finances aside, the
Veyron is such a huge technological achievement
that we chose to feature it on the jacket of this
year's *Car Design Yearbook*.

SUVs have been an increasingly popular
choice over the past ten years, in European and
especially US markets. As we can see by looking

Opposite
The Mini Concept Frankfurt previews the upcoming
station-wagon model for BMW's ultracool brand.

Above
The Cadillac Escalade shows that boxy American design
is alive and well in Detroit.

2006	The Car Design Yearbook **5**	**18**
2005	The Car Design Yearbook **4**	9
2004	The Car Design Yearbook **3**	5
2003	The Car Design Yearbook **2**	11
2002	The Car Design Yearbook **1**	8

Number of new SUVs launched in production

at the number of new SUVs launched over the past five years (see graph, left), the pace of new models coming onto the market is still quickening, with more being launched this year than at any time in the last five. Much of the increase is due to a greater appetite for platform-sharing between the different Ford and GM (General Motors) brands, though a counter-trend also shows focus shifting from conventional truck-based SUVs to the more comfortable and less thirsty car-based crossovers.

The world's reliance on oil is only now starting to be viewed with serious alarm as crude oil prices reach record highs. Some countries are now turning to ethanol to run their cars: Brazil leads in this field, with ethanol produced from home-grown sugar cane accounting for 40% of all fuel used by

consumer vehicles, and all gas containing by law a minimum of 20% ethanol. Even President Bush has talked of the United States's addiction to oil but, to date, talk is all it has been and no real policies to encourage the development of environmentally efficient cars have materialized. The rest of the world sees North American fuel as still being relatively cheap. Nevertheless, the steep rises at the end of 2005 were something of a wake-up call and there has been a discernible media and consumer backlash against the very biggest and heaviest conventional SUVs—though this may yet prove a short-lived panic and the market itself may return to big-business as usual.

The US industry is still suffering from serious over-capacity and from strong competition from Asian automakers, many of which build in North America. In February 2006 GM announced that it was slashing its dividend and making deep cuts to executive pay; the announcement followed word late last year that the world's largest automaker would close eight plants and cut 30,000 jobs. The troubles are not exclusive to GM. In January, Ford announced plans to lay off 30,000 workers and shut as many as fourteen plants. Probably the biggest winner in the US has been Toyota, with more than 400,000 Camrys sold in 2005; Toyota is expected soon to outsell Chrysler and become America's third-biggest car company in terms of sales, while, worldwide, it is poised to overtake GM to claim the global number one slot.

At the 2005 Frankfurt motor show Chinese manufacturers could already be seen planning

Opposite
The Bugatti Veyron is now the fastest production car in the world.

Above
The Chrysler Aspen, Chrysler's first-ever SUV, shows off its integrated styling, in which panels and features flow into one another.

their assault on Europe; with cars from China being launched in the US in 2008, this will only increase the pressure on the domestic brands. In the long run this could be a catalyst that leads to the elimination of one of the existing big players. Both the Chinese and the Indian automotive industries are steadily building up their output, in the first instance to satisfy growing demand in local markets and later to aim at export growth. Within a few years China is expected to replace Japan as the second-largest national market after the US, so the American and European businesses face challenging times ahead.

The industry is now seeing the effects of the big automotive mergers and takeovers that took place during the 1990s. The strategy of brand consolidation has not been entirely successful.

There are even examples to show that the more brands a firm owns, the less profitable it is, Fiat being one such instance. The grand idea was that platform-sharing between brands within a group would produce huge economies of scale. Reality has demonstrated, often painfully, that brands still need to be differentiated one from the other in order for brand equity to be preserved. This in turn has led some groups to limit their platform-sharing so as to minimize the risk of brand dilution.

GM has twice the number of brands as its closest competitor, Ford, yet it runs near the bottom in the profitability league. In contrast, Toyota is top of the tree for profitability. It has just four brands and a relatively small model range, but there are a large number of model

derivatives available. Toyota is still not quite the world's largest carmaker by number of units built, but given the speed at which it is growing and the speed at which GM is shrinking, the day when Toyota becomes the biggest must be close. Investors already recognize Toyota as the leader, and at the time of writing its market value is greater than that of GM, Ford, and DaimlerChrysler combined.

In 2000 GM struck a technical co-operation deal with Italian company Fiat, an arrangement that also included an option that would have obliged GM to buy the remainder of Fiat for two billion dollars. Concerned about taking on the ownership of another major liability, GM eventually decided to buy its way out of the obligation in 2005.

At DaimlerChrysler, top executives spent so much energy trying to turn Chrysler around that quality at Mercedes suffered. This led to an almost complete change in top management and Daimler and Chrysler together are now worth less in stock-market terms than Daimler alone was before the 1998 merger. As a result, the architect of the merger deal, Jürgen Schrempp, was nudged out of his chief executive's chair by leading shareholders.

So, while much remains to play for, one facet of the industry's future is certain: new Chinese and Indian manufacturers will both see the greatest growth and provide the greatest threat to the established brands. By setting up from scratch they can achieve world-class manufacturing efficiencies at low cost. And by working with Western designers and engineering experts they have the capability to create world-class products that, in the fullness of time, will certainly challenge Western and Japanese brands with long histories.

All the more important, then, for the established automakers to invest ever-increasing amounts in style, design, and engineering to enhance the one great advantage they already have over any potential upstart—the intangible character and qualities that define that precious brand identity.

Opposite
The Q7 is Audi's first-ever model for the luxury SUV segment.

Above
A beautiful example of coupé design, the Saab Aero X comes complete with exciting aero-related concept engineering.

Dashboard Design

Italian Design

Dashboard Design

Conventional wisdom has it that the exterior of a car is the most important aspect of its design, and that the interior, by contrast, is of only secondary significance. That reasoning might be crude, but it is also clear: after all, if the exterior does not connect with the customers' emotions and draw them in, no one will ever get close enough even to see the interior. Now, however, all that has changed.

Some companies—for example, BMW and Saab—have always been honorable exceptions to this rule, but it is only relatively recently that the great mass of carmakers has woken up to the fact that interior design can be just as important a factor in car purchase as exterior style. And as proof of this shift in attitude, such design-conscious producers as Renault have been working hard to attract the very best designers into interior work, convincing them that it should no longer be seen as a second-best occupation.

Many factors have fed into this trend. Rising levels of congestion mean that drivers and passengers are spending more time in their cars,

often at a standstill, making interior design a much more direct experience; growing numbers of women buyers bring very different preferences to the way the inside of their cars should look; and the spectacular explosion of electronic content in vehicles has both posed problems and provided opportunities for innovation in presenting information and operating controls.

The result has been heavy investment in interior design on the part of the carmakers, both in the controls and displays accessible to the driver and in the new technologies hidden beneath the dashboard surfaces. These changes, some of them radical, will feed into new cars with increasing momentum; many will be seen this year.

The possibilities opened up by electronics, as just one example, are limitless. Electronic displays can flick from digital to analog in an instant; the whole dashboard can be a giant screen, and what one moment is a conventional paired speedometer and rev counter could the next moment become an infrared view of the

road ahead. Patterns, colors and finishes can be generated electronically to match the driver's or passengers' prevailing mood, and calming films of, say, waves breaking or clouds passing can even be displayed in strategic areas. More than ever before, it is up to the individual carmaker to decide the image and the functionality to be projected through the dashboard design.

The photographs on these pages show beyond any possible doubt how distinct and varied dashboard design already is. Dark and conservative dashboard styles from Volkswagen; traditional wood-trimmed authenticity from Jaguar; discreet high technology from Mercedes; and the downright wacky concept designs from the Japanese manufacturers.

Whoever the manufacturer and whatever the style, the essential role of the dashboard is to communicate information quickly and clearly to the driver and passengers. The dashboard must also house many of the vehicle's most important controls and switches, again fulfilling a crucial safety responsibility. But beyond these practical

Opposite
Citroën C-SportLounge. The Citroën C-SportLounge uses geometric forms in black and yellow to dramatic effect, creating a slightly unnerving futuristic look.

Above
Jaguar XK. Traditional British values of craftsmanship are indelibly associated with the Jaguar brand, meaning that walnut and comforting leather remain the order of the day.

Left
Volkswagen Eos. This dark, functional dashboard from Volkswagen integrates conventional instruments and a central display screen. Aluminum accents enhance the perceived value and quality of finish.

roles is a further function: to represent the brand values of the car's manufacturer, and to bring to the inside a sense of the car's exterior style, thus connecting with the consumer both physically and emotionally.

This is becoming more and more of an issue for designers, who find themselves pressurized on the one hand to project strong brand values in their designs, and on the other hand to accommodate an ever-larger communication technology content. Navigation systems, CD autochangers, DVD players, mobile phones, PDAs, and iPods were virtually unknown just a few years ago, and there has never been a time when a car's dashboard has needed to integrate so many devices and communicate so much information. Those companies that win the design race and achieve true excellence in communication will become the new standard-bearers for twenty-first-century integrated interior design. And, as sure as BMW grew fast in the 1970s and 1980s on the strength of its ergonomic expertise, those firms will find

themselves gaining market share over their less info-savvy competitors.

Voice-activation technology is still in its infancy but is steadily becoming available in more and more mass-production applications. The opportunities within the car seem irresistible: imagine dashboards with almost no controls or switches, each climate control, entertainment, and navigation function being replaced by voice-command technology. Imagine a time in the future when, after buying a new car, instead of ploughing through the instruction manual learning what all the switches do, you teach your car to respond to voice commands—rather like teaching a puppy. For now at least, this is still in the future, but it is certainly a technical possibility.

Nowhere is the thirst for integrated technology higher than among young people—the people who tomorrow will be the biggest buyer group for new cars. Whether it is iPod docking stations, voice-recognition global positioning systems, or Earth-browsing systems where real-time street images are sent by satellite

to onboard screens, these new customers are capable of soaking up new technologies like no generation before them. And it is this quickening of the pace of technological innovation that is driving the real changes in interior design.

More and more cars have multimedia display screens mounted in the center console: these can control anything from navigation and in-car entertainment to air-conditioning, suspension settings, and even the telephone. The car industry is currently going through one of its periodic phases of familiarization, when customers are being encouraged to get used to the idea of using electronic screens to display information and control important functions: in the future we can expect these screens to become larger and provide much more information.

There is no reason, for instance, why screens could not be extended behind the steering wheel and incorporate the main instrumentation gauges. The Toyota Endo concept shows how this is possible: it has one large screen that replaces the conventional dashboard, and

displays all the information the driver and passengers need. Even as long ago as 2000 Ford showed its breakthrough 24:7 concept, in which the full width of the interior bulkhead lit up as a giant, reconfigurable computer screen. As display-screen technology develops further, screens will be able to be molded into different shapes, and this will again allow designers new freedoms. The Toyota Fine-X concept goes one step further, and has not only a large electronic dashboard screen for displaying familiar types of information, but also, across the lower dashboard, a curved screen projecting soothing images to induce a sense of calm within the cabin.

At the opposite end of the scale, BMW has continued to earn praise for its resolutely analog approach to information display. The dashboard in the new Mini projects a sense of youthfulness and fun, with a large centrally mounted dial jutting out from the horizontal dashboard beam. Other gauges and switches appear to sit on the main dashboard rather than be fully integrated into it. This makes for a more playful look, and

one that harks back to the original Mini of the 1960s. Different materials and textures of the same color give a sophisticated feel, appeal to the eye, and are pleasant to touch. The Toyota Yaris features a centrally mounted instrument window that projects its information to the driver through a system of lenses, thus saving space on the dashboard surface and simplifying its design.

Jaguar is at a key point in its history where it needs to adopt all the latest electronic systems, yet it cannot afford to lose sight of its tradition of rich, sumptuous interiors using exquisite leather and wood trim and projecting a clear message of heritage and craftsmanship. Having a large central display screen replacing the conventional dashboard is hard to imagine: the challenge for Jaguar in the future will be incorporating new technologies in a way that remains consistent with Jaguar values.

The new Mercedes-Benz S-Class has the closest thing yet to an intelligent dashboard display. The two high-resolution, photo-realistic screens are given equal prominence, one directly

Opposite top
Mercedes-Benz S-Class. Here a classic look is combined with up-to-the-minute technology.

Opposite bottom
Toyota Endo. The Endo hints at the future of dashboard screen technology.

Above
Mini Concept Frankfurt. Mini uses playful retro cues but implements them in a thoroughly modern way and with modern materials to sophisticated effect.

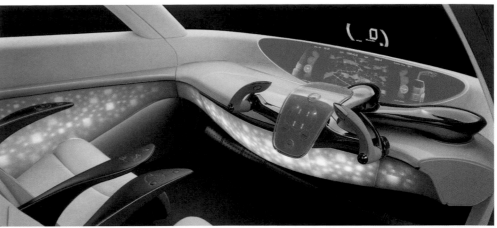

in front of the driver and the second at the same height toward the center of the car. The driver's display has a number of graphically animated instruments, resembling conventional analog devices. But their size and prominence varies according to which other functions are selected: for example, turning on the night-vision system shrinks and dims the main speedometer, speed readings now also being given below the grayscale road-ahead image produced by the infrared imaging system. In this way, information displayed can be automatically prioritized, be it navigation, audio, telephone, parking proximity detection, service messages, or even seat settings. It also allows Mercedes to pack lots of display information into a smaller space and still enable it to be clearly communicated.

At the absolute apex of the automobile pyramid stands the Bugatti Veyron, the Volkswagen Group's million-euro ultraluxury sports car capable of 400 km/h (250 mph), to be handcrafted in minute numbers. The dashboard of the Veyron is gently curvaceous and its horizontal form is slim so as not to look too heavy; the glitzy machined-aluminum panel in the center contrasts well with the thick brown matt leather, while valuable jewels are inset into the speedometer face. It is an exquisite combination of materials perhaps more familiar in Parisian *haute couture* than as car accessories.

As fuel-cell technology becomes more widely used, changes in the way vehicle components are packaged will have a knock-on effect on car interiors. In particular, more of the chassis and powertrain systems can be hidden under the car, allowing space to be freed up at the front; this in turn allows the interior to be lengthened to provide more internal space for a vehicle of a

conventional size. So-called "drive-by-wire" systems, which operate the brakes, steering, gears, and engine electronically rather than through direct mechanical links, will one day allow yet more space to be liberated inside the cabin. Designers will then be free to create dashboards that look a great deal more radical and very much more futuristic: the Nissan Pivo concept is just one such example. This concept car also has screens mounted on the inside of each A-pillar, displaying images of the view that the pillar blocks out—a very simple, practical safety solution.

Interiors, and dashboards in particular, are undergoing radical design changes brought about by technological innovation and the need to differentiate products from one another. At the center of the debate stand brand identity and the desire to create a strong and attractive

image in the eye of the consumer. At the same time, it must not be forgotten that the dashboard is the primary human–machine interface in a relationship that is becoming increasingly fraught and complex. It is the task of interior designers to simplify this acutely safety-critical aspect of the vehicle—and that is why investment in the design of car interiors is running at an all-time high level. All being well, it will be the consumer who reaps the rewards.

Opposite far left
Toyota Yaris. The center stack is topped with an instrument housing that projects driver information from a source hidden behind the dashboard.

Opposite top
Toyota Fine-X. The screens in Toyota's Fine-X concept are used for displaying information as well as for lighting the floor and changing the mood of the cabin.

Opposite bottom
Suzuki LC. Retro and minimalist, the Suzuki LC concept's dashboard is strikingly simple and echoes the exterior design of the car.

Above
Renault Egeus. Renault has pared down conventional dashboard design to a few simple forms where information appears on electronic displays behind the steering wheel. The system even includes a playful pop-up dial.

Italian Design

Italy's appetite for design and its long-established reputation for nurturing some of the world's most exciting designers is world-renowned. Italy as a country, of course, is awash with beautiful buildings, sculptures, and artworks, providing a feast of inspiration for any go-getting designer.

It is not only such iconic car brands as Ferrari and Maserati that create the aura around all things Italian: countless other products conjure up notions of Italian glamour and prestige, whether it be *haute couture* from the likes of Prada, Armani, and Versace, sleek contemporary furniture from such companies as Kartell, La Palma, and B&B Italia, or beautiful boats by Azimut. Italian style is recognizable the world over, with its sleek proportions and racy lines, and its sexy-looking modern feel and luxury materials. After World War II Italy saw a flourishing of small family-run businesses that made high-quality modern products without relying on mass production; other factors in the success of Italy's design industry included the increasing worldwide appreciation of Italian design, and the modern design movement of the 1960s.

The design of exceptional cars deep-rooted in motor-racing heritage is what has helped to make such makes as Ferrari, Alfa Romeo, and Maserati into the icons they are today. Turin in northern Italy is the center for Italian car design, with the best-known companies, including Pininfarina and Italdesign, being based there along with such less well-known design houses as Fioravanti, Bertone, Frua, and Scaglione. Historically such companies began as small coachbuilders, which, in the 1950s, tailor-made one-shot cars for the rich and famous. During the 1960s, carmakers moved to unitary construction, rather than the body and chassis being constructed separately, with the result that coachbuilders were unable to get chassis to work on. Some went out of business, but many went direct to the large manufacturers, effectively acting as design consultants, and in this way bringing the skills of smaller design companies to the mass market. Today, such companies as Pininfarina have developed into multi-faceted businesses not only focusing on design but also offering turnkey engineering and manufacturing

services to major car companies around the world. Fiat, Italy's largest mass-manufacturing company, which also controls Alfa Romeo, Lancia, Maserati, and Ferrari, often draws on the skills of Pininfarina, especially when designing sporty cars.

It is the design skills first and foremost that have made such consultancies so successful. The big car companies, especially those from outside Europe, often see the Italian design houses as a way of gaining acceptance in the European market owing to Italy's thorough understanding of the European customer and the cachet attached to designer-label products associated with Italian style houses. Pininfarina has also developed specialist expertise in convertible design, engineering, and manufacture, and has worked on recent products for Peugeot and Volvo. Pininfarina's long-term relationship with Ferrari means that the brand has an unshakeable association with performance styling, and Peugeot especially takes pride in sporting a Pininfarina emblem along the side of its cars.

Opposite
Ferrari F430 (2004). This athletic Ferrari replaced the best-selling 360 Modena at a time when Ferrari had won the Formula One constructors' championship for six consecutive years.

Above
Alfa Romeo Spider (2003). The facelifted Alfa Romeo Spider is an upgraded version of the 1995 original. Bold and true to its designer's vision, the Spider has won a loyal following with its distinctive styling. A new 2006 model has just been produced.

Right
Azimut 116 (2004). This beautiful boat resembles a Ferrari for the ocean, its sleek lines suggestive of speed, style, and the height of luxury.

Understanding the theory behind what makes Italian car design so special is more complex. The very careful development of vehicle proportions plays a vital part, together with a thorough understanding of how different intensities of light interact with surfaces at different times of the day. In deciding on the final detail treatments, Italian designers often appear to possess a confidence lacking in designers from other countries, and do not seem fazed about incorporating visually challenging features in their designs. Examples include the creases in the Fiat Coupé's wheel arches, and the stepped hood and high-mounted lamps on the first version of the modern Fiat Multipla.

If Pininfarina has a mantra it is probably that design is a harmony of proportions. Pininfarina designed the Maserati Quattroporte, which clearly shows this to be true. It is a sensual and elegant large sedan, but without any of the usual executive baggage: instead, it is more like a sports car, with complex flowing surfaces that create an enticing interplay of light and shadows. Its bold oval grille provides the backdrop for the

striking trident emblem, while the long hood and short overhangs are characteristic GT.

No feature about Italian design would be complete without considering Ferrari, the legendary supercar manufacturer that has become a symbol of Italy itself. The majority of Ferrari designs over the last forty years have been outsourced to Pininfarina, whose uncanny ability to communicate the Ferrari values of speed, sexiness, and handling goes unmatched. Current demand for Ferrari models is at an all-time high. Important factors in a Ferrari's makeup include everything from wheel design through to the way the visual masses are placed along the car.

Lamborghini is another famous Italian brand born out of the early racing era. It is now controlled by Audi, itself part of the German Volkswagen Group, although Lamborghini tries hard to maintain its association with Italy. Recent new models have all sold strongly, and the latest Miura concept featured in this book is a modern interpretation of the original 1960s Italian classic.

High-performance cars are by no means the only manifestation of Italian design; quite the

Above top left
Fiat Coupé (1995). This affordable mass-market sports car is given a unique look by its creased wheel arches.

Above left
Fiat Multipla (2000). The Multipla caused a stir when it was launched, many people thinking it was too odd-looking to sell. In 2005 it was given a facelift.

Above
Mk 1 Volkswagen Golf (1974). Giorgetto Giugiaro designed this iconic hatchback in the early 1970s. A whole range of similar hatchbacks from competitors soon took up the trend.

Opposite
Maserati Coupé (2002). The sumptuous cream Italian leather interior demonstrates that the warmth and vitality of this car run more than skin deep.

opposite, in fact. Take the Fiat Uno as an example—or the original Volkswagen Golf, which was designed by Giugiaro of Italdesign. Both were small everyday hatchbacks, widely accepted and sold in their millions; both set design trends that would pervade the whole industry. What hangs Italian design together is the ability to connect with the purchaser, being honest with the brand values and the fans of the brands. Whether it is the Daewoo Matiz, the Alfa Brera or a Ferrari, the new products that emerge from Italy's design studios are more likely to become latter-day classics than cars from any other country.

For those in the know, Giorgetto Giugiaro is synonymous with automobile design. Founder of Italdesign in 1968, Giugiaro is responsible for a wide variety of celebrated models, including examples from Ferrari, Oldsmobile, Maserati, BMW, and Volkswagen. Italdesign does not limit itself to automotive design; other projects have included helicopters for Agusta, and interiors for airplanes and motorboats for Tullio Abbate, Baglietto, and Comar. There have also been

bicycles, hiking boots, home furnishings, appliances, cameras, computers, and even pasta. The Italdesign business no longer fully reflects the artisan methods of Renaissance Italy; computers, virtual-reality visualization suites, and rapid modelmaking facilities now support the craft-worker's activities. Italdesign has grown its technology to fit with the large manufacturing organizations for which it works.

So why is Italy so intrinsically linked with design? Great art and design from many periods of history are, of course, widespread throughout the country, forming a rich backdrop that continues to inspire many forms of art and design today. With so much to feed from it is no wonder that so many design houses continue to flourish there. Italy's post-war emergence in small family businesses is another reason, aided by their being able to source leathers and metals locally, and having the technologies with which to use these materials to push design boundaries.

Like most of Italy's designers, the Turin car stylists continue to prefer to work in small studios rather than in large corporate design

centers. The Pininfarina design center is certain that it produces its best work when the team is not too big, and its designers pride themselves on being individuals.

One does not need to think too hard to come across other examples of iconic Italian design, the Vespa scooter being one. The Vespa (meaning "wasp") was created by Piaggio immediately after World War II, based on a rough scooter used by paratroopers and found in a German wreck. Soon after the Vespa came the Lambretta, named after the factory's location in the Lambrate quarter of Milan. Original models are now sought by collectors all over the world, and Vespas are still produced today.

It is clear that there is now an inbred passion and skill for design in Italy today, leading to the creation of a wide variety of products, cars probably being the most famous. That love of design is so deep-rooted and appreciated around the world that Italy has become synonymous with modern style.

Shown on these pages is a selection of vehicles that give a clear sense of Italian design.

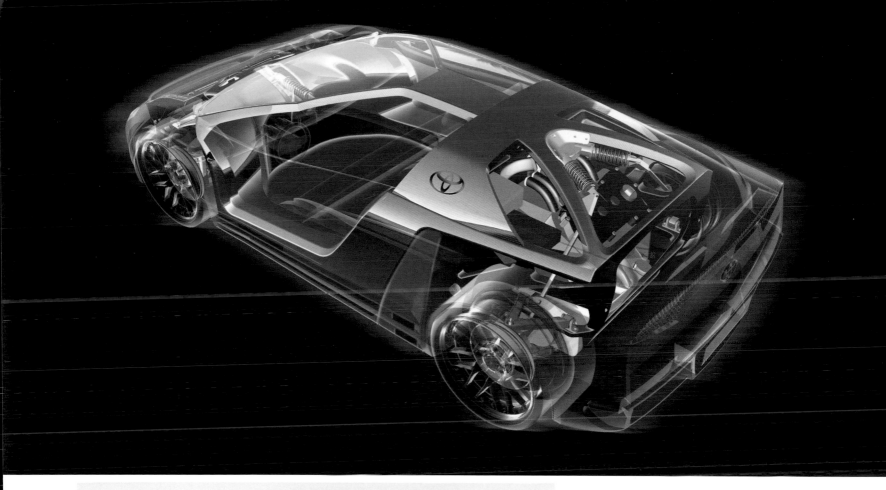

Opposite
Maserati Quattroporte (2003). An effortlessly beautiful modern sedan with bold sporting grille and retro undertones.

Above
Italdesign Toyota Alessandro Volta (2004) Italdesign's concept for Toyota mixes restrained Japanese surface language with unique Italian design elements, creating a striking appearance.

Left
Daewoo Matiz (1998). The cute-looking Matiz was designed by Giorgetto Giugiaro and first appeared in 1008. It has sold well, especially in southern Europe.

A – Z of New Models

Acura RDX

Design	Gary Evert
Engine	2.3 in-line 4
Power	179 kW (240 bhp)
Torque	353 Nm (260 lb. ft.)
Gearbox	5-speed automatic
Installation	Front-engined/all-wheel drive
Front suspension	MacPherson strut
Rear suspension	Multilink
Brakes front/rear	Discs/discs
Front tires	235/55R18
Rear tires	235/55R18
Length	4590 mm (180.7 in.)
Width	1860 mm (73.2 in.)
Height	1655 mm (65.2 in.)
Wheelbase	2650 mm (104.3 in.)
Track front/rear	1573/1586 mm (61.9/62.4 in.)
Curb weight	1815 kg (4001 lb.)
Fuel consumption	12.8 l/100 km (18.4 mpg)

Targeting the BMW X3 in the premium compact SUV segment, the new RDX from Honda's premium brand, Acura, went on sale in summer 2006. It comes fitted with the first turbocharged engine in Acura's history and is being sold as a luxurious model with the agile handling of a sports sedan.

The original RDX concept was launched at the Detroit show a year earlier: the overall proportions and design theme are retained, although there are many detailed changes to the grille, lamps, and bumpers, as well as a radical toning-down of the interior. Another, much more rugged RDX concept was shown in 2002, but its tough approach has clearly been abandoned in order to guarantee a more marketable mainstream production car.

The RDX is the first design to benefit from Honda's new global light truck platform: it has the important bonus of Honda's revolutionary Super-Handling All-Wheel-Drive system, first shown on the Legend sedan. This is able to alter torque from side to side and front to rear to improve cornering and straight-line stability.

The exterior design is decidedly soft and friendly, intended to appeal to both sexes in equal measure. The headlamp shape is geometric and eye-catching, as are the rear lamps. Viewed from the side, the focus is on the overall shape and practicality of the vehicle: the design is not one that draws the eye to specific details. A two-tone body trim running right around the car breaks up the height as well as giving it some off-road credibility.

Inside, the seats, doors, and dashboard are furnished in rich black leather, with aluminum-trim detailing creating a sporty, driver-oriented cockpit. The small, sporty steering wheel has gearbox paddle shifters, and the single large instrument panel, with smaller dials on either side, is an unusual feature.

Alfa Romeo Spider

Design	Pininfarina
Engine	3.2 V6 (2.2 in-line 4 also offered)
Power	194 kW (260 bhp) @ 6300 rpm
Gearbox	6-speed manual
Installation	Front-engined/all-wheel drive
Front suspension	Double wishbone
Rear suspension	Multilink
Brakes front/rear	Discs/discs
Length	4396 mm (173.1 in.)
Width	1830 mm (72 in.)
Height	1367 mm (53.8 in.)

The Spider is without question the most iconic car within the Alfa Romeo lineup—so the launch of any new generation is guaranteed to draw plenty of interest.

As with previous generations of the Spider, the new model accompanies a closely related coupé, so it comes as no surprise to find that the Brera coupé was used as the basis for the roadster. Much of the Brera has been carried over, the front three-quarter view below the waistline looking identical. The Brera's being one of the very prettiest cars on the market, this is clearly no bad thing.

The new Spider is much more aggressive than its GTV-based predecessor, with its triple headlamps and short overhangs front and rear. Historical references can be found, a clear example being the rear deck, where the raised rear fender shapes borrow from the Giulietta Spider of the 1950s.

Gone are the Brera's rear seats in favor of a small stowage shelf: the packaging space is needed to store the folded roof. While many similar roadsters are opting for a rigid folding roof, Alfa has chosen to stay loyal to the conventional canvas soft-top. Two neatly designed hoops are mounted behind the seats to offer protection in the event of a rollover, and the interior is of a much higher spec than the outgoing model. Luxurious materials, climate control, and steering-wheel-mounted radio controls all add up to a better driving environment.

As with all great Alfas, the new Spider stirs up emotions. It makes you want to get in, drive, and have fun. And it is not all just superficial looks: the top-of-the-range model comes fitted with a 3.2-liter V6 engine and an all-wheel-drive system, meaning that onroad performance is sure to match up to the gorgeous appearance.

Aston Martin Rapide

Design	Marek Reichman
Engine	6.0 V12
Power	357 kW (480 bhp) @ 6000 rpm
Torque	595 Nm (440 lb. ft.) @ 5000 rpm
Gearbox	6-speed automatic
Installation	Front-engined/rear-wheel drive
Front suspension	Double wishbone
Rear suspension	Double wishbone
Brakes front/rear	Discs/discs
Length	5000 mm (196.9 in.)
Height	1333 mm (52.5 in.)
Wheelbase	2990 mm (117.7 in.)
Curb weight	1940 kg (4268 lb.)
0–100 km/h (62 mph)	5.1 sec
Top speed	300 km/h (186 mph)

It is a mark of the growing strength of Aston Martin that it was able to present a proposal for a four-door, four-seater coupé to a Detroit show audience to unanimous praise. With the Rapide, Aston Martin is squaring up not only to Ferrari junior brand Maserati with its Quattroporte, but also to declared rival Porsche, with its announced Panamera four-door sports sedan.

The Rapide is based on a stretched version of the DB9's versatile aluminum platform: the roof is subtly raised and the wheelbase is extended to provide the extra space, but all the lithe elegance and sophistication of the Aston Martin profile remains. Unquestionably graceful and elegant, its strongly sporty persona and fabulously classy image combine to form the perfect advertisement for the luxury travel it seeks to provide.

The rounded shoulder running the length of the car is very prominent, and the front and rear themes are subtle developments of those on the DB9. Aston Martin's clay-modeling team worked alongside the computer-model team to ensure that the surfaces worked in harmony and played the light correctly.

Inside, the feeling of class and quality permeates every detail, from the plush leather adorning the seats and doors to the glass starter button, set in a wood panel surround, that is the first point of contact the driver has with the car. Even the trunk has a classy touch—a chiller cabinet designed to hold a single magnum of champagne, along with four flutes.

Aston Martin's designers said they would not have produced this car had it not looked perfect from every angle. The clear consensus is that they are 100% right.

Aston Martin Rapide **Concept** 41

Audi Q7

Engine	4.2 V8 (3.0 V6 diesel also offered)
Power	261 kW (350 bhp) @ 6800 rpm
Torque	440 Nm (324 lb. ft.) @ 3500 rpm
Installation	Front-engined/all-wheel drive
Front suspension	Double wishbone
Rear suspension	Double wishbone
Brakes front/rear	Discs/discs
Front tires	255/55R18
Rear tires	255/55R18
Length	5086 mm (200.2 in.)
Width	1983 mm (78.1 in.)
Height	1737 mm (68.4 in.)
Wheelbase	3002 mm (118.2 in.)
Track front/rear	1651/1676 mm (65/66 in.)
0–100 km/h (62 mph)	7.4 sec
Top speed	248 km/h (154 mph)
Fuel consumption	13.8 l/100 km (17 mpg)

It is one of the great ironies of the car business that Audi, the company that practically invented road-going four-wheel drive with its quattro system, has never built a dedicated SUV.

Not until now, at least. At last, Audi has conceded to the will of the market and developed a stand-alone SUV. The Q7 fits snugly into the upper reaches of the Audi lineup as a premium-class SUV to compete with the likes of the Mercedes ML and the BMW X5, not to mention Cadillacs and Lexuses in the United States.

The exterior is typically Audi, with a rounded nose and a deep crosshatch grille with chrome surround leading to the V-shaped hood, with its sculpted forms that then run outboard to the A-pillars. The windshield is steeply reclined and runs up onto the roof, which itself is arched, beginning at a point roughly above the driver's head to slope gradually downward toward the tailgate-mounted spoiler. From the side a tight crease line runs from the headlamps to the taillamps, visually lengthening the car. Above this line the doors roll over to the daylight opening line, making the doors look thick and protective. A midgray band runs around the circumference of the lower body, protecting the paintwork from stone chips.

There is no question that the ambience given off by the interior is that of a luxury car. Just like in top-of-the-range A6 and A8 sedans, the interior features the finest materials, including quality leathers and three wood-trim options.

The precursor to the Q7 was the Pikes Peak concept, shown at the Detroit Auto Show in 2003. Audi said it would not build that car, but the Q7 that has resulted has the same overall proportion—even though such features as the glass roof and LED rear lamps have been dropped in favor of more conventional solutions.

Audi Roadjet

Engine	3.2 V6
Power	221 kW (296 bhp) @ 7000 rpm
Torque	330 Nm (243 lb. ft.) @ 4500 rpm
Gearbox	7-speed DSG sequential
Installation	Front-engined/all-wheel drive
Front suspension	Four-link
Rear suspension	Trapezoidal-link
Brakes front/rear	Discs/discs
Front tires	245/45R20
Rear tires	245/45R20
Length	4700 mm (185 in.)
Width	1850 mm (72.8 in.)
Height	1550 mm (61 in.)
Wheelbase	2850 mm (112.2 in.)
0–100 km/h (62 mph)	6.4 sec
Top speed	250 km/h (155 mph)
Fuel consumption	8.7 l/100 km (27.1 US mpg)

The Roadjet takes Audi down a new design path in more ways than simply exploring a new set of proportions and testing the waters of a new market sector.

Its style is crisper and more sporting than has been seen of late from Audi, but the main shift has been in the balance of the masses that make up the overall impression it projects. Audi labels it a fastback sedan, but in reality it is more of a tall hatchback, with its forward-leaning rear screen extending to the rear bumper line.

The nose is dominated by the very deep grille that shouts about the V6 power lurking beneath, while lower meshed grilles on either side scoop in air to cool the brakes. The headlamps lead the sharp feature that runs, almost BMW-like, through the fender, creating tension as it overlaps the line that runs through the doors out to the rear. Yet the rounded rear speaks more of family-friendliness than sports performance.

Inside, the usual dark Audi colors are replaced with more soothing tones of gray and silver. The mesh pattern used on the individual seats and the air vents provides a visual link with the exterior, and the low daylight opening line makes for a spacious feel.

Technologies inside are many and varied: an espresso machine or a baby-carrier between the rear seats; sun visors replaced by a vari-light windshield the upper edge of which darkens in bright sunlight; an audio system that picks up when people are trying to talk to each other, then amplifying their voices through the speaker system; and a car-to-car communication system to warn of emergencies and even book parking spaces.

The Roadjet is certainly an interesting concept. Even if its intentions are not immediately clear, it may still signal the beginning of sharper, less weighty design language from Audi.

Audi Shooting Brake

Engine	3.2 V6
Power	250 kW (335 bhp) @ 6200 rpm
Torque	320 Nm (236 lb. ft.) @ 2500 rpm
Gearbox	6-speed manual
Installation	Front-engined/all-wheel drive
Front suspension	MacPherson strut
Rear suspension	Four-link
Brakes front/rear	Discs/discs
Front tires	245/40R19
Rear tires	235/40R19
0–100 km/h (62 mph)	6 sec
Top speed	250 km/h (155 mph)

Audi has dropped some pretty strong hints that its new Shooting Brake concept could eventually become a new Audi sports car. As a technology-laden design study it has all the right ingredients, and Audi has a strong track record of putting concept cars into production—as witness the A8, originally the ASF study; the TTS that became the iconic TT; and the Al2 that became the A2.

Design inspirations for the Shooting Brake are said by Audi to have included the A4 DTM racing car, the RSQ coupé conceived for the film *I, Robot*, and the recently launched RS 4 Quattro.

In design terms the rearward bias of the cabin is similar in some respects to the BMW 1 Series. The car looks very surefooted, with the upper cabin sitting inboard from the lower body. Pronounced wheel arches with wheels positioned as far out as possible give the Shooting Brake the look of a car that would go round corners as if on rails. The bold front grille with its vertical chrome bars may, however, be too overbearing and visually unbalanced ever to be considered for production.

Audi's standing as a sophisticated and sporty brand is signaled by the numerous driver aids and technological innovations. The suspension, for example, uses magnetic fluid in its dampers to give instant control over the ride by altering the fluid viscosity, while for braking, ceramic discs ensure that the car has race-car levels of braking performance.

Inside, the color combination is black, silver, and pearl-white. There is a multimedia interface with a touch-sensitive navigation screen on which the destination can be handwritten—even in Japanese—with the tip of a finger. Also new is the use of so-called "organic" light-emitting diodes in the chronograph instrument display, which, according to Audi, are easier to read in low light levels.

Bertone Suagnà

Italian design house Bertone has a long-standing relationship with Fiat, Italy's premier carmaker—and the stylist's latest concept car is developed around the new Fiat Grande Punto. *Suagnà* means "a job done painstakingly" in Piedmontese dialect, according to Bertone: judging by the design's eye-catching forms and lamp graphics, this does indeed appear to be what Bertone has succeeded in achieving.

The Suagnà is a coupé-cabriolet and has a fiercely individual style that is also classically Italian in origin. It uses very strong graphic elements, such as the large slash in the side, to create a dynamic and wedgelike profile; the sharp-edged hood is especially individual, with undecorated surfaces allowing the highly original headlamps really to stand out. The narrow, L-shaped lamp clusters are visually stimulating, and are set into a Z-shaped white trim that energizes the front and rear bumpers, linking left to right along the ground.

The design is echoed at the rear, with the lower crosspiece of the graphic shape rising in the center to accommodate the trapezoidal exhaust outlet. Because of the strong rising wedge graphic to the car's side profile the trunk line is high, meaning that with the rigid folding roof in place the rear window is very shallow and the rear pillars almost nonexistent.

The Suagnà has a youthful and sporty nature both outside and in; the seats, which claim to be anatomically shaped, have leather side strips with a crumpled effect, and a central strip in a high-tech fabric that appears to be woven with intertwined aluminum.

Although this car is not an obvious forerunner to a production Fiat, it will stimulate the debate in the fashionable coupé-convertible market-place. The concept may not have the media appeal of a supercar; what it certainly does provide is design ideas for the future.

Design	Bertone
Brakes front/rear	Discs/discs
Front tires	255/45R18
Rear tires	255/45R18
Length	4173 mm (164.3 in.)
Width	1773 mm (69.8 in.)
Height	1380 mm (54.3 in.)
Wheelbase	2511 mm (98.9 in.)

Bugatti Veyron 16.4

Design	Hartmut Warkuss
Engine	8.0 W16
Power	747 kW (1001 bhp) @ 6000 rpm
Torque	1250 Nm (921 lb. ft.) @ 2200–5500 rpm
Gearbox	7-speed double-clutch
Installation	Mid-engined/all-wheel drive
Front suspension	Double wishbone
Rear suspension	Double wishbone
Brakes front/rear	Discs/discs
Front tires	265/680ZR500A PAX
Rear tires	365/710ZR540A PAX
Length	4462 mm (175.7 in.)
Width	1998 mm (78.7 in.)
Height	1204 mm (47.4 in.)
Wheelbase	2710 mm (106.7 in.)
Curb weight	1888 kg (4162 lb.)
0–100 km/h (62 mph)	2.5 sec
Top speed	407 km/h (253 mph)
CO_2 emissions	574 g/km

Six years in the making, what is convincingly the world's most exotic car has finally arrived.

First shown at the Tokyo Motor Show in 1999, the Bugatti Veyron 16.4 has now become reality as the most powerful and most glamorous car ever built. The enormous technical headaches have been overcome and, at 407 km/h (253 mph), the Veyron is officially the fastest production car ever.

Such extreme performance expectations meant that Bugatti's owner, Volkswagen, had to draft a number of specialist companies to help solve such problems as how to cool the 1001 bhp midmounted sixteen-cylinder engine, how to get those 1001 bhp transferred to the road safely, and how to optimize the ride and handling performance, keep weight down, and minimize drag. High-speed stability is a critical issue—the Veyron is faster than most Formula One cars—and it must rank as the crowning achievement of Hartmut Warkuss, as VW's head of design, that the production Veyron has retained the design purity of the original concept with no unsightly spoilers or wings to detract from its lines.

The exterior is defined by two rounded, interlocking forms, highlighted by two-tone paintwork: the shape is smooth and simple, rather than complex and incoherent—a tribute again to a car for which much of the design work was carried out in the wind tunnel. Production of the Veyron is in Molsheim, near Strasbourg in France, the home of the original Bugatti Automobiles—surely the most luxurious customer service center on the planet.

Whichever way you look at it, the Veyron is a huge technical achievement. Sadly, it is so expensive that only a few hundred will be built—and even then, the development costs have been so high that the VW Group is unlikely to make a penny profit on this extraordinary machine.

Buick Enclave

Design	Jack Folden
Engine	3.6 V6
Power	201 kW (270 bhp)
Gearbox	6-speed automatic
Installation	Front-engined/all-wheel drive
Brakes front/rear	Discs/discs
Front tires	265/50R21
Rear tires	265/50R21
Length	5138 mm (202.3 in.)
Width	2006 mm (79 in.)
Height	1807 mm (71.1 in.)
Wheelbase	3023 mm (119 in.)
Track front/rear	1734/1759 mm (68.3/69.3 in.)

Trying to communicate an individual brand's DNA in a crowded market is invariably difficult—but it can be doubly difficult when that vehicle is an SUV. There is little freedom in the overall format, there are many practical requirements that need to be met, and function is often as important as form.

Buick's approach with the Enclave, its first car-derived SUV, has been to exploit its trademark curviness as well as lots of chrome to differentiate its newcomer from the established brands. The undulating, sculpted fender forms front and rear give a flowing movement to the Enclave's side view and distance it from any bland truck associations, while at the front the shape of the Buick grille, with its vertical slats, is distinctive and the large headlamps sweep flowingly into the fender feature line.

High-chrome finish ensures that the wheels really stand out, drawing the eye to their size and wide-set stance to emphasize the Enclave's surefooted look; chrome is also used liberally around all the side glass, around the taillights and as full-width accent strips across both front and rear bumpers.

Triple circular optical elements can be seen in the front and rear lamps, and the motif is taken up at the back of the hood as Buick's traditional portholes, creating a visual sense of power. The circular theme is gently carried through to the interior for continuity.

A considerable number of different materials, colors, and textures make up the Enclave's interior. Pale woods on the steering wheel, dashboard, and gearshift meet with black and gray plastics, chocolate-brown leather on the steering wheel and dash ends, a polished aluminum strip across the dashboard, and pale cashmere seats—as if Buick could not decide what image it wanted to project.

Cadillac Escalade

Engine	6.2 V8
Power	300 kW (403 bhp) @ 5700 rpm
Torque	566 Nm (417 lb. ft.) @ 4400 rpm
Gearbox	6-speed automatic
Installation	Front-engined/all-wheel drive
Front suspension	MacPherson strut
Rear suspension	Multilink
Brakes front/rear	Discs/discs
Front tires	265/65R18
Rear tires	265/65R18
Length	5143 mm (202.5 in.)
Width	2007 mm (79 in.)
Height	1887 mm (74.3 in.)
Wheelbase	2946 mm (116 in.)
Track front/rear	1731/1701 mm (68.2/67 in.)
Curb weight	2593 kg (5717 lb.)

For all its kudos as GM's latest and most prestigious SUV, the premium-nameplate Cadillac Escalade still has the look of a brutish American truck—something that is fast going out of fashion as the United States wakes up to higher fuel prices and an inkling of climate-change consciousness.

With its high hood, large wheel arches and generally heavy demeanor, the Escalade's design comes across as disappointingly utilitarian. This is not what one would expect from GM's blue-chip luxury brand, declared competitors of which include Lincoln, Infiniti, Acura, Mercedes-Benz, BMW, Range Rover, and Porsche. The comparison is all the more stark now that Mercedes has launched its very svelte GL-Class premium SUV at the top of the market.

Based on General Motors' full-size SUV platform, the Escalade shares its underpinnings with the fellow GM offerings from Chevrolet (Tahoe) and GMC (Yukon). Taking apparent inspiration from the huge Sixteen concept sedan of 2004, the Escalade has a more detailed Cadillac signature grille, vents in the front fenders, and chrome-accent trim along the side and above the rear bumper. The very taut surfaces add to its trucklike feel, an impression compounded by bumpers and side running boards that do not appear to blend in smoothly with the body.

The interior manages to avoid the overornamentation of many American designs, reflecting previous-generation Lexus styles. Its highlights include the first-ever powered fold-and-tumble second-row seats—handy if you have your hands full—and a powered open and close tailgate. The interior is claimed to use premium materials and comes in two color themes, ebony and cashmere.

This is a classic old-school SUV that will play well with the dwindling ranks of American buyers still subscribing to the gas-guzzler philosophy. For everyone else, there are plenty of other, more convincing choices.

Chevrolet Aveo

Engine	1.6 in-line 4
Power	78 kW (105 bhp) @ 5800 rpm
Torque	145 Nm (107 lb. ft.) @ 3600 rpm
Gearbox	4-speed automatic
Installation	Front-engined/front-wheel drive
Front suspension	MacPherson strut
Rear suspension	Torsion beam
Brakes front/rear	Discs/drums
Front tires	185/60R14
Rear tires	185/60R14
Length	4310 mm (169.7 in.)
Width	1710 mm (67.3 in.)
Height	1496 mm (58.9 in.)
Wheelbase	2480 mm (97.6 in.)
Track front/rear	1450/1430 mm (57.1/56.3 in.)
Fuel consumption	7.8 l/100 km (30 US mpg)

The new Chevrolet Aveo may be small, but there is a lot riding on it. As the replacement for America's bestselling entry-level vehicle the fresh model needs to keep up the momentum, not just in the United States but all over the world—for this is the Korean-built vehicle that will gradually take over from derivatives of the Opel Corsa as GM's staple global family model.

The new car has an all-new exterior and an interior that is more modern and grown-up than before. The body has a bolder face and overall crisper lines, emphasizing its more solid and substantial look. Starting at the front, the heavy chrome-framed grille has the characteristic twin Chevrolet openings and the gold bow-tie logo on its center bar; the headlamps are slightly set back and initiate a sculpted V-shaped form that runs up onto the hood. The angular surfaces catch the light in more defined ways, lending a contemporary appearance to the Aveo's structure. On the doors the upper pillars are matt black for an upmarket feel.

Inside, the cabin is simple—but this is not to the exclusion of useful contemporary touches such as the standard radio input jack for iPods and other music players. A wide selection of options includes a power sunroof, a six-CD-changer sound system, and steering-wheel-mounted audio and cruise controls.

It is only two and a half years since the last Aveo was launched in the US: this was based on the outgoing Daewoo/Chevrolet Kalos, which dated back to 2002. The new edition is a truly global car and will be known under different names in various markets, making its debut in the US as a 2007 model.

Chevrolet Camaro

Design	Tom Peters
Engine	6.0 V8
Power	298 kW (400 bhp)
Gearbox	6-speed manual
Installation	Front-engined/rear-wheel drive
Front suspension	MacPherson strut
Rear suspension	Multilink
Brakes front/rear	Discs/discs
Front tires	275/30R21
Rear tires	305/30R22
Length	4730 mm (186.2 in.)
Width	2022 mm (79.6 in.)
Height	1344 mm (52.9 in.)
Wheelbase	2806 mm (110.5 in.)
Track front/rear	1620/1607 mm (63.8/63.3 in.)

Few American icons from past decades are more vivid than the Chevrolet Camaro. Designed in the mid-1960s, the first-generation Camaro was GM's bid to counter the enormous success of the Ford Mustang: like the Mustang, it perfectly captured the optimism of an era and before long the pony-car ranks had swelled to include new heroes such as the Pontiac Firebird and the Dodge Challenger. This was a time when baby boomers were just teenagers, rock 'n' roll and Motown ruled the airwaves, and American culture was sweeping the globe.

Hardly surprisingly, the new concept does an excellent job of capturing the spirit of the original—the 1969 model, in fact, the version regarded as the best by Camaro aficionados. Other inspiration, says Chevrolet, came from the YF-22 aircraft, while the current Corvette was referenced to ensure that the design was consistent with contemporary Chevrolet brand identity.

The main proportions that made the original Camaro so distinctive are preserved, and indeed exaggerated: the hood is long and comes complete with power bulge, the rear wheel arches are strongly haunched, giving a powerful, propulsive look, and the shallow daylight opening line meets the rear fenders with the familiar signature angled C-pillar. The proportion clearly highlights the front-engined, rear-wheel-drive layout, but the design is more razor-edged than the original, with sharper body creases. The inset grille and headlamps emphasize the width of the car from the front, and help to give a menacing look.

The interior design is a less welcome 1960s throwback, with its period design shapes, large areas of bright metal, and garish orange highlights. The aluminum does, however, contrast well with the black leather trim, suggesting a no-nonsense dedicated sports car.

Of the many retro concepts turned out by US automakers in recent years, this is one of the most appealing and most convincing.

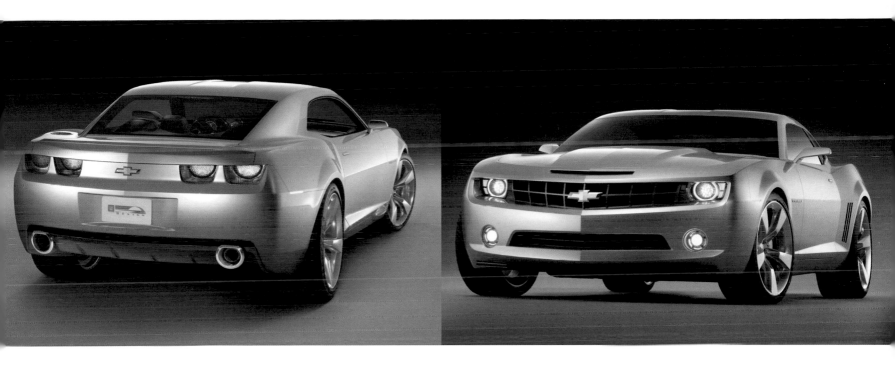

Chevrolet Captiva

The Captiva medium SUV, though tagged with the American Chevrolet brand, is in fact developed and built in Korea by GM Daewoo and sold globally under a variety of labels; later in 2006, Vauxhall and Opel versions will appear in Europe, and in North America Saturn will market a derivative as the Vue.

This latest model in GM's global grand plan is deliberately geared toward European tastes, currently the most fashionable in the car business. Major elements of the Captiva's style and design were previewed by the Chevrolet S3X concept shown in 2004; the production model makes only detailed departures from this appealing template.

It is a good-looking SUV that is neatly proportioned and detailed. It looks strong and solid, with crisp modern lines; GM has taken pains to ensure there are no quirky features that could scare off the middle-of-the-road SUV buyer. Well-resolved design points such as the gray body trim that encircles the car visually lower the body, making it look more like a tall off-road station wagon. In this it parallels—albeit in a smaller format—the very successful Volvo XC 90.

As with most SUVs, the Captiva majors in practicality: the generous interior space is easily extended thanks to seats that fold flat. Both five- and seven-seater versions will be marketed. The interior design is dark gray with plentiful aluminum trim, quite conservative in its treatment and with many square and circular features that recall current Volkswagen, BMW, and Mercedes thinking.

Designed to compete against the Toyota RAV4 and the Honda CR-V, the Captiva is not an innovative design. Rather, it comes across as Germanic in its appearance and could conceivably even worry premium products such as the BMW X3, as its pricing is expected to be very competitive.

Engine	3.2 V6 (2.4 in-line 4, and 2.0 diesel, also offered)
Power	169 kW (227 bhp) @ 6600 rpm
Torque	297 Nm (219 lb. ft.) @ 3200 rpm
Gearbox	5-speed manual
Installation	Front-engined/four-wheel drive
Front suspension	MacPherson strut
Rear suspension	Multilink
Brakes front/rear	Discs/discs
Front tires	235/55R18
Rear tires	235/55R18
Length	4635 mm (182.5 in.)
Width	1850 mm (72.8 in.)
Height	1720 mm (67.7 in.)
Curb weight	1710 kg (3770 lb.)
Fuel consumption	11.7 l/100 km (20.1 mpg)

Chevrolet Epica

Engine	2.5 in-line 6 (2.0 diesel also offered)
Power	115 kW (154 bhp) @ 5800 rpm
Torque	240 Nm (177 lb. ft.) @ 4000 rpm
Gearbox	5-speed automatic
Installation	Front-engined/front-wheel drive
Front suspension	MacPherson strut
Rear suspension	Multilink
Brakes front/rear	Discs/discs
Front tires	215/50R17
Rear tires	215/50R17
Length	4804 mm (189.1 in.)
Width	1807 mm (71.1 in.)
Height	1449 mm (57 in.)
Wheelbase	2700 mm (106.3 in.)
Track front/rear	1500/1500 mm (59.1/59.1 in.)
Fuel consumption	9.8 l/100 km (24 mpg)

Chevrolet is going all out to position itself as General Motors' entry-level brand in all key global markets—including, naturally, mainland Europe and the UK. Central to this strategy is the sourcing of value products from GM Daewoo in Korea—a move that GM is confident will allow Chevrolet to compete strongly on price and perceived consumer value for money.

The Epica, a medium-to-large four-door family sedan, is the latest model to join the fray, its mission being to defend GM's corner against other Korean brands and also the more conservative offerings from other Asian automakers. As such, it majors in size—especially trunk size—and specification. Style and sophistication come further down the Epica's priority list, though the inclusion of a straight-six-cylinder engine as the 2.5-liter gas powerplant adds an element of interest that would otherwise be lacking. The second engine choice is the same all-new 2-liter common-rail turbo-diesel as offered in the Captiva SUV. Transmissions, both manual and automatic, are five-speed.

The shape of the Epica, although hardly exciting, is not offensive either: crisp and simple lines, a gently rising waistline, decent proportions, and modern headlamps make it an effective sedan proposition. The slightly longer-than-average overhangs are all that could be considered to date it—but the benefit is seen in luggage space and, at the front, plenty of crush space for impact absorption.

The interior, likewise, does everything it needs to, but will not win any prizes for design or innovation. Chevrolet cites soft-trim furnishings and leather seat facings as notable features of the cabin. Factor in highly competitive pricing and the familiarity of the Chevrolet brand name—if only for large US cars—and the Epica could succeed where its Daewoo-branded predecessors have flopped.

Chevrolet Suburban

The Chevrolet Suburban has always been GM's most important full-size SUV. This latest evolution is based on GM's new full-size SUV platform, which incorporates a fully boxed frame and suspension. These developments, claims GM, result in better ride and handling. Yet, as an overall package, the nearly 6 meter (20 ft.) long giant has not felt the need to move with the times.

The Suburban's latest look is slightly more carlike, with the greater rake to the windshield forcing a move to curved front-door glass—and thus a less blocklike glasshouse. Even so, the rounded corners to the side windows give a feeling of reinforcement and fortification.

The new front is distinguished by single headlamp blocks instead of the previous double-decker units split by the grille's chrome band, and the bumpers and fenders now look more integrated into the overall shape. The Chevrolet gold bow-tie logo now nestles between two horizontal grilles, inset with dark mesh, which make up the Suburban's distinctive face. The hood now drops slightly toward the front, again lessening the boxiness of the design, and there is a prominent power hump to suggest the presence of a large engine. The characteristic flat-topped wheel arches remain but are less pronounced on the new model.

Inside, the freshly designed seats are easily folded and removed; there is a new HVAC system and a center console that boasts the largest storage capacity in the whole segment.

In some ways the new Suburban, though still vast and intimidating by any non-American standards of design, is a softer and slightly more friendly vehicle—not quite like a large car yet, but certainly less trucklike than in its previous macho guises. Something of an American icon, however, it still has not changed much—which is probably just how its loyal fans would like it.

Engine	6.0 V8 (5.3 V8 also offered)
Power	264 kW (354 bhp) @ 5400 rpm
Torque	504 Nm (371 lb. ft.) @ 4400 rpm
Gearbox	4-speed automatic
Installation	Front-engined/four-wheel drive
Front suspension	MacPherson strut
Rear suspension	Five-link
Brakes front/rear	Discs/discs
Front tires	265/70R17
Rear tires	265/70R17
Length	5648 mm (222.4 in.)
Width	2010 mm (79.1 in.)
Height	1950 mm (76.8 in.)
Wheelbase	3302 mm (130 in.)
Track front/rear	1731/1701 mm (68.2/67 in.)
Curb weight	2611 kg (5756 lb.)

Chevrolet Tahoe

Engine	5.3 V8 (4.8 V8 also offered)
Power	239 kW (320 bhp) @ 5300 rpm
Torque	461 Nm (340 lb. ft.) @ 4200 rpm
Gearbox	4-speed automatic
Installation	Front-engined/four-wheel drive
Front suspension	MacPherson strut
Rear suspension	Multilink
Brakes front/rear	Discs/discs
Front tires	265/70R17
Rear tires	265/70R17
Length	5129 mm (202.5 in.)
Width	2007 mm (79 in.)
Height	1955 mm (77 in.)
Wheelbase	2946 mm (116 in.)
Track front/rear	1731/1701 mm (68.2/67 in.)
Curb weight	2511 kg (5536 lb.)
Fuel consumption	13 l/100 km (18 US mpg)

The feeling of déjà vu evoked when contemplating the latest Chevrolet Tahoe is perfectly excusable, for this is quite simply the emblem-engineered twin sister of the Cadillac Escalade. With the same wheelbase, track, and overall width, the two big SUVs are identical in their proportions, and on closer inspection it can also be seen that the doors and the main body structure are the same, too. These are the fundamental parts of a vehicle's makeup, and thus very expensive to change.

Instead, the differences are seen in lamps, grilles, and trim, all of which cost several orders of magnitude less to vary. GM has certainly done a good job of achieving a reasonable differentiation between the two brands, especially from the all-important front view where most model identification takes place. And for Chevrolet, as GM's price-leading brand, the millions saved on development mean that the final ticket price can be that crucial few hundred dollars lower.

The Tahoe sits in the Chevrolet lineup below the massive Suburban, and has been the make's best-selling full-size SUV since 2001. The new model is built on an all-new platform that Chevrolet claims gives better refinement and driving feel. New door sealing, engine covers, and body developments that eliminate sound paths are adopted to reduce noise transfer into the cabin. Special features include a remote vehicle starting system, a rearview camera, touch-screen navigation, and powered running boards. Inside, the safety provision includes side-impact curtain airbags and rollover roof airbags.

Overall, the new Tahoe is improved and more sophisticated than the outgoing model; however, unfortunately for Chevrolet, the SUV segment is in free fall, and the market for big V8-powered SUVs—even if they have cylinder deactivation like the 5.3-liter Tahoe—may no longer be the cash generator that it once was.

Chrysler Akino

Design	Akino Tsuchiya
Length	3724 mm (144.6 in.)
Width	1799 mm (70.8 in.)
Height	1604 mm (63.1 in.)
Wheelbase	2413 mm (95 in.)

The Chrysler Akino is named after its designer, Akino Tsuchiya, a thirty-seven-year-old who was born in Japan and is based at the Chrysler Group's Pacifica Design Studios in California. She was solely responsible for designing the exterior and interior. The driving force behind the concept was Chrysler's imagining a small powertrain for a new vehicle, with the aim of finding out what would be possible if design were freed from the constraints of conventional powertrain packaging.

The result is a small cab-forward monovolume design with plenty of interior space. The body has two doors on the passenger side and one on the driver side, allowing space for a curved sofa-like rear bench seat and a swiveling front passenger seat, creating a sociable space. When viewed from the side the cant rail drops in an arc, eventually falling to the strong C-pillar. The roof is raised at the rear for more headroom and a semicircular glass panel bathes the passengers and the interior in natural light.

Akino means "autumn field" in Japanese, so it is no surprise that the interior of the concept vehicle uses a selection of autumnal colors and a variety of textures. The interior has a relaxing feeling for a group of friends to share, with an air almost of being in the comfort of one's own home. Material choices for the interior include synthetic fabrics and bamboo flooring. The blue suede driver cockpit area is visually separated from the rest of the interior, which is finished in cream suede.

Akino is an attractive contemporary design concept with many practical ideas. It will be interesting to see whether this study evolves into something more tangible than simply one designer's vision for the future.

Chrysler Aspen

Engine	5.7 V8 (4.7 V8 also offered)
Power	250 kW (335 bhp) @ 5200 rpm
Torque	502 Nm (370 lb. ft.) @ 4200 rpm
Gearbox	5-speed automatic
Installation	Front-engined/four-wheel drive
Front suspension	Upper and lower A-arms
Rear suspension	Live axle
Brakes front/rear	Discs/discs
Length	5101 mm (200.8 in.)
Width	1930 mm (76 in.)
Height	1887 mm (74.3 in.)
Wheelbase	3027 mm (119.2 in.)
Track front/rear	1636/1635 mm (64.4/64.4 in.)
Fuel consumption	14.7 l/100 km (16 US mpg)

Chrysler has chosen an inopportune moment to launch its first-ever SUV: the Aspen rolled onto the Detroit stage just as rising fuel prices were tipping the market into decline. And, worse, almost every other automaker was coming up with new or freshened products, eager to grab a slice of the fast-shrinking cake.

One look at the Aspen is enough to confirm how little innovation there is in contemporary volume-market SUV design: this is just another generic product, lightly brushed with just enough corporate identity treatments so that we can tell one brand from the next.

The huge grille and Crossfire-inspired hood ridges are what gives Aspen its token Chrysler look. This frontal treatment apart, there is nothing much else that makes the Aspen stand out: it would be difficult to name it from the side, for example, though Chrysler has thoughtfully added an emblem to the front door to reassure unconvinced onlookers.

The Aspen will seat up to eight adults and has all the functionality one would expect of a big SUV. The interior is less busy and brash than many American designs, with a combination of simple shapes, pale gray leather, pale wood insets, and dark gray finish to the top of the dashboard. The fit and finish of the interior has drawn criticism in some quarters: it is sometimes forgotten that this vehicle is priced toward the value end of the market and that, in the US at least, large size does not necessarily equate to top levels of quality.

SUV design is mostly about communicating size and practicality; the Aspen's Chrysler identity is here stamped on merely to draw in brand loyalists and maintain showroom traffic. It may represent the epitome of generic, inoffensive SUV design—but that could be precisely what America wants.

Chrysler Imperial

Design	Mike Nicholas
Engine	5.7 V8
Power	254 kW (340 bhp)
Gearbox	5-speed automatic
Installation	Front-engined/rear-wheel drive
Front suspension	Short and long arm
Rear suspension	Multilink
Brakes front/rear	Discs/discs
Front tires	245/45R22
Rear tires	245/45R22
Length	5439 mm (214.1 in.)
Width	1933 mm (76.1 in.)
Height	1615 mm (63.6 in.)
Wheelbase	3123 mm (123 in.)
Track front/rear	1623/1638 mm (63.9/64.5 in.)
0–100 km/h (62 mph)	5.7 sec
Top speed	258 km/h (160 mph)

Imperial has been Chrysler's traditional top-end nameplate for many generations, but the model has not figured in the Chrysler catalog since 1993. Now, however, the Imperial is back in grand style—as a concept, at least—and appears to have its sights set on the highest target of all: Rolls-Royce.

The concept has a deliberately stately look about it, with a bold grille and inset round headlamps that recall Rolls-Royce rather than past Chryslers. Rear-hinged rear doors are another point of similarity to the Phantom. Looking along the side of the Imperial, however, there is not the sheer sense of scale that the Rolls conveys.

The Imperial is tall for a sedan at 1.6 meters (5 ft. 3 in.): this gives it both visual presence and a commanding seating position. The front wheel arches are square volumes with a distinct crease line on the corner that gradually runs out through the doors. The wheels, with their large central discs and multi-spoked extremities, project a powerful limousine feel. A parallel line to the sill rises over the rear wheel arch, creating a very upright surface around the rear wheel. The trunk lid is raised and from above looks like a Gothic arch meeting at a point from which a vertical line drops through the winged Chrysler emblem. The rear lamps echo the "gunsight" design of previous Imperials.

The interior is a mix of modern and retro. A two-tone brown and cream color scheme gives it the feel of a luxury coffeehouse, while dashboard and floor lighting inspired by modern interior architecture is placed behind the floating elements of the instrument panel and doors, enhancing the sculptural elements of the interior.

This is an unusual and interesting concept from Chrysler, even if it is awkward from some angles; its suitability as a flagship model must right now be under scrutiny.

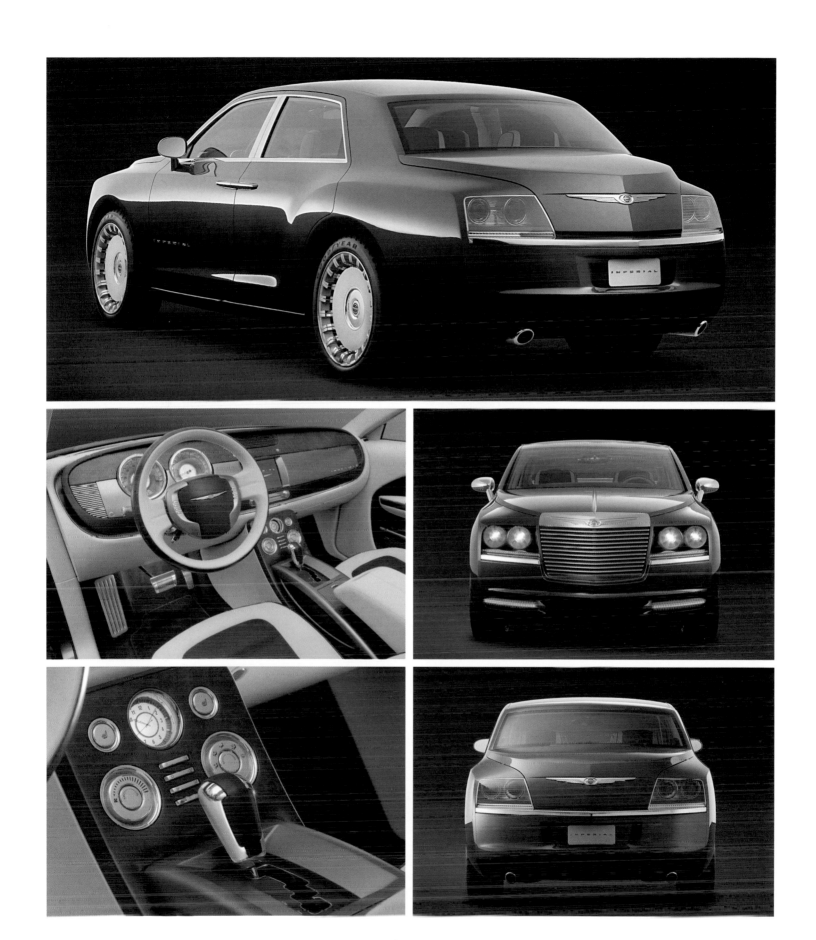

Citroën C-AirPlay

Power	82 kW (110 bhp)
Installation	Front-engined/front-wheel drive
Brakes front/rear	Discs/discs
Length	3300 mm (130 in.)
Width	1680 mm (66.1 in.)
Height	1390 mm (54.7 in.)
Wheelbase	2230 mm (87.8 in.)

Citroën's C-AirPlay is a playful new small-car concept designed to be fresh and exciting—which, on inspection, it indeed is. The idea behind the C-AirPlay is for a car that creates driving pleasure in terms of the physical and visual perceptions. The result, developed from a shortened version of the C2 compact supermini platform, is a friendly shape with plenty of curves, bulging wheel arches, and a roof with plenty of crown. Very short overhangs make it look nimble, while the large wheels, low ground clearance, and strong, arched body give it a sporty feel, even though speed is not the objective.

It is no coincidence that the body is finished in white. Designers at Citroën believe that by bathing the interior in more light the driver and passengers will feel better. The large windshield and roof are made of glass, with the center section of the roof being removable for a true open-air feel. Novel, too, are the porthole windows on the lower part of the doors to allow a direct view of the road, enhancing the feeling of speed as well as letting more light into the cabin.

The interior colors of white and bright red are designed for contrast, enhancing brightness and creating an impression of vitality and warmth in the cabin. The interior is designed for two people, and to reinforce this point, there are one large cosy bench seat up front and just two small seats in the rear.

Citroën has recently revived its reputation for designing spirited new cars, and the C-AirPlay makes a worthy addition to the list. Buyers today are looking for more from a car than simply a comfortable mode of transport—and if Citroën had the courage to build something like the C-AirPlay it could become the car of choice for fun seekers on a tight budget.

Citroën C-SportLounge

Power	149 kW (200 bhp)
Gearbox	6-speed Tiptronic
Installation	Front-engined/front-wheel drive
Brakes front/rear	Discs/discs
Front tires	255/40R20
Rear tires	255/40R20
Length	4510 mm (177.6 in.)
Width	1870 mm (73.6 in.)
Height	1520 mm (59.8 in.)
Wheelbase	2720 mm (107.1 in.)

The C-SportLounge is an intriguing vehicle that defies classification. It has the streamlined nose of something sports-car-like, and the long, sweeping roofline and big wheels of a crossover, while at the rear it could be a modern hatchback in the mold of the C4.

Citroën's official position is that the C-SportLounge "captures the true essence of a twenty-first-century Grand Tourer." Whatever that might mean in practice, the concept is a dedicated four-seater that in some of its aspects shares a visual relationship with more recent Citroëns such as the C4 and C6. But, true to its role as a concept vehicle, the SportLounge is more eye-catching by way of the high waistline and aluminum detailing that adorns the exterior.

Significantly, too, it has a deep, gaping grille mouth rather than the twin chrome strips forming the double chevron logo that Citroën has been establishing as the frontal identity for its road cars.

The C-SportLounge has a gorgeous proportion: smooth, protective, and visually stimulating. The curved body shape is soft and aerodynamic and has a friendly appearance. The long arched roof begins at the front over the middle of the front wheels. Toward the rear the roofline drops at the same point as the waist rail drops and then kicks up, creating a lovely rear quarter-window style.

The huge headlamps sweep right back alongside the hood, and the aluminum treatment that runs rearward from the headlamp and up the secondary A-pillar is an unusual but extremely effective design feature. The glazed roof ensures that plenty of light enters the cabin.

The interior is more futuristic, and modeled on a fighter-plane design, with padded leather seats that envelop the occupants. Though too bold for volume production, this car is a welcome sign that adventurous design is well and truly back at Citroën.

Dacia Logan

Design	Kenneth Melville
Engine	1.6 in-line 4 gas (1.4 gas and 1.4 diesel also offered)
Power	67 kW (90 bhp) @ 5500 rpm
Torque	128 Nm (94 lb. ft.) @ 3000 rpm
Gearbox	5-speed manual
Installation	Front-engined/front-wheel drive
Front suspension	MacPherson strut
Rear suspension	Torsion beam
Brakes front/rear	Discs/drums
Front tires	185/65R15
Rear tires	185/65R15
Length	4250 mm (167.3 in.)
Width	1742 mm (68.6 in.)
Height	1525 mm (60 in.)
Wheelbase	2630 mm (103.5 in.)
Track front/rear	1466/1456 mm (57.7/57.3 in.)
Curb weight	980 kg (2160 lb.)
0–100 km/h (62 mph)	11.5 sec
Top speed	175 km/h (109 mph)
Fuel consumption	7.3 l/100 km (32.2 mpg)
CO_2 emissions	175 g/km

Although the Dacia brand is not well known outside eastern Europe, its parent—Renault—is a household name across the whole continent. Dacia, based in Romania, was taken over by Renault in the 1990s and the Logan, which was actually designed at Renault's Technocenter near Paris, was born of a major policy move to provide a back-to-basics car costing just €5000 ($6400) for emerging markets. Soon, however, the idea grew in scope, and now Renault-branded Logans are on sale in established western European markets and the model is set to be produced in seven different countries.

The Logan is a car designed to be simple to construct, operate, and maintain. Every component and system has been designed to save money yet maintain effectiveness: for example, the glass is flatter than usual so as to reduce cost and complexity. The car's major mechanical components have been carried over from existing Renault models to keep cost down and ensure dependability and easy servicing in the field. The range of engines is deliberately restricted, too.

The same applies to the body design: to start with, only a four-door sedan is offered, though a pickup and station-wagon may follow later. Buyers at this level need space, ruggedness and simplicity: for its low starting price the Logan is a very big and roomy five-seater, with a large trunk, too. Taut surfaces and crisp lines with well-defined wheel arches reinforce the impression of dependability. The bright blue Dacia emblem (or the Renault diamond) sits in the center of the grille and is one of the few items of ornamentation on the exterior of the car.

The interior is understandably simple and sensible but, much to Renault's surprise, this has not prevented the car from being successful in western Europe too—albeit with options that push it well over its original low price tag.

Dacia Logan Steppe

The Romanian brand Dacia was little known in western Europe until it was used by Renault as the platform for building and marketing the audacious 5000 Logan. That model, despite its simple design and specification, has been an unexpectedly big hit right across Europe, and its success has empowered Dacia to look at other versions such as a pickup and a station wagon.

Now, a further boost appears in the shape of the Logan Steppe, an activity wagon concept designed around the theme of snow sports and giving a strong pointer to the format of an eventual production Logan wagon.

Basing itself on an extended Logan sedan platform, the Steppe has a practical yet fun-looking wagon body that completely changes the proportion of the original sedan: it is tall and boxy, yet also stylish, and the shape has a certain chunkiness about it.

Bumper, wheel arch, and door protection give it a clear sense of robustness, and the spacious interior succeeds in distancing itself from the very downmarket sedan while still making it clear that this is a practical car as well. The interior is modern, warm, and inviting, and uses a mixture of leather and tech-feel fabrics. The dashboard has an intriguing footprint on the passenger side that echoes track marks in the snow.

The design of this car is good enough to be a new Renault, bar the front end: this has a strikingly pointed grille that is much less friendly than the rear end, which is fun and youthful, and entered by two side-hinged doors. The roof system is designed specifically for the Steppe and includes a snowboard box and lockable ski clamps. The challenge for Dacia will be to maintain the feature content and consumer appeal while at the same time staying faithful to the brand's ultralow-price ethos.

Design	Kenneth Melville
Installation	Front-engined/front-wheel drive
Brakes front/rear	Discs/discs
Length	4470 mm (176 in.)
Height	1780 mm (70.1 in.)

Dacia Logan Steppe **Concept**   81

Daihatsu Costa

Engine	0.66 in-line 3
Installation	Front-engined/all-wheel drive
Front tires	175/65R15
Rear tires	175/65R15
Length	3395 mm (133.7 in.)
Width	1475 mm (58.1 in.)
Height	1575 mm (62 in.)
Wheelbase	2390 mm (94.1 in.)
Curb weight	750 kg (1654 lb.)

As a fun leisure concept with no doors, the Daihatsu Costa could in many ways be seen as a modern interpretation of the Mini Moke or Citroën Mehari. The European urban look is no accident, as the concept was designed and built in the UK. According to Daihatsu, one of the inspirations cited in its design is that of sandals. Simple curves, lozenges, and straight lines create an innocent- and youthful-looking vehicle with a strong affinity to contemporary product design, a factor reinforced by the visible aluminum structure and the brightly colored panels.

For a car that would want to be used on beaches and off-road, it comes with an all-wheel-drive system—although the very low ground clearance would probably mean that in fact it would get stuck in no time at all.

Inside, the whole interior is wipe-down and waterproof, including the wooden deck floor with its all-weather utility. There are mesh-covered hammock-like seats with fold-down armrests that offer a minimum of security, though the high side sill still gives a measure of protection in a side-impact collision. The Costa would make an ideal rental car for warm vacation island destinations: it would certainly be an interesting alternative to the regular A-segment hatchbacks or Suzuki 4x4s on offer.

It could be argued that the world needs a car like this, though any production version would need to have clever—and, inevitably, somewhat costly—solutions to guarantee passenger safety. It will be interesting to see if Daihatsu can convince itself that there is a decent business case to build it.

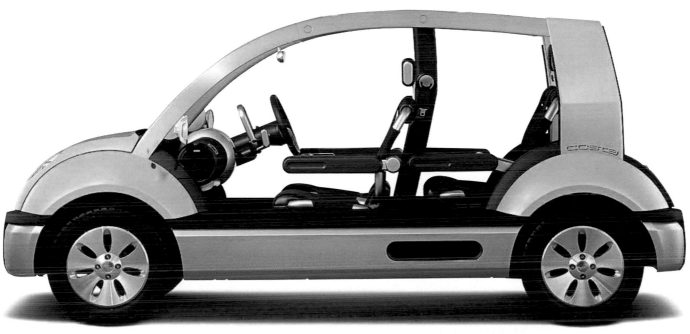

Daihatsu D-Compact 4x4

Engine	1.5 in-line 4
Power	77 kW (103 bhp) @ 6000 rpm
Torque	140 Nm (103 lb. ft.) @ 4400 rpm
Gearbox	5-speed manual
Installation	Front-engined/four-wheel drive
Front suspension	MacPherson strut
Rear suspension	Multilink
Brakes front/rear	Discs/drums
Length	4075 mm (160.4 in.)
Width	1745 mm (68.7 in.)
Height	1760 mm (69.3 in.)
Wheelbase	2580 mm (101.6 in.)
Track front/rear	1445/1480 mm (56.9/58.3 in.)
Curb weight	1230 kg (2712 lb.)
Fuel consumption	8.6 l/100 km (27.4 mpg)
CO_2 emissions	196 g/km

As manufacturers of baby SUVs go, few carmakers know more about the subject than Daihatsu, part of the Toyota group. The compact Daihatsu Terios, launched in the late 1990s, was billed as a model that would do for mini-4x4s what the Toyota RAV4 did for medium-size ones.

Now Daihatsu has shown the D-Compact 4x4 concept, a model that is being launched in a production version as the replacement for the Terios in June 2006. Like the Terios, the D-Compact is a neat little model targeted at the young and adventurous market. The front has an audacious appearance, with the large eyelike headlamps and twin circular spotlamps set low. Distinctive is the thrust-forward hood, which, says Daihatsu, incorporates a shock-absorbing structure and crushable fenders to help lessen pedestrian injuries—in line with a three-star rating in the European New Car Assessment Programme (NCAP) crash tests (three stars out of four being the most awarded so far for pedestrian safety by this independent body).

The body is raised to give useful ground clearance and make getting in and out easier. The contemporary overall feel is helped by an attractive rear-end design quite similar to that of the Suzuki Vitara. Blistered wheel arches trimmed in gray plastic help to break up the mass of the sides and make it clear that this is a 4x4 with off-road ambitions.

The interior design is somewhat disappointing, especially the cheap-looking steering wheel and the excessive use of aluminum-effect trim to break up large areas of black plastic.

The D-Compact 4x4 looks friendly and modern, and good enough to become a production model very soon. However, Daihatsu would be well advised to look again at the design and finishes of the model's interior: even at this budget end of the market there are competitors with markedly better perceived quality inside.

Daihatsu HVS

Though superficially it comes across as a competitor to the Mazda MX-5, the Daihatsu HVS claims to be something rather different: an environmentally friendly compact sports car.

The HVS's power comes from a hybrid system comprising a 1.5 liter gas engine and two electric motors, the rear motor being able to power each rear wheel independently. This makes the HVS an electrically powered four-wheel drive, giving it instant acceleration but also the added benefit of the gas engine for out-of-town performance.

On a visual level the HVS could be accused of being no more than a budget version of the MX-5; simple forms, bulging wheel arches, and the slim, nimble-looking body are all as one would expect of a small roadster. Such design touches as the headlamps and rear lamps appear to pay homage to the Toyota 2000GT of the 1970s, but do not look at home in the smoother, more modern shape; more troubling, however, is the general lack of excitement and originality.

Design has progressed in recent years and now exploits more complex forms to control the play of light on body surfaces. The HVS looks too obvious in comparison with other two-seaters—a format that, after all, is supposed to spell excitement and elegance.

In contrast to the exterior, the interior is more successful. A wraparound dashboard and well-proportioned vents and switches make it feel like an upmarket and exciting place to be. The gray carpet complements the satin aluminum console, which in turn is visually softened by the tan leather upholstery.

Hybrid cars have until now had a worthy but dull image. As more manufacturers open up to hybrid's potential for performance as well as ecological good citizenship, buyers are beginning to realize they can have excitement as well as fuel economy. And concepts like this Daihatsu are showing the way.

Engine	1.5 in-line 4 with 36 kW battery hybrid
Power	77 kW (103 bhp) @ 6000 rpm
Torque	140 Nm (103 lb. ft.) @ 4400 rpm
Gearbox	CVT
Installation	Front-engined/front-wheel drive/electric rear-wheel drive
Front suspension	MacPherson strut
Rear suspension	Torsion beam
Brakes front/rear	Discs/discs
Front tires	205/40R17
Rear tires	205/40R17
Length	3715 mm (146.3 in.)
Width	1695 mm (66.7 in.)
Height	1235 mm (48.6 in.)
Wheelbase	2235 mm (88 in.)
Fuel consumption	4.1 l/100 km (57.4 mpg)
CO_2 emissions	101 g/km

Daihatsu UFE-III

Engine	0.66 in-line 3
Gearbox	CVT
Front tires	115/65R16
Rear tires	115/65R16
Length	3395 mm (133.7 in.)
Width	1475 mm (58.1 in.)
Height	1200 mm (47.2 in.)
Wheelbase	2170 mm (85.4 in.)
Curb weight	440 kg (970 lb.)
Fuel consumption	1.38 l/100 km (170 mpg)

At the last three Tokyo Motor Shows, successive evolutions of Daihatsu's UFE concept have been unveiled. Tokyo 2005 was no exception, acting as the launch backdrop for the UFE-III—a concept that is more futuristic-looking than previous models and no longer has the appearance of a modified Daihatsu road car.

The dark canopy looks like something from a fighter plane and is extremely streamlined, while the long thin LED headlamps give a slippery impression and lie flush, well back into the fender. The canopy hinges at the front as a single large unit and opens up the cabin to display the 1+2 seating configuration. At the junction between the dark canopy and the silver body, a sinewy line runs rearward along the waistline and up over the roof in a dramatic curve. The futuristic design theme is continued through to the interior, with an instrument panel that moves up and down—an adjustment made possible by steer-by-wire technology.

With a weight of just 970 lb. and an aerodynamic drag of Cd 0.168, the fuel consumption of the tiny three-cylinder, 660 cc engine is incredible, at just 1.38 liters per 100 km, or 170 miles per gallon. This big achievement can be put down to significant engineering efforts aimed at reducing the aerodynamic drag of each external component, the development of special composite polymer body panels, the widespread use of aluminum in the vehicle structure, and new tires that further reduce rolling resistance.

UFE-III is clearly a leader in ultra-fuel-economy vehicles. It is powered by a small direct injection hybrid Atkinson engine and two electric motors. Daihatsu is obviously eager to be regarded as a leading innovator in fuel-efficient vehicles, which, longer term, could prove to be a shrewd business strategy.

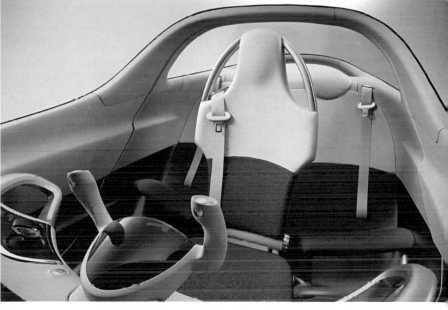

Dodge Challenger

Design	Micheal Castiglione
Engine	6.1 V8
Power	317 kW (425 bhp) @ 6000 rpm
Torque	570 Nm (420 lb. ft.) @ 4800 rpm
Gearbox	6-speed manual
Installation	Front-engined/rear-wheel drive
Front suspension	Short and long arm
Rear suspension	Short and long arm
Brakes front/rear	Discs/discs
Front tires	255/40R20
Rear tires	265/45R21
Length	5025 mm (197.8 in.)
Width	1997 mm (78.6 in.)
Height	1449 mm (57 in.)
Wheelbase	2945 mm (116 in.)
Track front/rear	1626/1654 mm (64/65.1 in.)
0–100 km/h (62 mph)	4.7 sec
Top speed	280 km/h (174 mph)

There is no better example of a design that symbolizes a past era than the Dodge Challenger muscle car. It is an automotive icon that everyone recognizes and respects. But this then raises the question, why has Dodge felt the need to remind everyone of its 1970s pony-car heritage?

One answer is the surprise success of Ford's new Mustang, a faithful reinterpretation of the car that kicked off the first pony-car craze. So perhaps Dodge, too, wants to inject spice into its present lineup by tapping into the excitement of the 1970s, when its models were more extreme and the brand had its heyday. Certainly Micheal Castiglione, principal exterior designer, believes that the original 1970s car symbolizes the most passionate era of automotive design.

So precisely have Dodge's designers reproduced the proportions and look of the original model that it is only such modern details as projector headlamps, cast-aluminum wheels, and flush glazing that reveal it as the new car. The signature side-view accent line that runs horizontally through the wheel arch and door and kicks up just forward of the rear wheel is accurately replicated, making the way the light hits the body from above very distinctive; the wide horizontal recessed forms at front and rear emphasize the car's width, again a key aspect of the original.

The interior is intentionally more modern in its design. It still mixes black and satin silver, but digital gauges, an on-board computer, and modern moulded panels bring it into the twenty-first century.

The decision to look back to go forward is perhaps the reaction of product planners playing safe in a difficult US car market. The Challenger is safer than most, for—by Dodge's own admission—it seeks to stir up emotions by correcting the imperfections of the original icon rather than by chasing innovation.

Dodge Challenger **Concept**   91

Dodge Hornet

Design	Mark Moushegian
Engine	1.6 in-line 4
Power	127 kW (170 bhp)
Torque	224 Nm (165 lb. ft.)
Gearbox	6-speed manual
Installation	Front-engined/front-wheel drive
Front suspension	MacPherson strut
Rear suspension	Semi-independent
Brakes front/rear	Discs/discs
Front tires	185/50R19
Rear tires	185/50R19
Length	3846 mm (151.4 in.)
Width	1737 mm (68.4 in.)
Height	1566 mm (61.7 in.)
Wheelbase	2534 mm (99.8 in.)
Curb weight	1409 kg (3106 lb.)
0–100 km/h (62 mph)	6.9 sec
Top speed	209 km/h (130 mph)

Presented at the 2006 Geneva show in order to gauge European attitudes toward potential new products from the American brand, the Dodge Hornet is something surprising from the US carmaker—a small hatchback, more compact than a Clio or a Punto, albeit dressed up in an aggressive rally-inspired set of sports clothes.

From the well-finished Geneva show car it was hard to tell how much of the Hornet's racy looks were wired into its basic design or whether the aggressive exterior was an extravagant party frock put on specially for the Geneva launch. Either way, the Hornet's imposing presence starts at the front with a dark menacing grille and twin stripes that run back over the hood, in well-understood racing style. Bold wheel arches with crisp creases and concave profiles in places separate the ambient light in a dramatic way. The waistline is high, giving the Hornet a strong overall look, helped by the machined-from-solid-looking sills. The rear also has a machined look, especially the sharp forms and the detailed features above the rear lamps.

Moving inside, the interior works in harmony with the exterior. Planar surfaces and regular geometric forms mix black and aluminum to striking effect. Blue-lit bars are used to divide the instrumentation gauges and help energize the dashboard still further.

The Hornet, as one would expect from its name, is certainly not easy on the eye. Instead, it is a car that shakes up the senses, a concept car designed to create enthusiasm for the Dodge brand. Its targets are Europe's youth, and in particular those following fashions in urban street culture. Parallels can be drawn with the Chrysler PT Cruiser, the Suzuki Swift, and even the Mini; your parents might not like it, but Dodge could be onto something big here.

Dodge Hornet **Concept** 93

EDAG Roadster

The EDAG Roadster was conceived to show the automotive world how EDAG, the German design and engineering company, could offer products that are very different from regular models yet are still derived from existing platforms and able to be produced at established production facilities.

The motive behind this is to help satisfy what is seen as a growing demand for niche products. In reality, however, deriving niche vehicles from volume sellers is something that has been done for years. The Mk 4 Volkswagen Golf and the New Beetle, for example, were both from the same platform, yet are strikingly different. But the practicalities of building different cars on the same production line can be complex, and it is not always very successful in practice.

Shown in bright green to attract maximum attention, the EDAG Roadster is a wedge-shaped rear-engined sports car based on the platform of the Smart Roadster, a model recently dropped—to some sadness—by the Smart company. The design is more aggressive than the Smart's, with the nose dropping right down to near ground level and ending at the sharp air splitter that directs air up through the radiator and out over the windshield. There is no roof, highlighting the fact that this design is aimed at seriously dedicated sports-car fanatics.

From a design point of view the styling is relatively simplistic—perhaps owing to the compressed timetable of this project. An example is the large fin at the back, which makes the car look unbalanced.

There are no plans to produce this car: its role is simply that of a skills demonstrator for EDAG. However, it does have a certain charm as a more extreme version of the Smart Roadster—and could even be taken seriously if any entrepreneur succeeds in restarting production of the sporty Smart.

Design	Johannes Barckmann

Ferrari 599 GTB Fiorano

Design	Pininfarina
Engine	6.0 V12
Power	456 kW (612 bhp) @ 7600 rpm
Torque	608 Nm (448 lb. ft.) @ 5600 rpm
Gearbox	6-speed manual
Installation	Front-engined/rear-wheel drive
Front suspension	Double wishbone
Rear suspension	Double wishbone
Brakes front/rear	Discs/discs
Front tires	245/40R19
Rear tires	305/35R20
Length	4666 mm (183.7 in.)
Width	1961 mm (77.2 in.)
Height	1336 mm (52.6 in.)
Wheelbase	2751 mm (108.3 in.)
Track front/rear	1689/1618 mm (66.5/63.7 in.)
Curb weight	1688 kg (3722 lb.)
0–100 km/h (62 mph)	3.7 sec
Top speed	330 km/h (205 mph)
Fuel consumption	21.3 l/100 km (11 mpg)
CO_2 emissions	490 g/km

The Ferrari 599 GTB Fiorano is the latest in a long line of classic V12 front-engined two-seater sports cars, following in the tire tracks of such heroes as the 275 GTB, the Daytona and, most recently, the 575 Maranello. The new car is named after the circuit Ferrari uses to hone the performance of both racing and road cars, and 599 loosely refers to the engine size of 6 liters. Self-evidently, the 599 has been designed to incorporate the very latest developments in Ferrari technology from both road and track, and—naturally—to provide intense driving pleasure.

Designed by Pininfarina, the 599's body is not as extreme as the mid-engined Enzo's. Unusually for a Ferrari, however, it does not look as sophisticated in two-dimensional photographs as it does in the reality of three dimensions.

There are rounded forms and a wide crosshatched meshed grille up front; the long hood has twin vents and a wide central power ridge. There are crisp lines too, noticeably those running over the front and rear fenders. Vents to the front and rear of the doors help to cool the huge engine and brakes. The stance is long, lithe, and potent.

Inside the cabin, leather and carbon fiber are mixed to create a sporty yet comfortable environment for two. Nevertheless, man-made carbon fiber and organic leather hide never quite sit comfortably together, creating in the Fiorano some ambiguity over whether this is a racing car or a road car.

In terms of technology there are the new superfast F1-inspired gearbox, the F1-Trac vehicle dynamics system, and a clever magnetorheological fluid suspension system that constantly fine-tunes the damping and stiffness characteristics.

Overall, the 599 GTB Fiorano is gorgeously proportioned and much more attractive than the Enzo. Whether it will one day be seen as a great Ferrari, however, is another matter.

Fiat Grande Punto

Design	Italdesign
Engine	1.9 in-line 4 diesel (1.3 diesel and 1.2 and 1.4 gas also offered)
Power	97 kW (130 bhp) @ 4000 rpm
Torque	280Nm (206 lb. ft.) @ 2000 rpm
Gearbox	6-speed manual
Installation	Front-engined/front-wheel drive
Front suspension	MacPherson strut
Rear suspension	Torsion beam
Brakes front/rear	Discs/discs
Front tires	205/45R17
Rear tires	205/45R17
Length	4030 mm (158.7 in.)
Width	1680 mm (66.1 in.)
Height	1490 mm (58.7 in.)
Wheelbase	2510 mm (98.8 in.)
Track front/rear	1473/1466 mm (58/57.7 in.)
Curb weight	1205 kg (2657 lb.)
0–100 km/h (62 mph)	9.5 sec
Top speed	200 km/h (124 mph)
Fuel consumption	5.8 l/100 km (40.6 mpg)
CO_2 emissions	154 g/km

The Grande Punto is the latest in a long line of big-selling Fiat family models, many of which have been significant design milestones in the small-car class. But as its name suggests, the Grande Punto is one up on the regular Punto in terms of size: indeed, the two will continue to sell in parallel for some while.

The skill of the Grande Punto's design is that it looks both compact and very sporty, yet is in fact surprisingly large and roomy inside. And, like the new Clio, it raises the size and the stakes in the supermini class.

The bold exterior has the flair one would expect from an Italdesign-Giugiaro-influenced design. Most distinctive of all is the elegant, elongated, and almost sports-car-like nose, with a shallow central grille and long, faired-in headlamps. Bold proportions and clever, subtle curves give it a Mediterranean feel, with feature lines that run along the doors and gain in intensity as they travel rearward toward the tailgate. Flanked by high-set taillamps mounted on the C-pillars, the tailgate itself is a wide body-colored panel void of unnecessary detail.

The dynamic look is skillfully reinforced by the subsidiary grille set in the front apron below the main grille, and through the side-sill forms that draw the eye to the ten-spoke wheels. It all adds up to a convincing sporty hatchback that has great appeal.

The interior, by comparison, is less distinctive in design; quality, however, marks a useful step up from Fiat's past efforts. Characterful small cars such as the 127, the Uno, and the Punto are what put Fiat on the map for a whole generation of European buyers—and, true to tradition, the new Grande Punto is a strong enough design to help pull the company out of its present business difficulties.

Oltre Fiat

Engine	3.0 in-line 4
Power	138 kW (185 bhp) @ 3700 rpm
Torque	456 Nm (336 lb. ft.) @ 1800 rpm
Gearbox	6-speed automatic
Installation	Front-engined/four-wheel drive
Brakes front/rear	Discs/discs
Front tires	315/40R26
Rear tires	315/40R26
Length	4870 mm (191.7 in.)
Width	2200 mm (86.6 in.)
Height	2050 mm (80.7 in.)
Wheelbase	3230 mm (127.2 in.)
Curb weight	7000 kg (15,432 lb.)
Top speed	130 km/h (81 mph)

The Oltre Fiat is something no one would have expected from Fiat: fittingly, its name is best translated as "beyond Fiat." As Italy's equivalent of the huge American Hummer terrain-crusher, it is totally untypical of a company most famous for its very small cars—but that is precisely what Fiat intended.

For the Oltre Fiat, the company turned to its commercial-vehicle arm Iveco and used as a starting point the military Light Multirole Vehicle that has won the Future Command and Liaison Vehicle contract for the British Army, as well as being chosen by the Italian Army. For Fiat, the rugged structure and bulletproof mechanicals of the military vehicle were a good guarantee of total integrity for the Oltre.

Though functionally based, the shaping of the Oltre Fiat manages to add an odd element of style to a set of solid, very square, and very straight surfaces. The flat windshield is shrouded by a heavy hood, and the inset square windows and the hard, boxy panels all spell armor-plated protection, but the white paintwork, blue glass, and chromed wheels help to soften the aggressive intent that the pseudomilitary profile would otherwise convey.

The brute-force functionality is emphasized by the huge clearances around the wheels, something that makes the body appear perched on top of the chassis. This clearance allows the Oltre Fiat to navigate through 85 cm (35 in.) fords, and Fiat claims that thanks to its three automatically locking differentials the vehicle can cope with lateral gradients of up to 40% and longitudinal gradients of 80%.

The interior design is both surprising and incongruous: a mixture of blue and white, and with a small sports steering wheel dwarfed by the massive center console.

The Oltre Fiat seems such a far cry from Fiat's car designs that it is difficult to see how consumers will be able to connect the two—other than to start to associate the qualities of toughness, durability, and adventure with the brand.

Fiat Sedici

Design	Italdesign
Engine	1.9 in-line 4 diesel (1.6 gas also offered)
Power	90 kW (120 bhp) @ 4000 rpm
Torque	280 Nm (206 lb. ft.) @ 2050 rpm
Gearbox	6-speed manual
Installation	Front-engined/front- or all-wheel drive
Front suspension	MacPherson strut
Rear suspension	Torsion beam
Brakes front/rear	Discs/discs
Front tires	205/60R16
Rear tires	205/60R16
Length	4110 mm (161.8 in.)
Width	1760 mm (69.3 in.)
Height	1620 mm (63.8 in.)
Wheelbase	2500 mm (98.4 in.)
Track front/rear	1495/1495 mm (58.9/58.9 in.)
Curb weight	1350 kg (2976 lb.)
Top speed	180 km/h (112 mph)
Fuel consumption	6.6 l/100 km (35.6 mpg)
CO_2 emissions	174g/km

Working in partnership with Japan's Suzuki, Fiat has been able to respond quickly to the growing market for compact 4x4s and has launched the Sedici—effectively Fiat's version of the Suzuki-developed SX-4. Both models are built at Suzuki's extensive Magyar Suzuki plant in Hungary.

The Sedici was designed at Italdesign in Turin and is an undeniably attractive car. Its cues are more those of a friendly family model than a macho SUV: it could easily pass for one of the currently fashionable tall hatchbacks such as the Opel Meriva or VW Golf Plus. The deep front grille leads down to an aluminum protection tray, the headlamps twist up and rearward to give a cheerful glow. A deep black plastic band runs around the car and, when viewed from the side, gives the Sedici a two-tier sandwich look.

Italdesign has managed to create a lot of interest along the side; the daylight opening line drops through the front door, creating enough space for a separate front quarter-light glass, and the angled upward line to the base of the screen is unusual. The upper pillars are black, working in harmony with the lower black trim. The rear corner of the cabin has dark wraparound glass that continues into the tailgate screen. The designers have been careful to use enough glass in the upper architecture to make the car visually light enough, but not so much that it begins to look flimsy. The rear lines are mostly horizontal to fit in with Fiat's design language; aluminum roof bars tie in with the front and rear skidplates.

Designed to compete in the segment below the Toyota RAV4, the Sedici—which means sixteen (or 4x4)—is the first crossover-like SUV in the compact class and could prove an important turnaround model for Fiat.

Fisker Coachbuild Latigo CS

Design	Henrik Fisker
Engine	5.0 V10 (4.8 V8 also offered)
Power	373 kW (500 bhp) @ 7750 rpm
Torque	521 Nm (384 lb. ft.) @ 6100 rpm
Gearbox	7-speed manual
Installation	Front-engined/rear-wheel drive
Front suspension	Double wishbone
Rear suspension	Multilink
Brakes front/rear	Discs/discs
Front tires	255/33R20
Rear tires	335/30R20
Length	4793 mm (188.7 in.)
Width	1895 mm (74.6 in.)
Height	1369 mm (53.9 in.)
Wheelbase	2779 mm (109.4 in.)
Curb weight	1710 kg (3770 lb.)
0–100 km/h (62 mph)	4.6 sec
Top speed	249 km/h (155 mph)

Fisker Coachbuild was founded at the start of 2005 by Henrik Fisker and Bernhard Koehler, two former executives who had previously worked at BMW, Ford, and Aston Martin. Constrained in what they could achieve within these large organizations, they have taken a bold step to create a new company offering coachbuilt cars direct to consumers. Initially at least, the new models are based on existing vehicles. In the case of the Latigo CS, the BMW 6 Series coupé provides the technical hardware beneath the skin.

With the Latigo, Fisker has aimed at a more exclusive car than the 6 Series on which it is based. A higher-priced car must look more exclusive, and Fisker has defined this look as dynamic, sculptural, and exotic. The result is a car with the perceived value of an Aston Martin coupled with still greater exclusivity. In terms of its proportions the car is similar to the 6 Series, but the detailing is crisper and the body mass of the car is much sleeker and more streamlined. The headlamps have piercing eyes and the black void for a grille looks rather menacing, as well as suggestive of the power that lurks beneath. Along the side there is a single horizontal crease line that leads through to the rear lamps. At the back the rear lamps seem to peer from under the trunk lid.

The interior looks less resolved, with quite simplistic surfaces compared to the exterior; with more time this can no doubt be developed. The Fisker Coachbuild team must have done its research: it is no surprise that the operation is based in California, where there is real hunger for this type of exclusive car. Yet by launching the designs at Frankfurt, Fisker also suggests that it is looking to be a global brand rather than restricting itself to the United States.

Ford Edge

Design	Doyle Letson
Engine	3.5 V6
Power	186 kW (250 bhp) @ 6250 rpm
Torque	326 Nm (240 lb. ft.) @ 4500 rpm
Gearbox	6-speed automatic
Installation	Front-engined/front-wheel drive
Front suspension	MacPherson strut
Rear suspension	Four-link
Brakes front/rear	Discs/discs
Front tires	235/65R17
Rear tires	235/65R17
Length	4717 mm (185.7 in.)
Width	1925 mm (75.8 in.)
Height	1702 mm (67 in.)
Wheelbase	2824 mm (111.2 in.)
Track front/rear	1656/1648 mm (65.2/64.9 in.)
Curb weight	1859 kg (4098 lb.)

In a world of generic SUVs, the new Edge from Ford brings a breath of fresh air. More crossover than traditional SUV, it is built on a unitary car platform rather than a heavy truck chassis, and its fresh silhouette—similar to that of a BMW X5, perhaps—bears this out.

The Edge is clean, smooth, and well proportioned, yet it is also able to carry an unmistakable American identity with its bold, three-bar Ford house-style chrome grille. The dynamic look of the Edge comes not only from its proportions but also from its high daylight opening line: the roof itself is made completely from glass, and incorporates a large opening panel—the first vehicle in its class to do so. From the rear the Edge looks very sporty, with its forward-leaning rear screen, crisp square lines, and neat roof spoiler. The taillamps sit right on the corners to allow for the largest tailgate possible. Wide-set wheels, placed close to each corner and set in large, well-defined wheel arches, give the Edge a sporty, firmly planted look.

Ford has designed in a large gray band that runs around the lower edges of the car to reduce the visual height of the body and to give the bodywork protection from stone chippings.

Moving inside, the Edge is well laid out, using sharp lines to continue the dynamic theme. The rear seats can quickly be folded to create a large luggage area, giving useful flexibility, but the perceived quality of the trim falls short of European standards. All in all, however, the Edge is a really good-looking new product. For customers who want a more dynamic vehicle with optional four-wheel drive but who want to buy American, this is the answer—especially if they are looking for a value purchase.

Ford F-250 Super Chief

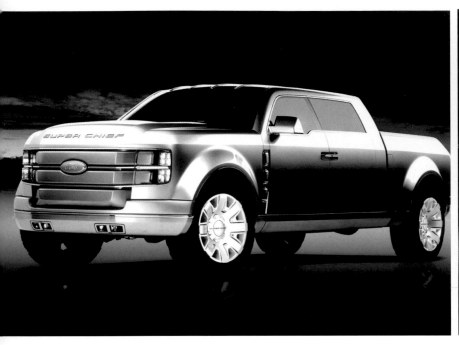

Design	J. Mays
Engine	6.8 V10
Power	231 kW (310 bhp) @ 4250 rpm
Torque	577 Nm (425 lb. ft.) @ 3250 rpm
Gearbox	5-speed automatic
Installation	Four-wheel drive
Front suspension	Twin-coil monobeam
Rear suspension	Live axle
Brakes front/rear	Discs/discs
Front tires	R24
Rear tires	R24
Length	6731 mm (265 in.)
Width	2343 mm (92.2 in.)
Height	1999 mm (78.7 in.)
Wheelbase	4445 mm (175 in.)
Track front/rear	2032/2032 mm (80/80 in.)

The F-250 Super Chief is the most extreme expression to date of an already extreme American automotive art form—the big, butch pickup.

At 6.7 meters (22 ft.) long it is hugely imposing; it has 24-inch wheels and stands 2 meters (6 ft. 6 in.) tall, giving it enormous presence. Apart from the overall dimensions, adding to the imposing look are the very high waistline, the even higher hood, and the boxiness of the proportions; the massive triple horizontal girders of the grille reinforce this. Appropriately, the inspiration for the frontal design came from the Atchison, Topeka, and Santa Fe Railway's Super Chief locomotive, say the truck's designers.

Yet the Super Chief is far removed from the familiar workhorse truck: as luxury, go-anywhere transport it has something of the feel of a Range Rover about it. The rear load bed has a wooden planked floor with raised metal strips, so again this comes across as a vehicle that places extravagance and excess above practicality and durability.

The interior is trimmed in brown leather and American walnut, and the distinctive square dials have a decidedly retro feel to their shaping. This mix of old with new is very interesting and creates an exciting look that is new to Ford. There is vast space for the rear-seat passengers, who benefit also from pop-up footstools when added relaxation is needed; access is eased by rear doors hinged at their rear edges.

Nevertheless, the Super Chief is not just about boldness: there is innovation too, in the shape of the world's first "Tri-Flex" fuel engine, which runs on ethanol, hydrogen, or gas; the massive V10 is topped by a dragster-style supercharger.

As a PR exercise the Super Chief is probably money well spent, given the fondness of the American press for the latest and largest new cars; as a design study it is both interesting and well resolved.

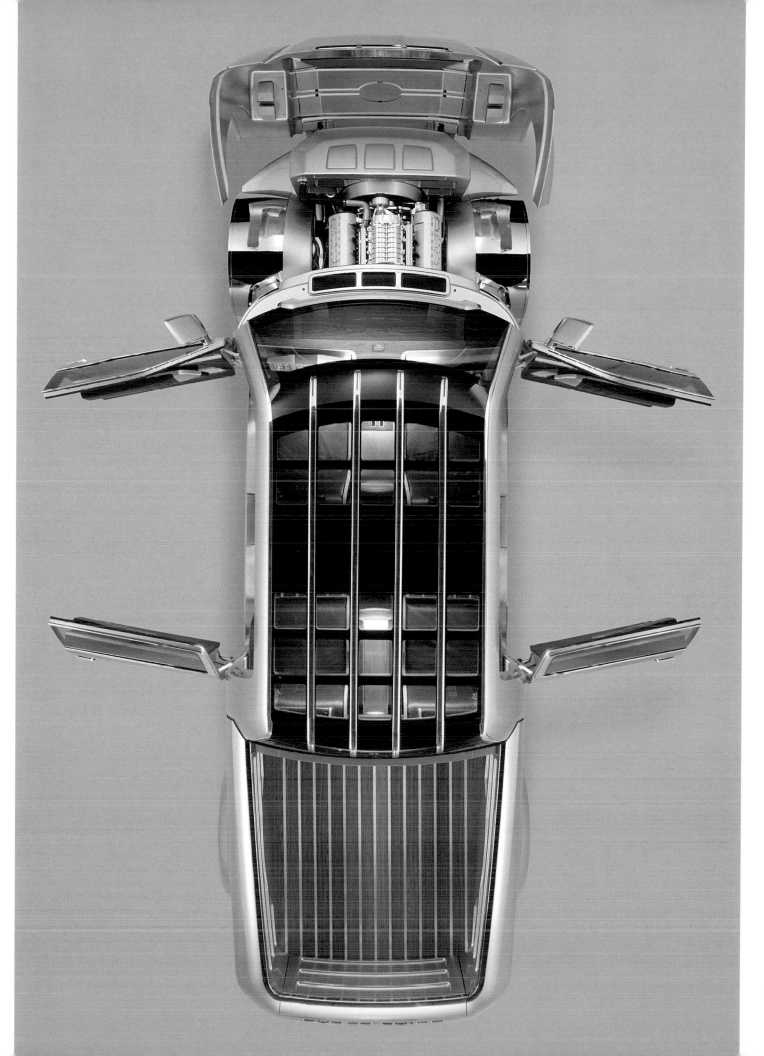

Ford Galaxy

Design	Martin Smith
Engine	2.0 gas (1.8 and 2.0 diesel also offered)
Power	108 kW (145 bhp) @ 6000 rpm
Torque	190 Nm (140 lb. ft.) @ 4500 rpm
Gearbox	6-speed manual
Installation	Front-engined/front-wheel drive
Front suspension	MacPherson strut
Rear suspension	Semitrailing arm
Brakes front/rear	Discs/discs
Front tires	215/60R16
Rear tires	215/60R16
Length	4820 mm (189.8 in.)
Width	1884 mm (74.2 in.)
Height	1764 mm (69.4 in.)
Wheelbase	2850 mm (112.2 in.)
Track front/rear	1578/1600 mm (62.1/63 in.)
Curb weight	1697 kg (3741 lb.)
0–100 km/h (62 mph)	10.9 sec
Top speed	193 km/h (120 mph)
Fuel consumption	8.2 l/100 km (28.7 mpg)
CO_2 emissions	197 g/km

The 2006 Galaxy gives just a small nod to Ford's new "kinetic design" philosophy. The new car replaces the multiseater people-carrier that has been a familiar part of the landscape for many years. As such, it responds with crisper and much more modern styling, but is not so different as to risk alienating old customers. Ford's SAV concept, previewed a year earlier and featured in *Car Design Yearbook 4*, is similar in size to the Galaxy but will become the sportier addition to the Ford lineup when it is added later in 2006. This leaves the Galaxy as the more practical model, focusing on comfort, space, and flexibility.

Visually the Galaxy is a large monospace vehicle just like the old model, with the hood and windshield running straight to the roof with its multiple glass panels. The high waistline and roof are complemented by the high 'command' seating position for all passengers—a powerful selling point among today's customers. The crisp feature lines and sharp corner details give the Galaxy plenty of visual energy, a useful antidote to the general image of people-carriers as worthy but dull vehicles that no one looks forward to driving.

Well-defined wheel arches draw the eye down to the wheels to give the whole vehicle a more planted stance on the road; at the front, the distinctive sharp headlamps feature a moving halogen system whereby the bulb swivels by up to 12 degrees to help navigate corners on tight country roads. From the rear view, the five-sided taillight units are similarly distinct features.

Inside, technical colors (shades of gray) mix with a wood-veneered panel on the passenger side. The effect avoids van overtones and is deliberately carlike, with a conventional hooded instrument cluster in front of the driver and a standard center-tunnel position for the gear lever.

Ford Iosis

Recent Fords such as the Fusion and the new Focus have been criticized for having boring exteriors—but such criticism is instantly swept away by the dramatic Iosis concept.

Unveiled at the 2005 Frankfurt show by incoming design director Martin Smith, the Iosis is intended to signal a whole new design direction—the so-called "kinetic design" philosophy—that will inspire future models from the company. And judging by the Iosis, the results promise to be remarkable.

The Iosis has the lithe, low stance of a coupé but is in fact a four-door sedan, possibly even a future Mondeo. It looks powerful and muscular, with striking trapezoid air intakes below the front bumper and a strong shoulder line that rises through the rear door. Along the sides there are complex forms and undercut lines that run through the doors, playing with the light in the way an Alfa, rather than a Ford, more usually might.

The swept-back headlamps sit in recessed shoulders ahead of blistered wheel arches that could have been lifted from a design of Mazda, Ford's Japanese stablemate. Gorgeous 20-inch wheels fill the large wheel arches, which themselves have shapes that echo the front air intakes. The Iosis uses the rising curve as a common feature, for the top of the headlamps, for the daylight opening line, and at the base of the doors.

Twin gullwing doors on each side are eye-catching in themselves but also provide a good view of the radical interior. Bathed in gray with bright orange trim, the interior stirs the senses. The air vents mimic the shape of a jet fighter's afterburners, and there is an innovative electroluminescent foil lighting concept.

If the Iosis is indeed the template for Ford's future European design, car buyers will have every reason to be very excited indeed.

Design	Martin Smith and Andrea di Buduo

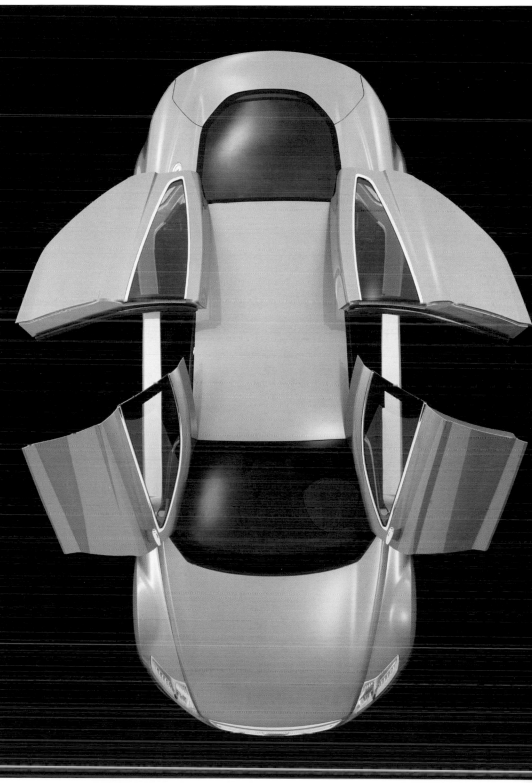

Ford Reflex

Design	Freeman Thomas
Engine	1.4 diesel in-line 4 and twin electric motors
Power	116 kW (155 bhp) @ 6000 rpm
Torque	175 Nm (129 lb. ft.) @ 4000 rpm
Gearbox	6-speed manual
Installation	Front-engined/all-wheel drive
Front suspension	Double A-arm
Rear suspension	Double A-arm
Brakes front/rear	Discs/discs
Front tires	R20
Rear tires	R20
Length	3958 mm (155.8 in.)
Width	1786 mm (70.3 in.)
Wheelbase	2548 mm (100.3 in.)
Track front/rear	1516/1506 mm (59.7/59.3 in.)
Fuel consumption	3.6 l/100 km (65 US mpg)

Car designers often try to convey the sense of an athlete's muscles as a way of humanizing their designs and building a sense of energy into sculptural forms. The Ford Reflex, a compact sports coupé boasting strong environmental credentials—including sound insulation made from recycled Nike running shoes— is a case in point.

The inswept cant rails at the rear of the roof create plenty of opportunity for sculptural forms over the rear wheels, giving the Reflex a strong-haunched look. The front of the car is rounded and smooth, with a three-bar grille made from extruded matt aluminum and L-shaped headlamps of which the horizontal elements are solar panels that deliver energy to the hybrid system and store it for the headlamps to use after dark. The rising waistline at the B-pillar creates a strong visual identity and is central to the name Reflex.

The concept has remarkable rear-hinged butterfly doors, made possible by the large tumblehome of the door glass. As well as the solar-panel-powered headlamps, technologies include inflatable rear safety belts that reduce the risk of chest injuries, and of course a novel hybrid powertrain that unites contemporary turbodiesel engineering with the latest hybrid control systems.

The interior has a young feel to it, with mesh-covered seats that encourage airflow, save weight, and take up less space. With no wood or leather in sight, it is a truly modern treatment, warm and cool colors replacing more traditional dark shades. The pop-up instrument cluster and cabin controls light up in a cool blue powered by light-emitting diodes.

The Reflex is part of Ford's campaign to prove to North American consumers that small can indeed be big: it is attractively conceived, engineered, and executed, and shows how sustained investment in design can lead to a rethink of what is possible.

Ford S-Max

Engine	2.5 in-line 5 (2.0, and 1.8 and 2.0 diesel, also available)
Power	162 kW (217 bhp)
Torque	320 Nm (236 lb. ft.)
Installation	Front-engined/front-wheel drive
Brakes front/rear	Discs/discs
Length	4768 mm (187.7 in.)
Width	1854 mm (73 in.)
Height	1607 mm (63.3 in.)

A year after Ford's sporty SUV concept was shown under the name SAV, the company has launched the production version of the car, bearing the name S-Max.

The "Max" label gives a perhaps misleading clue to the model's positioning; it is much more than just a taller cousin to the Mondeo, as the Focus C-Max is to the standard Focus. The S-Max sits above the Mondeo, but this time there is also the Galaxy SUV at the top of the lineup. Both the S-Max and the Galaxy are seven-seaters, but the former takes a more sporting approach in order to draw in customers who reject full-size MPVs because they believe them bulky and dull to drive.

The S-Max uses Ford's current "kinetic" design language to good effect. It is taut and dynamic, the short hood rising in an almost straight line onto the windshield, from where the roof begins to drop gradually toward the rear. Gills in the front wheel arch add a real touch of character to a car that desperately does not want to be regarded as just another MPV. The side glass is extensive, visually lengthening the car and adding to the overall dynamic look with the kickup line at the rear. Sharp body creases give the S-Max a thoroughly contemporary feel. The exterior is almost identical to the concept version, bar the chrome trim running around the side glass, which has been ditched in favor of glass black-out, while the sill and front bumper profiles have been toned down in favor of a slightly less aggressive look.

The interior is changed quite considerably from the SAV concept: it is now a more conventional Ford interior with black circular dials and an aluminum center console. Orange highlighting remains, but muted colors more acceptable to the mass market are predominant.

Honda FCX

Competition between technology leaders Toyota and Honda has always been intense—and now it extends to jostling for position as to who can develop the best fuel-cell technology. The FCX concept is actually an evolution of the Kiwami study shown in Tokyo two years earlier: visually, the side profile at the front is loosely similar, as is the wheel treatment.

In terms of proportion the FCX is one unbroken volume, with a silhouette that has forward poise and suggests luxurious, refined travel. Deliberately, the look has been kept only moderately futuristic: Honda does not want its fuel-cell technology to be thought of as relevant just for some distant future.

Underneath, the platform consists of a chassis frame encircling the three key modules needed for fuel-cell power: hydrogen tanks, battery, and motor. Because these are all packaged flat under the body, it is possible to have a flat, low floor and a low center of gravity.

At 4.7 meters (15 ft.), the FCX is a big car that will seat four in space and comfort. Because it comes laden with hidden technology that requires less input from the driver, it is possible to simplify the interior and make more space for extra-large seats to maximize comfort. Apart from driver recognition for door unlocking, technology on board includes an instrument panel that senses the driver's line of sight so as to make possible hands-free operation of audio, air conditioning, and other systems. The interior style is much more futuristic than the exterior, signaling how new technology can free designers to create new interior shapes; here, a leather-clad wing wraps from side to side to support the instrument binnacle and steering wheel. A genuinely novel touch—though one of questionable usefulness—is lights in the floor that change according to the cabin temperature.

Engine	Hydrogen fuel cell
Brakes front/rear	Discs; regenerative
Length	4720 mm (185.8 in.)
Width	1870 mm (73.6 in.)
Height	1430 mm (56.3 in.)
Wheelbase	2900 mm (114.2 in.)

Honda Sports4

Installation	Front-engined/all-wheel drive
Length	4580 mm (180.3 in.)
Width	1850 mm (72.8 in.)
Height	1360 mm (53.5 in.)
Wheelbase	2700 mm (106.3 in.)

The Sports4 is a good-looking sports sedan, loosely based on the Accord. The exterior uses crisp lines and corners to make it look contemporary and dynamic, while the bold wheel arches and high waistline combine strength and power.

The front end is curved rearward to the front wheel arches, setting the headlamps back into the hood and over the front wheels. The A-pillar is angled back steeply and, as soon as it reaches the roof, it immediately begins its descent toward the trunk lid and into a widening C-pillar. The small upper canopy also adds to the Sports4's streamlined look and gives it the appearance of having a low center of gravity.

The taut surfaces through the doors have a twisted plane running above them back over the rear wheels, creating a strong shoulder line. Honda's designers refer to this new design language as "keen edge dynamics," and its influence is clearly visible in other areas of this vehicle too. The rear end, with its high trunk lid, dramatic rear lamps, and triangular exhaust outlet, creates a visible energy even at rest. This is clearly a conceptual preview of things to come from Honda—a brand that in certain market segments could benefit from shaking off its frequently bland image. Moreover, the new language succeeds in positioning the brand more highly in relation to its competitors.

As in the larger Legend, technology abounds—from the all-wheel-drive powertrain underneath to the interior, where there is a night-vision pop-up display and each occupant has an electrically controlled skylight. The interior is in fact more futuristic than the exterior, yet also perhaps less upmarket. The steering wheel in particular lets the sophisticated impression down and, interestingly, this even extends to the use of the Honda logo in the center.

Honda WOW

The Tokyo motor show can be relied upon to produce a regular crop of truly outrageous concept vehicles—and this wild idea from Honda is a leading contender for the way-out award.

As the first concept car to consider the ultimate comfort of one's dog, the Honda WOW is unique. WOW stands for Wonderfully Open-hearted Wagon and its avowed aim is to bring dog and owner closer together when on the road.

To enable your canine friend to travel in more comfort, a number of original features have been designed. The seats can be transformed into crates in which you can safely leave a dog, and there are flexible vents that stream fresh air into the cabin, benefiting both canine and human occupants. The flat open wooden floor allows a walk-through area for the dog, although the smooth finish is likely to mean that the dog skids all over the place, not only scratching the woodwork but also, ironically, becoming a bit of a driving hazard.

Slotted glass panels low in the doors allow the dog to see the road whizzing past from its cosy home in the soothing, natural-wood interior. In the dashboard there is a special lidded compartment so that a small dog can be right by your side.

Viewed from the front there is even a dog theme in the exterior design, the headlamps set back from the nose in the way that a dog's eyes are, and the roof domed like a dog's back. Honda's idea of making a dog's life on the road more comfortable is an honorable one—but how great a driving distraction would even a contented canine in fact be?

As so many dogs do travel in cars, it would be good to see the ideas in the WOW develop into a more serious concept, perhaps within a conventional vehicle, that considers pet transportation.

Installation	Front-engined/front-wheel drive
Length	3980 mm (156.7 in.)
Width	1720 mm (67.7 in.)
Height	1680 mm (66.1 in.)
Wheelbase	2680 mm (105.5 in.)

Hyundai Accent

Engine	1.6 in-line 4
Power	82 kW (110 bhp) @ 6000 rpm
Torque	144 Nm (106 lb. ft.) @ 4500 rpm
Gearbox	5-speed manual
Installation	Front-engined/front-wheel drive
Front suspension	MacPherson strut
Rear suspension	Torsion beam
Brakes front/rear	Discs/discs
Front tires	185/65R14
Rear tires	185/65R14
Length	4280 mm (168.5 in.)
Width	1694 mm (66.7 in.)
Height	1471 mm (57.9 in.)
Wheelbase	2499 mm (98.4 in.)
Track front/rear	1471/1461 mm (57.9/57.5 in.)
Curb weight	1073 kg (2366 lb.)
Fuel consumption	8.5 l/100 km (27.7 mpg)

The new Hyundai Accent is essentially all about providing a value-for-money car that can be sold in huge numbers to people who want simple and inexpensive motoring. This is the third generation of the Accent line and, like previous models, it will be offered in five-door and three-door versions.

The outgoing model was hardly known for its style; with some crisp lines the new Accent has been just about brought up to date, but it still remains a design with little distinction. The most notable feature on the exterior is the moulding applied just below the feature line, itself high up on the car's side. This runs the length of the doors but little further, suggesting that its function is practical—as a rubbing strip— rather than aesthetic.

While the front conveys an impression little different from that of the old model, the rear does at least have a modicum of added personality. Such details as a chrome grille, large headlamps, 14-inch wheels and a variety of body-colored trim all try, albeit with limited success, to raise the look to that of a more upscale model.

New to the Accent, though commonplace in many other modern cars, are such technical features as four-wheel antilock disc brakes, electronic brake force distribution, and a total of six airbags, including side curtain airbags. Yet from an aesthetic point of view the interior is an odd mix of nicely detailed instruments and very cheap-looking trim, made worse by the color combination. The atmosphere is sadly let down by the wide range of colors and plastic components with a lot of different curvatures to them, making the interior resemble a design from the late 1970s. Surely something more of a contemporary feel would be welcomed, even by Hyundai's conservative customers.

Hyundai Accent **Production**   125

Hyundai Azera/Grandeur

Engine	3.8 V6
Power	196 kW (263 bhp) @ 6000 rpm
Torque	346 Nm (255 lb. ft.) @ 4500 rpm
Gearbox	5-speed automatic
Installation	Front-engined/front-wheel drive
Front suspension	Double wishbone
Rear suspension	Multilink
Brakes front/rear	Discs/discs
Front tires	225/60R16
Rear tires	225/60R16
Length	4895 mm (192.7 in.)
Width	1849 mm (72.8 in.)
Height	1491 mm (58.7 in.)
Wheelbase	2779 mm (109.4 in.)
Track front/rear	1580/1565 mm (62.2/61.6 in.)
Curb weight	1646 kg (3629 lb.)

Replacing the XG350, the Azera—or Grandeur, as it is known in Europe—is the third of seven new models to be launched by Hyundai within two years. The Azera is an aspiring premium sedan competing against the Buick LaCrosse, the Toyota Avalon, and the Ford Five Hundred in North America; in Europe it will have to do battle with the likes of Volvo, Lexus, BMW, and even Mercedes-Benz.

The Azera has looks that seek to raise its fairly generic style to that of a premium sedan. Key elements that make it look upper class are its grand proportions (it is almost 5 meters/16.4 ft. in length), the chrome trim running along the bumper rubbing strips, and still more chrome encircling the side glass. The thrust-forward grille is also a clear bid to project a certain brand identity. The front end is clearly Hyundai, with lamps and grille similar to those used on the Sonata.

The overall proportions are stately, with the upright grille, long upper architecture, and simple curved surfaces devoid of much decoration. The pronounced curves to the front and rear fenders are the main distinguishing feature.

Underneath the hood is a 3.8-liter V6 powerplant to ensure the Azera is not left behind. As one would expect, the interior is much more upmarket than the new budget-class Accent; the design is certainly more contemporary, with crisp lines and tighter radii featuring on all elements, but the impression is still last-generation Lexus rather than the very latest in interior thinking.

Despite not being a truly memorable design, the Azera will certainly advance the Korean manufacturer as a serious contender for quality sedan sales in the US. This it achieves by focusing on not being offensive, instead offering generic design and decent value for money.

Hyundai HCD9 Talus

Design	Joel Piaskowski
Engine	4.6 V8
Power	234 kW (340 bhp)
Gearbox	6-speed automatic
Installation	Front-engined/rear-wheel drive
Brakes front/rear	Discs/discs
Front tires	265/40R22
Rear tires	265/40R22
Length	4667 mm (183.7 in.)
Width	1932 mm (76 in.)
Height	1578 mm (62.1 in.)
Wheelbase	2800 mm (110.2 in.)
Track front/rear	1592/1640 mm (62.7/64.6 in.)

The Hyundai HCD9 Talus concept is one of a growing number that seek to stake out new crossover ground—but this time it is not the already well-trodden territory between station wagons, SUVs, and people-carriers, as in the Mercedes R-Class. Instead, Hyundai is looking to bridge the gap between two even more disparate car types—the sports car and the SUV.

Accordingly, Hyundai's design studio in California has given the HCD9 the ground clearance and off-roading ability of an SUV, yet the upper body is not at all SUV-like. Instead, it has a much racier look, with a swept-back windshield, a sleek roofline, and a forward-leaning tailgate. The effect is that of a sports coupé perched unnaturally high on a set of oversized wheels.

The exterior uses muscular surfaces and the large grille makes no apology for the 4.6-liter V8 packaged behind it. At the rear there is a powered clamshell tailgate that opens up wide to allow easy access to the trunk space. There are many different shapes, organic surfaces, and shut lines, especially at the rear, which make it difficult for the eye to rest. The coupé profile brings a clear penalty in terms of interior space: despite its bulk, the Talus is no more than a 2+2 seater.

The interior mixes rounded, organic shapes, chrome accenting, and brown chestnut leathers, chosen for their warmth; the effect will be too rich and gaudy for many. Technology inside includes wireless Internet and a night-vision system.

Hyundai appears to be exploring an opening in the market between two different vehicle types so far apart that it is hard to see the logic of combining them. This sports–SUV cross is an uneasy compromise and, rather than finding synergies between the two, it risks suffering the disadvantages of both.

Hyundai HCD9 Talus **Concept** 129

Hyundai HED-2 Genus

It is a sign of the growing maturity of Korea's Hyundai corporation that it is producing much more exciting designs; indeed, it appears to be pushing the importance of car design up its corporate priority list. Proof comes in the HED-2 Genus, the latest in a series of concepts from Hyundai design studios around the world. Exploring the potential for a new D-segment model—that is Laguna/Vectra/Audi A4 territory in Europe—the Genus is essentially a large sports wagon but, as one would expect from a show concept, it is much more flamboyant in its design than any production cars we have seen recently from Hyundai.

The energy of this design starts from the large grille and flows round to the headlamps and then along the side of the car. The headlamps, scarily long as they extend to the center line of the front wheels, lead to sharp creases and a strong concave shoulder form that runs the length of the car, exiting through the rear lamps. The ridge along the side of the hood runs up into the A-pillars and gives the HED-2 the look of a car that is strong and safe. By contrast, the central area of the hood is simple and undecorated, and helps draw the eye across to the imposing headlamps.

Large seven-spoked wheels add to the sense of dynamism that this concept seems to ooze. Along the side the upper pillars and glass run flush for a very sleek look. Inside, unusual innovations include a retractable bench seat that, claims Hyundai, can double up with a sliding deck concealed in the bumper to form an outside seating area.

The HED-2 Genus is still very conceptual, but it is exciting to watch Hyundai explore interesting shapes and more dynamic forms of expression for its potential future mainstream products.

Design	Thomas Bürkle
Engine	2.2 in-line 4 diesel
Gearbox	5-speed automatic
Installation	Front-engined/four-wheel drive
Brakes front/rear	Discs/discs
Front tires	R20
Rear tires	R20
Length	4750 mm (187 in.)
Width	1870 mm (73.6 in.)
Height	1565 mm (61.6 in.)
Wheelbase	2850 mm (112.2 in.)

Hyundai Neos-3

Hyundai's Neos-3 concept is the third in a series exploring ideas for near and medium-term future models. This time, the design is a sporty SUV in its flavor, effectively a fastback wagon crossover offering four-wheel drive.

It is unusual in its proportions, with a high, arched beltline and much emphasis placed on the heavy wheel surrounds. Viewed from the side, the visual mass leans toward the rear, thanks to an extremely fast windshield angle, which forms a continuous arc with the cant rail. This arc is reflected in the sills and echoed in the door handles. The wheel arches are slightly squared off, presumably to help with off-road tire clearances. Five surfaces meet at a point at the rear lamps, creating an unusual rearward-facing arrow effect; the result is a perhaps overcomplicated set of feature lines, especially the one that runs out toward the wheel arch.

The frontal theme uses lateral slats in the headlamps and grille, an effect echoed in the rear lamps. The front lamps have built-in advanced technology sensors that determine precrash situations through proximity control using high-frequency radar. For improved nighttime visibility, forward-facing infrared cameras extend the angle of view, and the conventional lighting system uses steering input to orient the headlamp beams.

The rear treatment is on the whole more successful than the front, the cleaner lines setting off the strong graphical design of the rear screen. Inside the vehicle, the design themes are sculptural and, says Hyundai, reflect the visual energy of the exterior. The interior is split into what Hyundai calls the excitement zone at the front, the comfort zone for the second row, and the versatile zone in the rear, where passengers or luggage can be accommodated. Overall, the Neos-3 may not be beautiful, but it is an interesting study.

Design	Chiba Design Center in Korea
Engine	4.6 V8
Gearbox	5-speed automatic
Installation	Front-engined/four-wheel drive
Length	4978 mm (196 in.)
Width	1961 mm (77.2 in.)
Height	1674 mm (65.9 in.)
Wheelbase	2985 mm (117.5 in.)

Hyundai Santa Fe

Engine	3.3 V6 (2.7 V6, and 2.2 diesel 4, also offered)
Power	172 kW (230 bhp)
Torque	299 Nm (220 lb. ft.)
Gearbox	5-speed automatic
Installation	Front-engined/front-wheel drive
Front suspension	MacPherson strut
Rear suspension	Trailing arm
Brakes front/rear	Discs/discs
Front tires	235/60R18
Rear tires	235/60R18
Length	4675 mm (184.1 in.)
Width	1890 mm (74.4 in.)
Height	1725 mm (67.9 in.)
Wheelbase	2700 mm (106.3 in.)
Track front/rear	1615/1620 mm (63.6/63.8 in.)

The existing Santa Fe has been successful in establishing Hyundai in the growing market for medium SUVs, proving a popular—and often better-value—alternative to the Toyota RAV4 and Land Rover Freelander. The job of the new model is to capitalize on that support base and bring the vehicle to a broader and more discriminating clientele.

Pretty much identical to the outgoing model in terms of its proportions and overall message, the new design succeeds in projecting a better-quality impression. The exterior is much smoother and tidier, and the integrated bumpers and wide headlamps give it a much more grown-up face. The grille is deep and strong, and makes a welcome contrast to the old model's clumsy stuck-on affair.

Crucially for brand building, the new face of the Santa Fe fits snugly with the rest of the Hyundai range, with their signature wide headlamps coming off at a diagonal from the grille. Along the side the windows now flow into one another and the pillars are blackened to make the side glass appear as a single, coherent area.

The interior is less impressive. Its mixture of synthetic-looking wood and plastic textures not only is out of keeping with modern preferences, but also fails to convey the impression of quality that is increasingly important to buyers—especially in the V6 market where the Santa Fe now competes. If, as it has recently declared, Hyundai is to migrate its position upmarket into near-premium territory, it will need to be more convincing when it comes to interior design.

The new Santa Fe is a much more harmonious and confident design than before, and thus deserves to be taken seriously by the drivers of RAV4s, Honda CR-Vs, and Land Rover Freelanders it is aimed at. A better interior would help its cause considerably.

Infiniti Coupé

The Infiniti Coupé concept shown at the Detroit show is more than just a concept: in the tradition of many Japanese companies, it is a pretty accurate preview of the next volume-production G35.

In keeping with Infiniti's position as Nissan's upscale North American nameplate, this new coupé is an evolution rather than a radical redesign of the current car. In terms of their proportions the two cars are fundamentally the same: the differences are in the detail. The surfaces on the concept, especially around the wheel arches, are more subtle. The 20-inch wheels fill the wheel arches very effectively—but this is a concept-car trick performed for maximum visual impact and is not practical on a showroom model. Smaller wheels are sure to come as standard when the G35 is launched.

The large projector headlamps sit in the wrap-over wheel arches, and wide boomerang-shaped rear lamps are not only striking features in themselves but also very effective at complementing the dynamic nature of the car. There is a full-length glass roof panel; compact cameras instead of door mirrors handle rear vision; and the door handles are hidden.

The interior has a high center console to separate the front occupants. A metallic aluminum band splits the dashboard and runs back into the doors, breaking up the sculptural shapes and visually bringing the cabin together as one space. This band is specially textured to evoke the image of traditional Japanese "Washi" paper, giving a sense of warmth and crispness. The use of violet lighting with satin aluminum gives a futuristic look to the instruments.

Whether or not this concept marks a step forward for car design, it is clearly distinctive and Nissan has been eager to retain the identity of the current model.

Design	Koji Nagano

Inovo Lirica

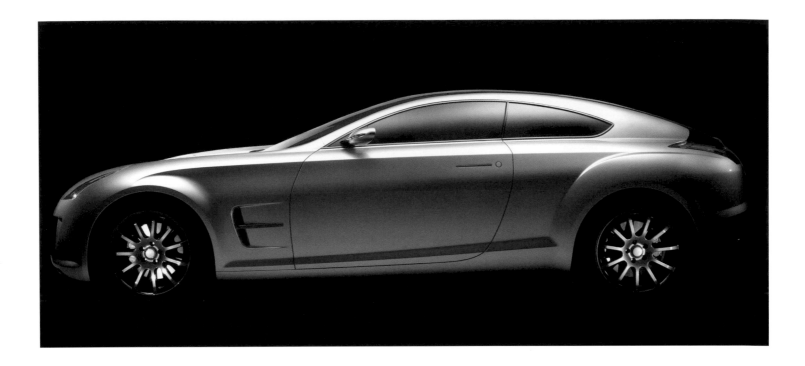

Inovo Design presented a large coupé at the 2006 Geneva show, describing it as "a new concept for a performance 2+2 coupé with an innovative man–machine interface inside." Inovo is an automotive and product design consultancy based in Turin and was set up in 1995 by Maurizio Ficcadenti; Lirica is a name that comes from the Greek word indicating song with musical accompaniment.

The design philosophy was to create a car that is thoroughly modern but also classically inspired. The result is a large and well-proportioned coupé, with great visual presence. The Lirica is graceful yet powerful, more monolithic and less balanced than a Ferrari, but not as avant-garde as a Lamborghini.

A huge gaping grille and massive wheels leave one in no doubt as to the power within, but the long arched roof extending right to the back of the car moves the visual mass rearward and serves to highlight its aggressive poise. The emphasis on the rear wheel arch suggests that most power lies there, pushing the car along from the rear. A shoulder line emanating from the front wheel arch gradually widens rearward to incorporate the rear lamp cluster in an intelligent way, neatly finishing off the high tailgate. The rear lights themselves are almost horizontal, being formed from outward extensions of the tailgate glass.

The interior is less well finished, confirming that this is a show prototype majoring in exterior style rather than engineering or cabin sophistication. Despite Inovo's claims to innovation in the man–machine interface, the Lirica in its present form is disappointing in this respect: the interior plainly does not complement the exterior.

The Lirica is intended to demonstrate how Inovo Design can help to transform products from other organizations by giving them a fresh injection of design. A smart company will recognize the potential there.

Design	Maurizio Ficcadenti
Engine	V8
Installation	Front-engined/rear-wheel drive
Brakes front/rear	Discs/discs
Length	4968 mm (195.6 in.)
Width	1976 mm (77.8 in.)
Height	1405 mm (55.3 in.)
Wheelbase	3068 mm (120.8 in.)
Track front/rear	1656/1656 mm (65.2/65.2 in.)

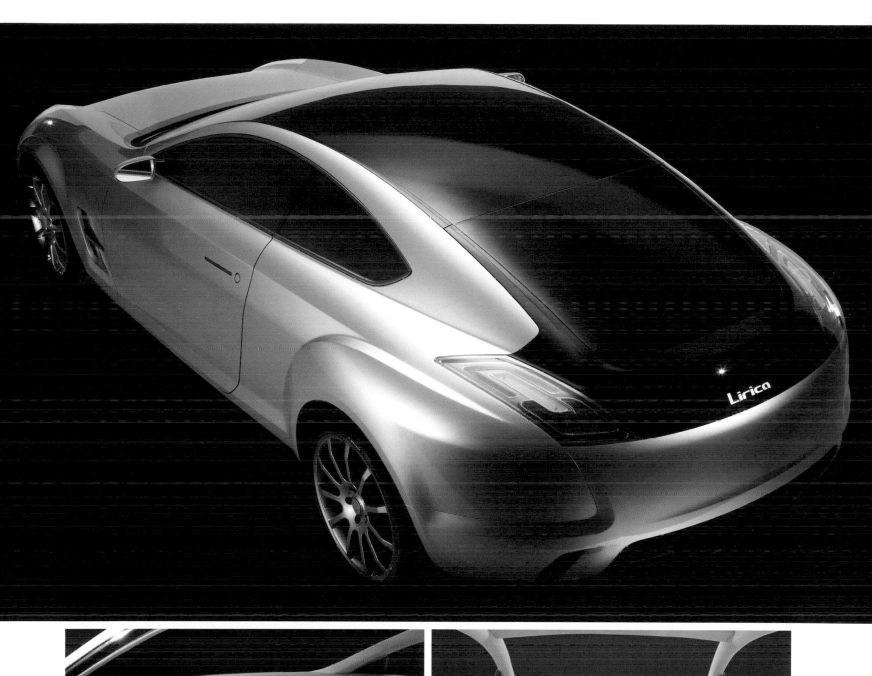

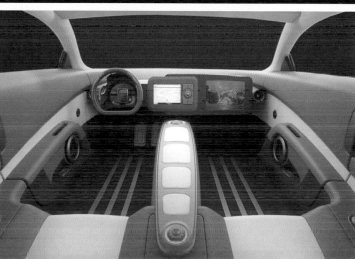

Inovo Lirica **Concept**   139

Italdesign Ferrari GG50

Design	Giorgetto Giugiaro
Engine	5.7 V12
Power	403 kW (540 bhp) @ 7250 rpm
Gearbox	6-speed automatic
Installation	Front-engined/rear-wheel drive
Front suspension	Double wishbone
Rear suspension	Double wishbone
Brakes front/rear	Discs/discs
Front tires	245/35ZR20
Rear tires	305/35ZR20
Length	4810 mm (189.4 in.)
Width	1950 mm (76.8 in.)
Height	1347 mm (53 in.)
Wheelbase	2950 mm (116.1 in.)
Track front/rear	1677/1643 mm (66/64.7 in.)

Based on the Ferrari 612 Scaglietti, the GG50 celebrates fifty years of Giorgetto Giugiaro's working in the car design industry, hence the car's initials. The GG50 is Giugiaro's expression of where Ferrari should be today, and he has had this car designed and built for himself to enjoy.

This idea is said to have come about at a meeting between Giugiaro and the president of Ferrari at the Paris Motor Show in 2004, where the Ferrari boss made only three stipulations: the design should be developed from the 612 Scaglietti, should be in keeping with Ferrari tradition, and should transmit a sense of compactness. Otherwise Giugiaro was given a free hand.

The overhangs of the 612 were reduced but the wheelbase maintained, and a reshaped roof structure carries a top-hinged tailgate at the rear. The front, too, has been subtly reshaped so that the grille appears to protrude more, an effect enhanced by the narrow headlamps that make the hood look much wider. The slight rounding of front and rear corners of the body helps to make the design look lighter and more nimble. Viewed from the side, the air vent behind the rear wheel contains feature lines that visually break up the doors and connect the front wheels to the rear. Curved quarter-window glass and curves on the rear screen are in contrast to sharp linear features lower on the body.

Inside, the fuel tank has been repositioned from behind the seats to under the floor, so that the rear seats can fold to accommodate more luggage. In other respects the interior is similar to the 612 production car, bar a new navigation system. Yet, though the GG50 is a personal reflection of a great designer's vision, it is unlikely to go down in history as a great Ferrari.

Jaguar XK

Design	Ian Callum
Engine	4.2 V8
Power	224 kW (300 bhp) @ 6000 rpm
Torque	420 Nm (310 lb. ft.) @ 4100 rpm
Gearbox	6-speed automatic
Installation	Front-engined/rear-wheel drive
Brakes front/rear	Discs/discs
Length	4791 mm (188.6 in.)
Width	2070 mm (81.5 in.)
Height	1322 mm (52 in.)
Wheelbase	2752 mm (108.3 in.)
Curb weight	1595 kg (3516 lb.)
0–100 km/h (62 mph)	5.9 sec
Top speed	250 km/h (155 mph)

The new Jaguar XK is very closely related to the Advanced Lightweight Coupé concept that was first unveiled at the Detroit Auto Show in January 2005 and was featured in *Car Design Yearbook 4*. Compared to the outgoing XK production car the new model is even sportier, with tauter surfaces that stretch over the mechanical components. In this regard it has become more similar to the epochal 1960s E-type. The hood power bulge and the tailgate all have echoes of the E-type, with the oval grille owing its roots to the racing Jaguar D-types of the 1950s.

To quote the words of Ian Callum, Jaguar's design director, "the new XK has clean lines, a purposeful stance, and exquisite proportions. We took influences from our heritage and evolved them to produce a car that is beautiful, visually fast, yet undeniably modern."

The body construction is also very modern, the structure being lightweight aluminum—just like the XJ sedan, it is riveted and epoxy-bonded together, but also features castings and extrusions in the crucial nodal points in the construction.

The sharp points to the lamps at front and rear hint at some of the styling devices currently employed by Jaguar's parent company, Ford. This need not be an inhibition as by any standard the new XK looks breathtakingly good. With its long hood, small upper cabin, and huge wheels, the car has classic coupé proportions, a near-perfect mix that makes it look both lithe and securely planted on the road.

Inside the new XK, a contemporary rich mix of finely stitched leather contrasts with a choice of high-tech trim surfaces such as metallic finishes. In a break with Jaguar tradition, the central slab of wood has made way for a more modern layout centered on a 7-inch touch screen that allows selection of all key vehicle functions.

Jeep Commander

Engine	5.7 V8 (4.7 V8 and 3.7 V6 also offered)
Power	246 kW (330 bhp) @ 5000 rpm
Torque	508 Nm (374 lb. ft.) @ 4000 rpm
Gearbox	5-speed automatic
Installation	Front-engined/four-wheel drive
Front suspension	SLA
Rear suspension	Live axle
Brakes front/rear	Discs/discs
Front tires	245/65R17
Rear tires	245/65R17
Length	4787 mm (188.5 in.)
Width	1900 mm (74.8 in.)
Height	1826 mm (71.9 in.)
Wheelbase	2781mm (109.5 in.)
Track front/rear	1589/1589 mm (62.6/62.6 in.)
Curb weight	2361 kg (5205 lb.)
Fuel consumption	17.7 l/100 km (13.3 mpg)

The new Commander celebrates nearly sixty-five years of the Jeep brand's producing sport utility vehicles. Fittingly, it will serve as the largest model in Jeep's lineup and, equally appropriately, it harks back to many classic Jeeps in the detail of its design.

As one would expect, the new model comes with the seven-slot grille, trapezoidal wheel arches, planar body surfaces, and steep windscreen and rear end that are all classic Jeep features. The headlamps are round, though encased in bright rectangular housings. Key sources of design inspiration came from Willys Station Wagons (1946–1962), the Jeep Wagoneer (1963–1991) and, lastly, the Jeep Cherokee (1984–2001).

The Commander is the first Jeep to feature three rows of seats: each row sits higher than the previous one, improving rear passengers' visibility, and the roof is stepped up to maintain headroom. There are also two skylights and a powered sunroof, ensuring that the cabin is well filled with light. At the rear the roof rack follows down the D-pillar to present two assist handles: these, and the rear step below the tailgate, are practical features that fulfil the utilitarian mantra.

Yet the very square design also presents a bulky impression, with none of the elegance of, say, the Land Rover Discovery (LR3 in North America): the screw-on wheel arches are a particularly crude attempt at a rugged look.

Inside, the dashboard features a two-tone gray color scheme, the upper half of which uses Allen-headed bolts to make the interior look securely bolted together. On upmarket models, chrome trim complements wood veneer, reminding the driver that this is not a luxury car but a road car with an off-road heritage. Using the same powertrain options and wheelbase as the Grand Cherokee, the Commander presents itself as the more utilitarian, more family-oriented option.

Jeep Compass

Engine	2.4 in-line 4 gas
Gearbox	5-speed manual
Installation	Front-engined/four-wheel drive
Brakes front/rear	Discs/discs
Front tires	255/50R19
Rear tires	255/50R19
Length	4405 mm (173.4 in.)
Width	1761 mm (69.3 in.)
Height	1631 mm (64.2 in.)
Wheelbase	2635 mm (103.7 in.)
Track front/rear	1520/1520 mm (59.8/59.8 in.)
Curb weight	1472 kg (3245 lb.)

Given the rock-solid values of the Jeep brand, it is surprising that this most all-American of companies has for so long resisted diversifying into other types of vehicle where its brand equity could be exploited to commercial advantage.

But now, with the arrival of the Compass, Jeep is at last entering the broader market—in this case that for the current buzz configuration, the crossover. With strong brand values, youthful and rugged elements, and a more affordable mass-market price point, the Compass should find a strong customer base.

Back in January 2002 Jeep showed a different Compass as a concept, which was much more of a sporty off-roader, with a neat, rounded profile and only three doors. In 2005, a further concept was shown—and this forms the basis for this final production model. Today's Compass remains true to Jeep's signature design cues such as the seven-slot grille and round headlamps, but apart from these details it would be hard to recognize it as a Jeep.

The reason is that it is built on a car platform rather than a tall off-road chassis; it is in fact the sister model to the Dodge Caliber, also reviewed in *Car Design Yearbook 5*, and has a transverse engine and a tacked-on four-wheel-drive system. Power units will include Jeep's 2.4-liter gas and 2.0-liter diesel engines coupled with a CVT transmission.

Trevor Creed, Jeep's chief designer, describes the Compass as "an all-new kind of Jeep." It certainly is. This latest evolution has five doors and is longer than the 2002 concept, as well as being more practical. The final Compass has been toned down slightly from the earlier concept versions but still retains enough ruggedness to be considered a true Jeep. One thing is for sure, however: there will be plenty of potential Jeep buyers eager to find out whether a car-derived platform can really deliver the authentic Jeep values they crave.

Jeep Patriot

In terms of size, the Jeep Patriot is similar in many respects to the Compass concept, and both were unwrapped at the same time—at the 2005 Frankfurt show. Both are based on the same platform, too. But the aim of the Patriot is somewhat different, as it is targeting a different market sector by being more utilitarian in style. It is immediately recognizable as a classic Jeep, for a start.

Higher ground clearance gives plenty of space between the tires and body, something important for greater wheel articulation in serious off-road driving. Additionally, the Patriot's more upright stance suggests a more practical off-road design than the lower-riding Compass, which has firmer suspension to match its road-car ambitions.

Pronounced wheel arches, an upright windshield making a definite corner to the roof panel, horizontal cant rails, and recessed square side windows: these are all features typical of the traditional Jeep. But in contrast to Jeep's much larger and more powerful models such as the Liberty and the Cherokee, the Patriot—like the Compass—is planned for a global market. Essential, therefore, is a choice of 2.4-liter and 2.0-liter diesel power options.

The Patriot at the Frankfurt show was painted armor green, with black accents and dark-tinted windows—a fitting color scheme for a practically oriented vehicle. Together with the strong horizontal shoulder line that runs right through from the headlamps to the taillamps, this helps to give it the look and feel of an authentic 4x4 with rugged credentials.

The Patriot is only one of a large number of recent concepts presented by Jeep: each explores subtly different ground in bringing the Jeep message to a broader public. This model is closer to the core of what the Jeep brand currently stands for, so expect to see its influence in forthcoming volume production models.

Front tires	235/65R17
Rear tires	235/65R17
Length	4412 mm (173.7 in.)
Width	1755 mm (69.1 in.)
Height	1666 mm (65.6 in.)
Wheelbase	2634 mm (103.7 in.)
Track front/rear	1519/1519 mm (59.8/59.8 in.)

Jeep Wrangler

Engine	3.8 V6
Power	153 kW (205 bhp) @ 5200 rpm
Torque	325 Nm (240 lb. ft.) @ 4000 rpm
Gearbox	6-speed manual
Installation	Front-engined/four-wheel drive
Front suspension	Live axle
Rear suspension	Live axle
Brakes front/rear	Discs/discs
Front tires	225/75R16
Rear tires	225/75R16
Length	3881 mm (152.8 in.)
Width	1872 mm (73.7 in.)
Height	1801 mm (70.9 in.)
Wheelbase	2423 mm (95.4 in.)
Track front/rear	1572/1572 mm (61.9/61.9 in.)
Curb weight	1706 kg (3761 lb.)

The Wrangler is the modern product that is closest to the original wartime Jeep, which is now sixty-five years old: fittingly, even in its latest incarnation, the renewed Wrangler comes across as one of the most familiar vehicles on—and off—the road. If there was any vehicle the design of which was inseparable from its name, then this is it. The strength of the Wrangler is that this is precisely what people first think of when the Jeep brand is mentioned.

Despite having been subject to umpteen revisions, the Wrangler remains cool and iconic; it has a no-nonsense, honest design, one that is function-led. The distinctive styling comes as a result of planar surfaces, boxy proportions, and plastic wheel arches, all of which symbolize basic functionality rather than design to create some other emotion. The off-road ability of the Wrangler is ensured by generous ground clearance and short overhangs: even the sill is short, allowing the chassis rails and suspension arms to be exposed on view from the side.

The Wrangler's core values of freedom, adventure, mastery, and authenticity are clearly retained. The classic must-have features of the round headlamps, seven-slot grille, trapezoidal wheel cutouts, and exposed forged door hinges are all in place. Jeep maintains that its Wrangler customers are of virtually any age: what characterizes them, says Jeep, is that they are all adventurous outdoor people seeking excitement, physical challenge and freedom.

The new model, slated for launch during the autumn of 2006 and built at the Chrysler assembly plant in Toledo, Ohio, has moved from the classic straight-6 engine to a more modern V6. Its dimensions are slightly larger than the old model and the interior is more spacious, but for most buyers these details are irrelevant—what they are interested in is the iconic concept.

Karmann SUC

Design	Jörg Steuernagel
Engine	4.4 V8
Power	235 kW (315 bhp)
Gearbox	6-speed automatic
Installation	Front-engined/all-wheel drive
Brakes front/rear	Discs/discs
Front tires	295/45R22
Rear tires	295/45R22
Length	4638 mm (182.6 in.)
Width	2180 mm (85.8 in.)
Height	1750 mm (68.9 in.)
Wheelbase	2820 mm (111 in.)
Track front/rear	1649/1695 mm (64.9/66.7 in.)
Curb weight	2634 kg (5807 lb.)

The German engineering, manufacturing, and roof systems specialist Karmann joined up with chassis and transmissions expert ZF to produce this concept for the 2005 Frankfurt Motor Show, with the intention of displaying each company's expertise—and showing solutions that might be attractive to mainstream carmakers.

Karmann was conscious that women were an essential factor in the SUV boom, in part because they especially appreciated the additional protection afforded by the larger vehicle. Combining high levels of passenger protection with the appeal of open-top motoring thus seemed a good idea, leading Karmann to coin the phrase "Sport Utility Cabrio" for this latest niche in car design.

From a styling standpoint the strong, sharp features of the SUC make it immediately eye-catching enough to hold one's attention, though it will not ever be remembered as the most beautiful piece of automotive design. This concept is of course more about the technical partnership between the two companies, and ZF showcases its latest electronic chassis control system, which co-ordinates damper settings, stability protection, and antilock brakes to give better driving comfort, higher safety, and a reduction in vibration.

Karmann's contribution is no less innovative. As the world moves away from soft-tops toward folding hard roofs, Karmann has chosen to develop what is by far the largest fully automatic powered soft-top in the world. At 4 square meters (43 sq. ft.) it spans both the occupant and the luggage compartments, something that would have been impossible with rigid roof sections.

Karmann and ZF see the US and western Europe as offering the largest sales potential for a vehicle like the SUC. All Karmann now needs is a carmaker to build it—or at least the innovative roof concept—into a mainstream product plan.

Kia cee'd

Design	Gregory Guillaume
Installation	Front-engined/front-wheel drive
Brakes front/rear	Discs/discs
Front tires	265/30R19
Rear tires	265/30R19

The cee'd, pronounced "seed," is an important model for Kia. Launched at the 2006 Geneva show, it is based on the forthcoming new C-segment model that Kia will be building from December 2006 at its first-ever European assembly plant, in Slovakia. With its brand-new production facility Kia will be looking to expand its model lineup, increase its volumes, and exploit the potential of the platform. The new range will be central in this strategy.

The cee'd concept is clearly a dynamic hatch with performance aspirations; its large wheels and deep front bumper are evidence enough. The pronounced shoulder line through the doors gives it visual strength and solid looks, despite a rather out-of-place-looking depression at the base of the doors.

The rear is unusual and impressive, too: large, triangular rear lights sweep outward to meet the side feature line at their apexes, while the top points of the lights rise to blend with the dark rear window. In side profile the window graphic is highly distinctive, with tiny triangular quarter-lights set high on the C-pillars, following the steep upswing of the window baseline.

Kia has been eager to highlight its European influences and the fact that this car is a creation of its German studio. The exterior paintwork is even described as "English pewter," designed, says Kia, to give a unique lustre, while the interior is a dramatic combination of large areas of jet-black Italian leather with bright metal fittings and cream-colored contrast on the doors, lower dash, and carpeting.

In Europe especially, Kia has yet to find itself a clear visual identity in the market-place; this will only come once the design philosophy is clearly explained and followed through the range. The cee'd is a step in the right direction but, for true impact, more originality is still needed.

Kia Magentis

Design	Chang-Sik Min
Engine	2.7 V6 (2.0, and 2.0 diesel, also offered)
Power	138 kW (185 bhp) @ 6000 rpm
Torque	247 Nm (182 lb. ft.) @ 4000 rpm
Gearbox	5-speed automatic
Installation	Front-engined/front-wheel drive
Front suspension	MacPherson strut
Rear suspension	Multilink
Brakes front/rear	Discs/discs
Front tires	215/50VR17
Rear tires	215/50VR17
Length	4735 mm (186.4 in.)
Width	1805 mm (75.1 in.)
Height	1480 mm (58.3 in.)
Wheelbase	2720 mm (107.1 in.)
Track front/rear	1558/1552 mm (61.3/61.1 in.)
Curb weight	1490 kg (3285 lb.)
0–100 km/h (62 mph)	9.1 sec
Top speed	220 km/h (137 mph)
Fuel consumption	9.2 l/100 km (25.6 mpg)

The new Kia Magentis has been completely rethought in every detail. Designed for the European market, it is longer, wider, and higher than the Magentis model it replaces. The new car is aimed squarely at the Mazda6, Ford Mondeo, Peugeot 407, and VW Passat; Kia clearly does not—yet—command the same brand appeal as the others, instead seeking to offer a good value choice for those customers who cannot stretch to the more upmarket brands.

The new design is a notable improvement on the style that went before: it is stronger and tauter, in fact quite Mondeo-like in many ways. There are no superfluous details: the Magentis stands for sensible and practical motoring in a package that is designed neither to overexcite nor, even more importantly, to disappoint. Evidence of longer-term brand-building can be seen in the Kia face on the Magentis, which is similar to the treatment on the smaller Rio model; this time, however, the grille is chromed to provide a more upmarket persona.

The designers have created an inoffensive, well-proportioned modern car, yet have at the same time successfully integrated an imposing frontal view by using large square headlamp units. The sloping C-pillar could have made the overall aspect more sporty, but the effect is sabotaged by a lower body void of skirting; this leaves it looking more like a standard modern sedan, even though there is a sporty GLS model that comes fitted with a V6 engine.

The target customer group is thirty- to forty-five-year-old family men with young children and a dynamic lifestyle. While many of these customers would, deep down, no doubt prefer a more prestigious brand, Kia is steadily becoming more attractive despite designs that, in the sedan sector at least, are very safe.

Kia Soul

Design	Tom Kearns
Engine	2.0 in-line 4
Gearbox	5-speed automatic
Installation	Front-engined/four-wheel drive
Brakes front/rear	Discs/discs
Front tires	245/45R20
Rear tires	245/45R20
Length	4040 mm (159.1 in.)
Width	1850 mm (72.8 in.)
Height	1620 mm (63.8 in.)
Wheelbase	2550 mm (100.4 in.)

The Kia Soul is a boxy, fun car for young people, similar in many ways to the Skoda Yeti. Basically a compact SUV in its format, the Soul has enough ground clearance to take adventure-seekers over beaches or up rutted tracks, for example. Yet its compact dimensions would make it handy in town, too.

Moulded black bumper guards at front and rear give it a suitably tough look, and chunky wheels and bulging wheel arches reinforce the sense of adventure. The blackened lower body and the wedge-profiled glasshouse create a sandwich effect with the titanium-colored body.

The wraparound windshield is highly distinctive and adds to its personality, as does the broad, flat hood that extends over the sides to meet the wheel arches and air vents, and down the front to form the grille and the vehicle's characteristic facial expression. This is a car that would be understood as much in an urban environment as out of town, and few cars can offer this flexibility.

With a boxy shape such as this, interior space is good and access is easy too, as the rear doors are rear-hinged, eliminating the B-pillar. In the rear there is a compartment for housing wet sportsgear. Mood-setting nighttime lighting comes from around each sunroof and from the door panels, similar to the effect found in limousines. The dashboard is the only major disappointment: it is stuffed full of every conceivable communications device but looks cheap and dated.

The whisper is that a production version of the Soul could be in the offing. When Toyota launched the RAV4 back in the early 1990s it quickly gained a strong following among young and adventure-hungry buyers. Handled correctly, the characterful Soul could easily do the same thing for Hyundai—although it would surely do even better with a different name.

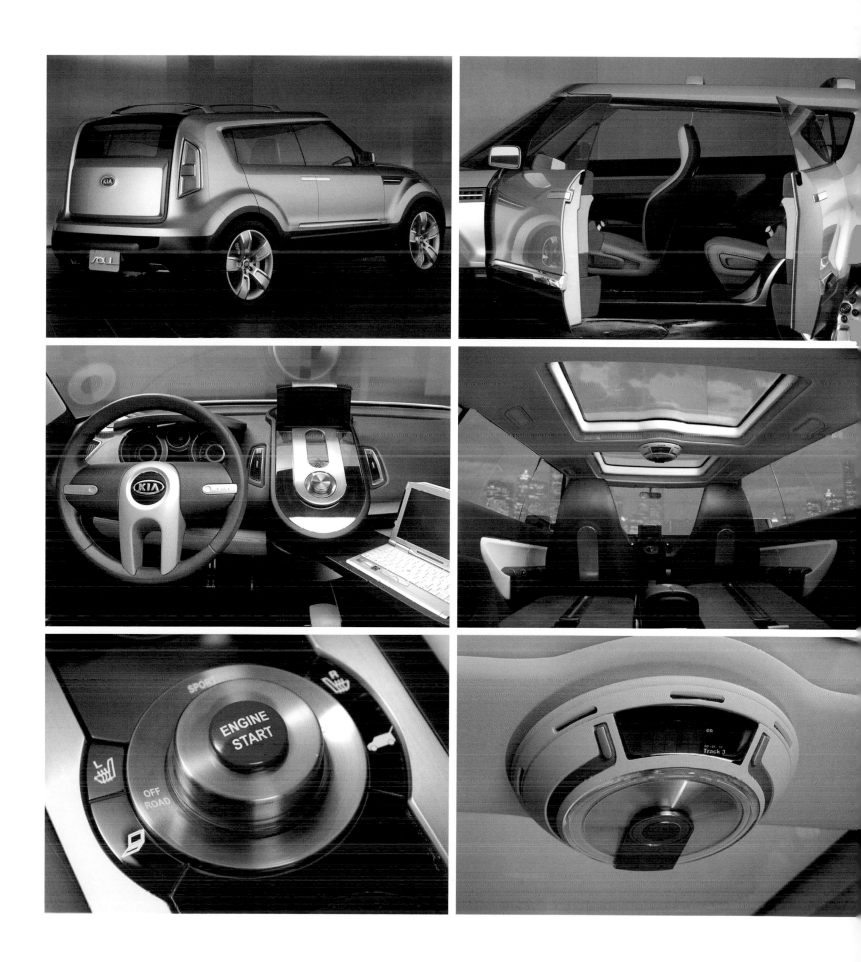

Lamborghini Miura

Like movie directors who remake classic films with modern casts and techniques, car designers seeking to reinterpret four-wheeled favorites from earlier eras do so at great peril. The new version almost always falls sadly short of the original, rendering the remake an embarrassingly pointless exercise.

With the 1966 Miura widely regarded as the most beautiful Lamborghini of all time, reshaping it for a modern audience could be seen as little short of artistic heresy. Yet with Ford reviving its GT from the same era, Lamborghini could not resist the temptation to do the same. When the original Miura was first shown forty years ago, today's Lamborghini design director Walter de' Silva was just sixteen. Perhaps the redesign of the Miura was his dream project, but despite his considerable skills the result must be judged a disappointment.

The proportions of the new concept have been kept very similar to the original but, as with the Ford GT, scaled up somewhat. In the 1960s, design and manufacturing technologies were less effective at smoothly integrating parts together, so that such components as headlamps, grilles, and bumpers looked like add-ons. Cars such as the Miura showed off their fantastic proportions but were limited by imperfect detailing. The difference today with the new concept is that it looks like a precision-engineered product, but the downside of this is that it lacks some of the raw human spirit that would make it really exciting.

The huge level of interest in the latest production Lamborghinis—the Gallardo and the Murciélago—shows that design innovation is a powerful seller. Only radical shifts such as the new Mini have managed to find a comfortable place while making a nod to the past—so it is hard to understand why looking backward, even to something as fantastic as the Miura, should suddenly make sense for Lamborghini.

Design	Walter de' Silva
Installation	Mid-engined/rear-wheel drive

Lexus LS460

Engine	4.6 V8
Power	283 kW (380 bhp)
Torque	502 Nm (370 lb. ft.)
Gearbox	8-speed automatic
Installation	Front-engined/rear-wheel drive
Front suspension	Multilink
Rear suspension	Multilink
Brakes front/rear	Discs/discs
Length	5151 mm (202.8 in.)
Width	1875 mm (73.8 in.)
Height	1476 mm (58.1 in.)
Wheelbase	3091 mm (121.7 in.)
0–100 km/h (62 mph)	5.5 sec

This fourth generation of Lexus's LS luxury flagship was previewed in concept form at the 2005 Tokyo show as the LF-Sh, the designation indicating the presence of a hybrid drive system. Less than three months later the production version made its debut at the 2006 Detroit show, minus the hybrid technology but boasting another exclusive, in the shape of the world's first eight-speed transmission.

As befits the top model from the Toyota group's top brand, the LS460 offers the last word in sophistication, refinement and, thanks to an all-new body profile, status. Compared with the previous generations of LS, the new car is considerably less conservative in its design language, with a smooth, streamlined front, a thrust-forward Lexus-signature grille, and swept-back headlamps.

Designed to sit at the very top of the Lexus sedan range, above the IS and GS models, the LS uses closely related design language to create a progressive luxury car with a clear connection—especially at the rear—to its smaller peers. Viewed from the side, the new LS looks smooth and elegant, with strong forms along the waistline that run through to the rear lamps and to the tip of the trunk lid. The long doors and black pillars again visually lengthen the car. Subtly flared wheel arches cuddling the large wheels make the vehicle appear powerful and well grounded; the chrome trim at the base of the doors gradually widens toward the rear, its arrow shape projecting speed.

Given that its target competition is the German luxury brands, it is inevitable that the LS incorporates some of their gravitas and presence. But this generation of the LS goes an important step further than its predecessors: the design cues are contemporary and fresh rather than borrowed from obsolete models. At last, Lexus is showing that it can develop its own distinctive brand identity in the luxury class.

Lincoln MKS

Design	Patrick Schiavone
Engine	4.4 V8
Power	235 kW (315 bhp) @ 4500 rpm
Torque	434 Nm (320 lb. ft.) @ 3000 rpm
Gearbox	6-speed manual
Installation	Front-engined/all-wheel drive
Front suspension	MacPherson strut
Rear suspension	Multilink
Brakes front/rear	Discs/discs
Front tires	245/45R20
Rear tires	245/45R20
Length	5176 mm (203.8 in.)
Width	1912 mm (75.3 in.)
Wheelbase	2906 mm (114.4 in.)
Track front/rear	1656/1666 mm (65.2/65.6 in.)

The MKS concept is the precursor to a new luxury Lincoln sedan due out soon to replace the LS and sit below the large Town Car in the Ford premium brand's lineup. As such, the MKS gives an excellent hint as to the future design of top Ford-group models in North America.

The design of the MKS has a strong, contemporary flavor, with a bold signature waterfall grille finished in satin silver. Just below the grille is a broad horizontal slatted air intake that emphasizes the width of the front and lessens its visual weight. The wheel arches are attractively sculpted, with a crisp feature line that goes on to form the high shoulder along the side and runs out through the rear lamps. When viewed from the side the MKS has more than a sense of Volvo about it, though the air outlets behind the front wheel arches lend a touch of Jaguar and Aston Martin too. At the rear the car looks more American than from any other angle, the wide trunk lid and the bumper dropping slightly to highlight the center line. The titanium-colored band that encircles the lower body adds subtly to the look of sophistication.

The interior of the MKS is really beautiful. It mixes a range of generally pale-colored luxury materials in a harmonious manner; Ford designers say it was inspired by luxury interior furnishings from the Milan furniture fair. The switches on the center console and door casings have a high perceived-quality finish and are set in a contemporary way.

Lincoln is very eager to become seen as America's luxury car. Now, with its design direction being overseen by Peter Horbury, who built up Volvo's distinctive current identity, the Lincoln brand can look forward to a much stronger future.

Lincoln MKS **Concept** 165

Lincoln MKX

Design	Doyle Letson
Engine	3.5 V6
Power	186 kW (250 bhp) @ 6250 rpm
Torque	326 Nm (240 lb. ft.) @ 4500 rpm
Gearbox	6-speed automatic
Installation	Front-engined/front- or four-wheel drive
Front suspension	MacPherson strut
Rear suspension	Trailing arm
Brakes front/rear	Discs/discs
Front tires	245/60R18
Rear tires	245/60R18
Length	4737 mm (186.5 in.)
Width	1925 mm (75.8 in.)
Height	1707 mm (67.2 in.)
Wheelbase	2824 mm (111.2 in.)
Track front/rear	1656/1648 mm (65.2/64.9 in.)
Curb weight	1914 kg (4220 lb.)

Unlike the Lincoln MKS concept, the MKX is already planned for production in 2006 as a 2007 model. Based heavily on the Ford Edge, also shown at the Detroit show but in production form, the MKX is to become the new midsize SUV for Lincoln and to fly the group's flag in the medium premium crossover segment against such competitors as the BMW X3 and Honda CR-X.

Why such emphasis on the crossover utility vehicle (CUV) segment? It is the fastest-growing market in North America and, in common with all other US automakers, Lincoln needs to cash in on the growth to compensate for the collapse of the market for traditional full-size SUVs.

It is unfortunate, therefore, that the Ford group's development budget did not run as far as providing a distinct exterior to differentiate the MKX from the cheaper Edge: effectively, the structure and much of the exterior panel work is in common with the Ford.

While the Edge is undoubtedly a handsome vehicle, the MKX's prominent full-width close-mesh grille and tailgate-width horizontal lighting panel at the rear may still not provide enough instant differentiation to give the Lincoln a strong identity of its own. The wide chrome band that breaks up the body-colored tail door from the dark rear screen is perhaps the strongest identification point.

Fortunately, the MKX and the Edge do differ more substantially inside. Here, development costs are lower and the Lincoln version is able to mix modern quality soft leathers, woods, and metals to stylish effect; the square instrument dials and display housing hint at designs more common in the 1930s.

Peter Horbury, executive director of design for Ford in North America, believes consumer attitudes concerning the display of luxury are shifting away from ostentation and toward discretion. Subtlety in the colors and textures, as in the MKX, is the word.

Lotus APX

Design	Russell Carr
Engine	3.0 V6
Power	224 kW (300 bhp) @ 6250 rpm
Torque	360 Nm (265 lb. ft.) @ 4500 rpm
Installation	Front-engined/four-wheel drive
Brakes front/rear	Discs/discs
Length	4697 mm (184.9 in.)
Width	1852 mm (72.9 in.)
Wheelbase	2700 mm (106.3 in.)
Track front/rear	1554/1556 mm (61.2/61.3 in.)
Curb weight	1570 kg (3460 lb.)
0–100 km/h (62 mph)	5.4 sec
Top speed	245 km/h (152 mph)
Fuel consumption	8.7 l/100 km (27 mpg)

It is not often that Lotus unveils a new concept car; and it is even less often that that concept car is not a sports car but what could be termed a conventional, family-oriented car. But the APX concept is different: for a start, it is not the forerunner to a Lotus-emblem production car, nor is it an indication of the future direction of Lotus aesthetic design.

Instead, the APX is the work of the Group Lotus engineering department, and its role is that of a technology demonstrator—the function of the style is to give potential engineering customers a more concrete example of what can be achieved with the underlying technologies. The technologies in question are those in the Lotus-designed 3-liter supercharged engine and, of most interest to designers, the "Versatile Vehicle Architecture." VVA is Lotus's innovative modular aluminum construction, a system that the company believes allows automakers to bring niche vehicles to market faster and build them more profitably; it also gives the vehicle its APX designation, for Aluminum Performance Crossover.

The objective in the APX's design was to create a car that was not only practical but also highly focused as a driver's car. A 2+3+2 seating configuration was chosen, though the taut V-shaped body design at front and rear communicates more dynamic ability than might be expected from a three-row vehicle. The sports-proportioned cabin sits toward the rear, while flared wheel arches and racy wheels complete the look.

The interior is modern in its theme, mixing gray leather with aluminum trim for a highly technical feel that is also luxurious. Visually the whole car is very conceptual—the rear seats, for example, are painfully small. Yet it is still a good demonstration of the potential for Lotus's new platform technology, with its claimed weight of just 1570 kg (3460 lb.) being perhaps its most impressive statistic.

Lotus Europa S

Design	Russell Carr
Engine	2.0 in-line 4
Power	149 kW (200 bhp) @ 5400 rpm
Torque	263 Nm (194 lb. ft.) @ 4200 rpm
Gearbox	6-speed manual
Installation	Mid-engined/rear-wheel drive
Front suspension	Double wishbone
Rear suspension	Double wishbone
Brakes front/rear	Discs/discs
Front tires	175/55R17
Rear tires	225/45R17
Length	3900 mm (153.5 in.)
Width	1714 mm (67.5 in.)
Height	1120 mm (44.1 in.)
Wheelbase	2330 mm (91.7 in.)
Track front/rear	1457/1490 mm (57.4/58.7 in.)
Curb weight	995 kg (2194 lb.)
0–100 km/h (62 mph)	5.5 sec
Top speed	225 km/h (140 mph)
Fuel consumption	9.3 l/100 km (25.3 mpg)

With the lightweight Elise sports car having enjoyed so much critical acclaim and commercial success, it is surprising that Lotus has been so slow to build on its position as a leader in sports-car design. During the last few years, while Porsche sales have climbed steadily upward, Lotus has done little to enhance its relatively aged product range.

The larger, V6-powered M250 shown in 1999 was meant to change all that; it made a lot of sense as a follow-up product, but financial problems at Lotus and the company's takeover by Malaysia's Proton meant the program was eventually shelved. The fixed-head version of the Elise—the Exige—moved the range in an even more hard-core direction, again missing an opportunity with a clientele wanting to combine at least some element of comfort with the famous Lotus dynamic experience.

Addressing the gap, at last, is the Europa S, previewed at the 2006 Geneva show. (The name Europa was used on Lotus's first mid-engined sports car in 1966, which ran in production until 1975, but there is no connection between the two.) Based on the Elise but larger and more usable as an everyday car, the Europa S is in effect a business-class derivative. The new car uses a similar aluminum structure and mid-engined layout, but entry and exit are easier and the interior is clad in full leather. It comes with a range of features that an Elise driver could only dream of: satellite navigation, air-conditioning, driver and passenger airbags—and carpets. It has a similarly low seating position as the Elise but the exterior design language is toned down somewhat. Yet, in the softening of the features, some of the purity of the Elise and the Exige has been lost; worse, against such competitors as the Porsche Boxster and BMW Z4 the design could come across as too toylike.

Maybach Exelero

Design	Fredrik Burchhardt
Engine	5.9 V12 bi-turbo
Power	522 kW (700 bhp) @ 5000 rpm
Torque	1020 Nm (752 lb. ft.) @ 2500 rpm
Installation	Front-engined/rear-wheel drive
Front suspension	Double wishbone
Rear suspension	Multilink
Brakes front/rear	Discs/discs
Front tires	315/25ZR23
Rear tires	315/25ZR23
Length	5890 mm (231.9 in.)
Width	2140 mm (84.3 in.)
Height	1390 mm (54.7 in.)
Wheelbase	3390 mm (133.5 in.)
Curb weight	2660 kg (5864 lb.)
0–100 km/h (62 mph)	4.4 sec
Top speed	351 km/h (218 mph)

Of all the new concept cars launched at the Frankfurt Motor Show, the Exelero was the most impressive. At nearly 6 meters (20 ft.) long, the Exelero, at present just a one-shot exercise bearing the Maybach emblem, is one huge coupé.

Painted black to show off every crease and surface, it packs a whopping 700 horsepower from the V12 bi-turbo engine packaged under its massive hood. The body is shaped with aerodynamic flow at the forefront of the designers' minds. The front bumper and grille lean right back, allowing the air to flow smoothly over the hood and windshield, while at the rear the roof gradually sweeps down to the rear bumper to ensure minimal turbulence and drag.

Based on the large Maybach limousine, the Exelero was built for tire manufacturer Fulda as a one-shot effort for the testing of a new generation of high-performance tires. There is a historical precedent for this, as Maybach last built a coupé for Fulda for the very same reason way back in 1939.

So often, one-shot concept cars are just models that look great in pictures. The Exelero is different: it is a fully running vehicle and has even been tested at the Nardò high-speed circuit in Italy, where it reached a top speed of 351 km/h (218 mph). Inside the car, acres of dark-gray quality leather combine stylishly with detailed red pinstriping on the seats, steering wheel, and safety harnesses.

Maybach is now positioning itself to offer customers specially built limousines on request, but there are no plans for a production version of the Exelero, which was designed in partnership with students from Pforzheim College in Germany and built at Stola in Turin. Nevertheless, who is to say that Maybach might not be persuaded if enough millionaires came forward with blank checks?

Maybach Exelero **Concept** 173

Mazda CX-7

Design	Iwao Koizumi
Engine	2.3 in-line 4
Power	182 kW (244 bhp) @ 5000 rpm
Torque	350 Nm (258 lb. ft.) @ 2500 rpm
Gearbox	6-speed automatic
Installation	Front-engined/all-wheel drive
Front suspension	MacPherson strut
Rear suspension	Multilink
Brakes front/rear	Discs/discs
Front tires	235/60R18
Rear tires	235/60R18
Length	4675 mm (184.1 in.)
Width	1872 mm (73.7 in.)
Height	1645 mm (64.8 in.)
Wheelbase	2750 mm (108.3 in.)
Track front/rear	1617/1612 mm (63.7/63.5 in.)
Fuel consumption	10.2 l/100 km (23 US mpg)

The Mazda CX-7 is effectively the production version of the MX-Crossport unveiled at the Detroit show a year earlier, and is designed specifically for the North American market. The changes for the production version are limited to practical enhancements such as larger front-door handles, visible handles for the rear doors, and small embellishments like the chrome strip that now runs along the base of the doors. Other details, such as the front fog lights set into the lower side grilles, are simplified.

It can be difficult to translate the visual character of a sports car into an SUV/crossover model, but this is what Mazda has succeeded in doing with the CX-7. Despite the much greater length, height, and bulk of the 4x4 vehicle, the designers have managed to blend dynamic shapes with characteristic SUV boldness to bring the distinctive sports feel of the RX-8 sports coupé to this curvaceous crossover. The CX-7 has an aerodynamic screen swept well back at 66 degrees, clearly spelling speed, and an interesting stepped-up waistline over the rear door that makes the rear quarter-window small and the roof appear to drop, even though it does this only a little, in the interests of maintaining good headroom in the rear.

The interior is contemporary, with cream and black layers interspersed with aluminum trim. The dashboard features an extra layer extending across the whole width of the cabin. Mazda's classic three-dial meters and triple vents at the top of the center stack provide continuity throughout the range. Mazda claims to have paid particular attention to ensuring that the leather trim, steering wheel, gear knob, and ventilation dials all have their own tactile feel, with soft-grained leather ensuring minimal reflectivity.

The CX-7 arrived in North America in spring 2006 and will appear at a later date in Europe.

Mazda Kabura

Design	Franz von Holzhausen
Engine	2.0 in-line 4
Installation	Front-engined/front-wheel drive
Front suspension	Double wishbone
Rear suspension	Multilink
Brakes front/rear	Discs/discs
Front tires	245/35R19
Rear tires	245/35R20
Length	4050 mm (159.4 in.)
Width	1780 mm (70.1 in.)
Height	1280 mm (50.4 in.)
Wheelbase	2550 mm (100.4 in.)

The Kabura, a compact coupé based on a stretched version of the MX-5's rear-wheel-drive platform, is the first new car from Mazda's new US design director Franz von Holzhausen. The proportions of the Kabura created a sensation at the Detroit show where it was first displayed, not least because the design explores many new and fascinating ideas.

Particularly distinctive is the way the very low tapered hood makes the wheels appear to be wrapped outside the main body mass. The front end design looks very dynamic, visually lightening, and more like a classic sports car than anything in the current Mazda range. It is complex, however.

Innovations include the asymmetric interior seating layout, which places a small jump seat behind the driver and two full-size seats on the passenger side, with the front passenger positioned 15 cm (6 in.) forward of the driver. Mazda, which has the second-youngest average buyer age in North America, commissioned research that found that most younger people mainly use three seats in their car and only very occasionally the fourth: the Kabura is the interpretation of that research.

Unusually, too, there is an extra short door on the passengers' side: this disappears cleverly into the rear wheel arch to give access to the rear passenger seat. The very modern feel of the cabin is reinforced not only by the dramatic black and white color scheme but also by details such as a cabin floor made from a woven leather substitute derived from industrial waste.

The name Kabura comes from the Japanese term *kabura-ya*—referring to an arrow that makes a howling sound when fired and that, historically, was used to signal the start of a battle. Franz von Holzhausen has certainly created something new with this sports-car concept, but whether this will be the start of a new battle for Mazda remains to be seen.

Mazda Sassou

Design	Luca Zollino
Engine	1.0 in-line 3
Gearbox	6-speed manual
Installation	Front-engined/front-wheel drive
Front suspension	MacPherson strut
Rear suspension	Torsion beam
Front tires	225/40R18
Rear tires	225/40R18
Length	3890 mm (153.1 in.)
Width	1740 mm (68.5 in.)
Height	1370 mm (53.9 in.)
Wheelbase	2490 mm (98 in.)

The Mazda Sassou, designed in Europe but based on Japanese principles, is a supermini-class concept aimed squarely at European Generation Y buyers. The car reflects the notion of the *shoji* screen—rice-paper screens common in Japanese houses that partially conceal what is behind, leaving a surprise when they are finally opened. The name "Sassou" is a Japanese term indicating a positive state of mind—and the two principles interact in a very interesting way in this attractive and sporty concept.

At the front of this young, vibrant coupé is a large five-point grille cover that is designed to move in and out electronically to optimize the airflow; another innovation at the front is the LED headlamps that are integrated beneath translucent plastic but treated to blend in with the body panels. When on, the lighting appears to come from behind the body panels. With further development this could be the start of a new trend that has the potential literally to change the face of car design.

From the side a strong crease runs through the door and is indicative of Sassou's sporty nature. The lack of an upper B-pillar visually lengthens the car and improves visibility for the rear passengers, and the rear quarter-window wraps inboard, making the rear wheels look wider and more securely planted on the ground.

The dashboard is dramatic in its smooth simplicity. Instead of a conventional key, a USB key inserted in the center console unlocks all the controls necessary to drive the Sassou, and a circular screen, controlled by a joystick, gives vehicle information in graphic form.

There are many interesting new ideas built into the Sassou. However, Mazda will need to find a cost-effective way of producing this car if it wants to test the market—which might, regrettably, be more conservative than people at the company expect.

Mercedes-Benz F600 Hygenius

Engine	Hydrogen fuel cell with hybrid battery
Power	86 kW (115 bhp)
Torque	350 Nm (258 lb. ft.)
Brakes front/rear	Discs/discs
Front tires	215/45R20
Rear tires	215/45R20
Length	4348 mm (171.2 in.)
Fuel consumption	2.9 l/100 km (81.1 mpg)

The F600 Hygenius is, on one level, a research vehicle for fuel-cell technology; on another level, it is an opportunity for Mercedes-Benz engineers to create a futuristic body and a high-tech interior while demonstrating their most recent advances in hydrogen drive. The latest fuel-cell system in the F600, they claim, is more compact, starts better in the cold, and runs more efficiently.

Apart from the dramatic visual differences such as the very low waistline and the large side glass area, there are construction advances as well. The front doors swing upward at a slant, meaning that they take up less space to the side; the tailgate also has a unique mechanism, the lower half hinging inward so that it can be opened in restricted spaces. As the tailgate opens, the rear bumper drops and the floor panel of the luggage compartment slides rearward, simplifying loading.

Videocameras on the outside cover the driver's blind spots and, when opening doors, warn of vehicles close by. Inside, the high-resolution color displays in the dashboard are also projected as a head-up display to lessen driver fatigue. The cabin—spacious for a vehicle of this size—has a remarkable degree of originality and versatility throughout, especially in its seating arrangements.

The obvious zero-emissions benefits of hybrid hydrogen fuel cells are already well known; the F600 is exceptional in offering a range of 400 kilometers (250 miles) on one tank filling. There are spin-off benefits too: as an example, the cup holders in the F600 use electrical power from the fuel cell to keep drinks chilled or hot.

The design concept of the F600 is as exciting as the technology it holds within. It is such concepts as this that make car design stimulating and that bring us the most enticing glimpses into the future.

Mercedes-Benz GL-Class

Design	Steve Mattin
Engine	5.4 V8 (4.6, and 3.0 and 4.0 diesel, also offered)
Power	285 kW (382 bhp) @ 6000 rpm
Torque	530 Nm (390 lb. ft.) @ 2800–4800 rpm
Gearbox	7-speed automatic
Installation	Front-engined/four-wheel drive
Front suspension	Double wishbone
Rear suspension	Multilink
Brakes front/rear	Discs/discs
Front tires	275/55R19
Rear tires	275/55R19
Length	5088 mm (200.3 in.)
Width	1920 mm (75.6 in.)
Height	1840 mm (72.4 in.)
Wheelbase	3075 mm (121.1 in.)
Track front/rear	1645/1648 mm (64.8/64.9 in.)
Curb weight	2370 kg (5225 lb.)
0–100 km/h (62 mph)	6.6 sec
Top speed	240 km/h (149 mph)
Fuel consumption	13.9 l/100 km (16.9 mpg)

The old Mercedes G-Class was an honest, boxy design; much like the classic Land Rover Defender, it was perfect for the utilitarian use for which it was originally designed. Unlike the Defender, however, because of its large size, high price, and increasing equipment content, it came to be seen as Mercedes' 4x4 flagship.

The new GL-Class supplements the G-Class but follows a very different design path: built on the same platform as the ML- and R-Class crossovers, the GL is as luxurious and upmarket as its predecessor was stark and simple. And in using a monocoque body construction rather than a separate chassis frame, the Mercedes follows the trend set among its European competitors.

The exterior design has clear cues from both the ML-Class—in its frontal treatment—and the R-Class, especially noticeable around the window line. The strong features start at the front, with the two horizontal louvres running through the grille to frame the large three-pointed star set prominently in the center. Powerful elements include large lamp units sitting at each of the car's four corners, as well as vents and bulges in the hood, chunky door handles, and the slightly squared-off wheel arches that hint at the potential for off-roading.

The interior design is luxurious and a mile away from that of the old G-Class. A two-tone dashboard with quality wood and leather trim gives a true upscale feel: this even extends to three different types of wood veneer.

Like the R-Class, the GL offers a range of gas and eco-friendly diesel engines, and accommodation for seven; the difference between the crossover and the SUV is best illustrated by the GL's Off-Road Pro option pack, which provides an additional low-ratio transfer gearbox, differential locks, and even more sophisticated AirMatic suspension, which can give 30 cm (12 in.) ground clearance and a wading depth of 58 cm (23 in.).

Mercedes-Benz R-Class

Engine	5.0 V8 (3.5 V6, and 3.2 V6 diesel, also offered)
Power	228 kW (306 bhp)
Torque	460 Nm (339 lb. ft.) @ 2700–4750 rpm
Gearbox	7-speed automatic
Installation	Front-engined/all-wheel drive
Front suspension	Double wishbone
Rear suspension	Four-link
Brakes front/rear	Discs/discs
Front tires	255/55R18
Rear tires	255/55R18
Length	5157 mm (203 in.); 4922 mm (193.8 in.) for Europe
Width	1922 mm (75.7 in.)
Height	1656 mm (65.2 in.)
Wheelbase	3215 mm (126.6 in.)
Track front/rear	1643/1636 mm (64.7/64.4 in.)
Curb weight	2240 kg (4938 lb.)
0–100 km/h (62 mph)	7.0 sec
Top speed	245 km/h (152 mph)
Fuel consumption	13.3 l/100 km (17.7 mpg)

Previewed in 2004 as the GST Grand Sports Tourer concept, the innovative Mercedes-Benz R-Class has now reached the market in production form. Europeans receive this US-built luxury wagon–SUV crossover in its shorter version, measuring just over 4.9 meters (16 ft.) from bumper to bumper, whereas Americans get the full-size edition, longer by 235 mm (9 in.). These two lengths reflect the twin incarnations of the GST concept.

The production models, to Mercedes' great credit, remain faithful to the concept's style and ambience. At the front the hood edge steps down onto the headlamp, creating a shoulder that runs into the door mirror and making the car look sure-footed and dynamic. There is a central ridge featuring in the front bumper and grille and running up onto the hood, again enhancing the look of agility.

Sweeping curves and forms define the R-Class. The aerodynamic nature of the car is highlighted in particular by the coupé-like silhouette, the lines running through the doors, and the arched roofline connecting the A-pillar to the D-pillar. The line that rises from the front wheel arch to the rear lights becomes more defined as it travels rearward, accentuating the wedge shape of the body and therefore the dynamic character. The window pillars are black along the side, stressing the impression of length.

The R-class is designed to seat six in comfort in a luxury cabin. The trim is a warm two-tone affair with touches of aluminum and wood to break up the larger areas and offer a sophisticated, sporty feel. One key new feature is the steering-column-mounted transmission selector system that eliminates the need for the traditional console-mounted lever and instead gives space for useful extra stowage.

Mercedes-Benz claims that the R-Class represents a whole new motoring experience. For the fortunate few who can afford it, that claim could well be justified.

Mercedes-Benz S-Class

Engine	5.5 V12 (3.5 V6 and 5.5 V8, and 3.0 V6 diesel, also offered)
Power	386 kW (517 bhp)
Torque	830 Nm (590 lb. ft.) @ 1900–3500 rpm
Gearbox	5-speed automatic
Installation	Front-engined/rear-wheel drive
Front suspension	Four-link
Rear suspension	Multilink
Brakes front/rear	Discs/discs
Front tires	255/45R18
Rear tires	255/45R18
Length	5206 mm (205 in.)
Width	1871 mm (73.7 in.)
Height	1473 mm (58 in.)
Wheelbase	3165 mm (124.6 in.)
Track front/rear	1600/1606 mm (63/63.2 in.)
Curb weight	2180 kg (4806 lb.)
0–100 km/h (62 mph)	4.6 sec
Top speed	250 km/h (155 mph)
Fuel consumption	14.3 l/100 km (16.4 mpg)

A new S-Class from Mercedes is always a major event in the luxury car class, setting the tone for the sector for many years to come. This new S-Class is visually impressive, just as the previous model was, but does not appear to take such a big step ahead in design.

The new car has a more prominent V shape at the front, with headlamps that wrap further rearward. When viewed from the side there are large, gently flared wheel arches that make the wheels appear smaller than perhaps they should. The rear screen angles sharply back in coupé-esque style, leaving a short trunk lid that sits above the rear haunches. The whole tail appears to lean forward, which is perhaps the new car's most distinctive feature.

The chrome trim that runs along the top of the windows curves downward and recalls the curves found on the CLS; a single gentle feature line runs from the headlamps to the rear lamps, rising through the doors to create a feeling of dynamism.

As one would expect from a car costing up to $190,000, the interior is one of comfort and opulence. Wood mouldings combine with digital screens and fine nappa leather trim, and there is even an analog clock nestled between the air vents—this is perhaps somewhat out of place in what is otherwise a technical interior.

The S-Class was always the technology pioneer in the Mercedes lineup; this generation launches infrared night vision that can see beyond the reach of its normal headlamps, alerting the driver to cyclists, pedestrians, and animals. Other systems include collision avoidance, precrash conditioning (automatically tightening the seatbelts, among other things, before a crash) and, of course, comprehensive airbag provision.

The new S-Class is a technological marvel, but its exterior design is not as pleasing or as skillful as its predecessor's—with the result that it may not enjoy such a timeless appeal.

Mini Concept Frankfurt

Design	Dirk Müller-Stolz and Ulrike Schafmeister
Engine	1.6 in-line 4
Gearbox	5-speed manual
Installation	Front-engined/front-wheel drive
Brakes front/rear	Discs/discs
Length	3980 mm (156.7 in.)
Wheelbase	2540 mm (100 in.)

The Mini Concept Frankfurt is one concept car that looks likely to reach production before too long—if in a somewhat diluted form. With the massive popularity of the existing Mini range across the world, Mini parent BMW is set to capitalize on its success by marketing a new version of the original Traveller station wagon, launched first time round forty-five years ago.

Compared to the current Mini, the Concept Frankfurt has a longer wheelbase, giving better storage capacity and improving the visual proportions of the wagon. Novel design features that fit with the Mini spirit include retractable aluminum headlamps, air vents that turn into cup holders, and a central navigation screen that flips round to be replaced by a Jules Verne-style globe. Most hatchback cars today have top-hinged rear hatches, but the Mini stays true to its origins and comes with two small side-hinged doors. On the concept they are on elaborate hinges that allow them to swing right round to the side—a solution sure to be too costly for volume build.

When the original Mini was first launched the glass in the front doors slid fore and aft. As a nod to the past, the new concept has its rear side windows sliding rearward rather than down. This also allows the concept to forgo an upper B-pillar, making the rear passengers feel less enclosed. The interior looks more conceptual than the exterior but the Concept Frankfurt clearly demonstrates how Mini interiors designed to be fun will always be an intrinsic part of the brand's ethos.

BMW is in the enviable position of having a much-loved global brand where customers constantly crave more Mini treats. The Traveller (or whatever name the wagon eventually adopts) will certainly be warmly welcomed—but how long must we wait for the Moke to be resurrected, too?

Mitsubishi Concept D:5

Engine	2.4 in-line 4
Power	125 kW (168 bhp)
Torque	226 Nm (167 lb. ft.)
Gearbox	6-speed CVT
Installation	Front-engined/four-wheel drive
Front suspension	MacPherson strut
Rear suspension	Multilink
Brakes front/rear	Discs/discs
Front tires	255/55R20
Rear tires	255/55R20
Length	4735 mm (186.4 in.)
Width	1815 mm (71.5 in.)
Height	1875 mm (73.8 in.)
Wheelbase	2850 mm (112.2 in.)
Track front/rear	1540/1540 mm (60.6/60.6 in.)

The Mitsubishi Concept D:5 is the forerunner of the next generation Delica model sold in Japan. The Delica is a family of minivans and light commercial vehicles that for many years has been based on the platform of the Pajero off-roader.

The D:5 makes the switch to a new platform—that of the Outlander and the Concept Sportback. It combines a four-wheel-drive chassis with a monovolume cabin and, in so doing, shifts into a kind of minivan/SUV segment. The design is made up of rectangular elements with small radii to soften the appearance. The body surfaces are taut and free of unnecessary decoration: the D:5 is functional above anything else and, claims Mitsubishi, is very safe. This safety promise is communicated in the design language by the solid looks, high waistline, and bluff nose.

High ground clearance suggests useful terrain-crossing abilities, even if it makes the Concept D:5 look awkwardly poised at rest. The safety message permeates almost every aspect of the design: new technologies include a range of ten sensors that detect pedestrians and obstacles and audibly warn the driver to take care, while onboard cameras monitor the lane markings on the road and the system corrects the steering trajectory when it senses that the vehicle is starting to depart from its lane. This, says Mitsubishi, helps to alleviate driver strain and fatigue. An advanced cruise-control system uses radar technology to monitor the distance to the vehicle ahead and regulate engine power so as to maintain a safe distance, again with the aim of reducing the driver's workload.

The interior creates an awkward tension between the amount of cold-looking aluminum—designed to make the internal structure look strong—and the warm dark-brown leather for the seats. The theme is severe, blocky, and solid, and not as well resolved as the exterior.

Mitsubishi Concept Sportback

The Concept Sportback is Mitsubishi's ambassador for a new range of sports hatchbacks that will be aimed at the European market. As such, it shows a bold, aggressive stance, suggesting that distinctive design will play a key role in Mitsubishi's European—and global—renaissance.

Mitsubishi's redevelopment program will see the launch of large numbers of new cars over a three-year period. This concept gives dramatic momentum to that program by making a very clear visual connection between the company's successful motorsport heritage and both its high-performance and its everyday road cars. Thus the Concept Sportback previews both the new-generation Golf-sector hatchback from Mitsubishi, as well as the dynamic shape of the eventual replacement for the rally-winning Evo 8 roadburner.

At first glance the Concept Sportback looks mean, especially from the front, where its inverted gaping grille was inspired by jet-fighter air intakes. This front-end design contrasts with such current models as the Colt and the Grandis, which use the three-diamond logo as the focal point. The hood features a shallow step that runs rearward into a shoulder line through to the rear lamps. The cant rail forms a continuous arch that meets the window line at a sharp point above the rear lamps. Flared wheel arches are tightly filled with huge wheels and have crisp detailing around the edges.

This car is confident and well resolved and has a strong stance on the road. The nose is its most striking feature, but the rear is distinctive, too, with its narrow strip of lights (mimicking the headlamp shape) and a bold though perhaps overaggressive spoiler shadowing the rear window. Mitsubishi still has an excellent reputation for durability: now, with the advent of the new-generation models, it may at last have the visual design to draw in buyers who are interested in aesthetic performance too.

Design	Omer Halilhodzic
Power	149 kW (200 bhp)
Installation	Front-engined/four-wheel drive
Length	4500 mm (177.2 in.)
Width	1795 mm (70.7 in.)
Height	1450 mm (57.1 in.)
Wheelbase	2630 mm (103.5 in.)

Mitsubishi Concept-X

Engine	2.0 in-line 4
Gearbox	6-speed auto-manual
Installation	Front-engined/all-wheel drive
Front suspension	MacPherson strut
Rear suspension	Multilink
Brakes front/rear	Discs/discs
Front tires	255/35R20
Rear tires	255/35R20
Length	4530 mm (178.3 in.)
Width	1830 mm (72 in.)
Height	1470 mm (57.9 in.)
Wheelbase	2650 mm (104.3 in.)
Track front/rear	1565/1565 mm (61.6/61.6 in.)

Similar in many respects to the Concept Sportback shown at the Frankfurt show, the Concept-X is more the conventional three-box sedan, a future take on the forthcoming Lancer Evolution. The addition of the trunk gives the Concept-X a greater visual mass at the rear, balancing the front end and making for a more orthodox overall profile—spoilers apart, of course.

For the Concept-X has every performance styling treatment one could possibly want, starting with the 20-inch wheels, working up to the huge front bumper complete with multiple air intakes and a gray-colored air splitter. Two vents and a recessed intake are cut into the hood; at the rear a large aerofoil manages the airflow over the top, while the lower diffuser, with its aggressive-looking vertical splitter plates, encourages air to speed under the car and help hold it to the road. Vents behind the front fender help air to escape along the side of the car, and are used as the starting point for a rising dynamic feature line that runs through the door handles to the rear lamps. The headlamps and taillamps use LED technology and are tightly packaged within the body, giving the Concept-X a menacing look at the front.

The interior is functional and, like the exterior, overtly masculine: the focus is solely on the driver and his machine. There are new technologies on-board: for example, a multimedia system with a high-definition LCD monitor provides a real-time status on the all-wheel-drive system, navigation maps and DVD audio. Rear passengers can also share the driving experience, with their own LCD displays mounted on the back of the front seats.

Overall this is an intentionally extreme version of what is a fundamentally functional and honest design. Production versions will reach world markets in 2007.

Mitsubishi CT MIEV

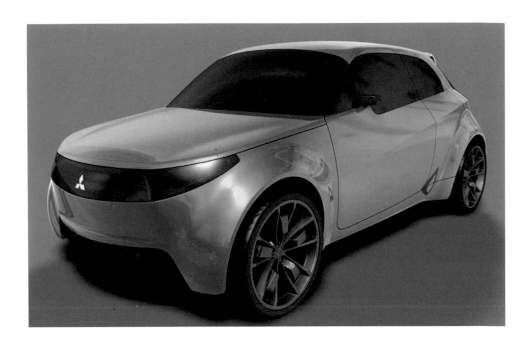

Design	Mark Kim
Engine	1.0 in-line 3 hybrid with four 20 kW in-wheel motors
Power	50 kW (67 bhp)
Gearbox	None
Installation	Mid-underfloor engine/all-wheel drive
Length	3800 mm (149.6 in.)
Width	1700 mm (66.9 in.)
Height	1430 mm (56.3 in.)
Wheelbase	2600 mm (102.4 in.)

This is a subcompact that oozes attitude. Cast in a dramatic wedge shape, the CT MIEV is certainly unique in its design, and as a series hybrid (with an underfloor engine generating current for each of the four in-wheel electric motors), it is technically novel too.

The bright gold color of the CT's stubby body contrasts well with the black details and aluminum wheels. Clearly visible through the large wheels are the electric motors—again gold—which allow the engineers to dispense with gearboxes, axles, and driveshafts. At the front the turned-down bumper at the edges echoes the look of an ugly fish and creates an unnerving contrast with the smiling grille. The surfaces are voluminous in general, blistered wheel arches hugging wheels positioned at the outer reaches of the car to create a sense of maneuverability, performance, and handling.

The edge of the hood creates a strong feature line that runs straight back into the door cheater area (the triangular area where the mirror is attached to the door). The line then follows a hockey stick path and drops before running out at the rear lamps. There is plenty of tumblehome on the upper architecture, especially at the rear, which adds to the design's firmly planted appearance on the road.

The rear window is especially unusual. Not only is it a complex shape, swelling outward at its base to follow the contours of the car's flanks, but it also incorporates the LED rear lights—a triangle and two L-shaped swooshes at each side—fused directly into the glass.

Access to the interior is through four doors, the rear pair hinging upward from their rear edge. Equally innovative, though not especially attractive, is the steering-wheel rim, which rotates around a fixed center containing gold-colored displays and black switches.

Mitsubishi EZ MIEV

Engine	Lithium-ion battery, four in-wheel motors
Power	80 kW (107 bhp)
Torque	1600 Nm (118 lb. ft.)
Gearbox	None
Installation	Two- or four-wheel drive using wheel motors
Front tires	225/30R20
Rear tires	225/30R20
Length	3700 mm (145.7 in.)
Width	1800 mm (70.9 in.)
Height	1750 mm (68.9 in.)
Wheelbase	2750 mm (108.3 in.)
Curb weight	1200 kg (2645 lb.)
0–100 km/h (62 mph)	11 sec
Top speed	150 km/h (95 mph)

With the world premiere of the EZ MIEV at the 2006 Geneva Motor Show, Mitsubishi launched its vision of future automotive transport. Designed around a pure electric drive system, the EZ MIEV's vehicle architecture is conceived to maximize the specific packaging benefits that this system provides.

The key advantage of the Mitsubishi MIEV (Mitsubishi In-wheel-motor Electric Vehicle) drive system is that the four electric motors power the wheels directly—thus doing away with the requirement for transmissions, driveshafts, or any form of differential; this in turn frees up more space than on a conventional vehicle, especially one requiring four-wheel drive.

The pure monovolume shape uses glass and a two-tone pearl-white and silver body scheme, leaving one in no doubt that this is a futuristic concept. The effect of these different-colored panels is very graphical, especially on the roof where the black windows contrast so strongly with the white. Loosely based on elements of the Se-ro and "i" concepts of the two previous years, the EZ MIEV is a much better-resolved package: it has a freshness and a modernity that are immediately appealing, and thanks to its novel powertrain configuration it makes remarkably efficient use of its footprint on the road.

For the interior, Mitsubishi started by defining three so-called "mood modes." The first is a driving mode, where the 4+1 seating configuration gives class-beating levels of comfort and spaciousness; secondly, a transport mode has removable luggage containers and rear seats that sink into the floor; thirdly, the lounge mode sees the seats folded into reclining benches and relaxed lighting and music giving the appropriate ambience.

Although the EZ MIEV is some way off production readiness, it provides an exciting glimpse into the future and shows clearly how electric vehicles can shake up the design rulebook.

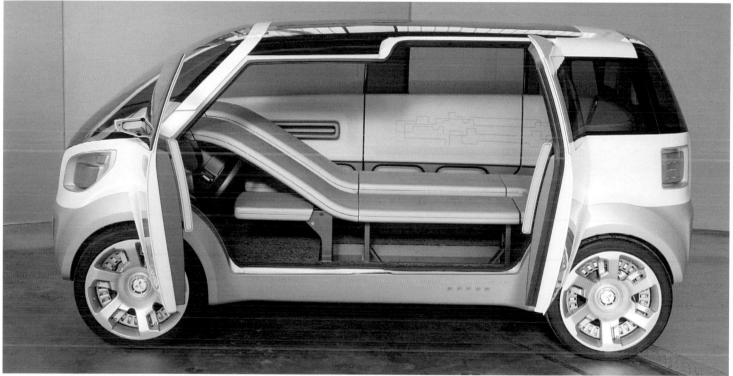

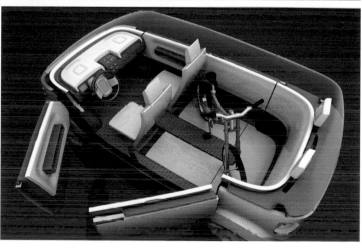

Mitsubishi i

Engine	In-line 3
Power	47 kW (63 bhp)
Installation	Mid-engined/rear-wheel drive
Front tires	145/65R15
Rear tires	175/55R15
Length	3395 mm (133.7 in.)
Width	1475 mm (58.1 in.)
Height	1600 mm (63 in.)
Wheelbase	2550 mm (100.4 in.)
Track front/rear	1310/1270 mm (51.6/50 in.)

The funky i is Mitsubishi's new "*kei*-class" minicar and replaces entirely the Minica/Toppo range. The design is one of the most innovative seen in the minicar field for many years, not least because of the engineering freedom that led its designers to place the engine under the floor, just ahead of the rear axle. This in turn allows a long wheelbase for good ride comfort and, as the occupants can be moved further forward, maximizes interior space. This is what gives the i its unique, almost elliptical, exterior proportion.

The whole shape feels tight and encompassing, with the doors set inboard slightly at the sill to make them look like a distinct and separate entity. The body surrounding the doors appears to swirl round in a loop, giving an effect similar to the Smart. Again like the Smart, the front wheel arches are drawn forward ahead of the center section of the hood. The large windshield and relatively high seating position give a commanding view of the road.

The interior is pleasantly designed, with warm two-tone colors and some orange lighting and trim features to inject more youthfulness and vibrancy. The center console is cut short, enhancing the feeling of space around the feet.

Mitsubishi claims that the i is a new type of minicar that offers a premium level of reliability, material quality, and design. The mid-engined layout offers clear packaging benefits and promises good safety ratings, too.

With a cheerful appearance that makes it look as if it wants to be driven round twisty city streets, this will be a desirable low-cost car for many people. Mitsubishi is at present evaluating the business case for marketing it outside Japan, the market for which it was designed.

Mitsubishi Outlander

Engine	2.4 in-line 4
Power	125 kW (168 bhp)
Torque	226 Nm (167 lb. ft.)
Gearbox	6-speed CVT
Brakes front/rear	Discs/discs
Front tires	225/55R18
Rear tires	225/55R18
Length	4640 mm (182.7 in.)
Width	1800 mm (70.9 in.)
Height	1680 mm (66.1 in.)
Wheelbase	2670 mm (105.1 in.)
Track front/rear	1540/1540 mm (60.6/60.6 in.)

The new Outlander from Mitsubishi is a key model for the company. Based on the same platform as the Concept Sportback and Concept-X, its role is that of the now-fashionable crossover—a vehicle with car-type underpinnings for good refinement, low costs, and efficient manufacture, but with a useful degree of four-wheel-drive ability to draw in the more adventurous customer.

Considering what Nissan has achieved with its rakish Murano in the same category, the Outlander shown at Tokyo appears to have little immediate design interest. The shape is unresolved and undemanding of attention: of its few notable features only the reverse rake to the D-pillar stands out as memorable. The LED lamps at the rear that form the transition between rear screen and tailgate are an exception, too.

Otherwise, there are so many different surfaces, lines, curves, and angles that the eye is left confused, with no idea what the visual theme is. In terms of its proportions, the design has to tread carefully between the characteristics of a performance car and those of a utility vehicle. Rugged features that confirm its SUV pedigree include the chunky five-spoke wheels, front stone guard, pressed lines in the roof panel, and lower dark-gray body trim. The ride height is raised, too. But where it misses an opportunity is that it gives equal prominence to numerous individual elements of its exterior, thus preventing the design from creating a strong identity in any way.

Against this it should be borne in mind that Japanese models aimed at Japan's domestic market are frequently cautious and conservative in their design: the version for Europe is expected to have a much more adventurous frontal treatment, for example.

Nissan Amenio

The Amenio is a preview of the next generation of the Nissan Elgrand, a large MPV dating back to 2002 and sold only in Japan and the United States.

In a design clearly influenced by the Renault Espace, the extensive use of glass in the upper body makes the vehicle look interestingly futuristic and light up top. The lower body is deeply sculpted and forms a shelf that creates the rear wheel arch. From the front the LED headlamps sit flush in the nose and form the starting point for a line running along the waistline right around the back of the car, briefly rising and falling with a heartbeat-like kink as it passes from the front door to the rear. The body surfaces are bold and go from being crisp at the front and rear to being slightly unwieldy in the center, especially in the front door.

The interior is just as wild as the exterior: bright red seats adorn the cabin and a combination of brown fabrics and aluminum trim on the center stack serves to stimulate the senses. Materials used in traditional Japanese architecture, such as rosewood, also feature. The cabin environment is intended to reflect the ambience of a living room, with comfortable seats and lots of light, but the result is simply too hard on the senses to be considered a relaxing place to be. An extra-wide monitor displays local information in City Browsing mode, and, implausibly, there is also an Earth-browsing mode that lets the driver look down from outer space at cars traveling on the Earth's surface—perhaps not that incongruous in a car that looks as if it was designed on another planet.

Clearly, although the Amenio is a welcome relief from the boxy van type of MPV, some of Nissan's wilder ideas will have to be toned down for this to be a suitable production-car proposition.

Front tires	R20
Rear tires	R20
Length	4900 mm (192.9 in.)
Width	1900 mm (74.8 in.)
Height	1830 mm (72 in.)
Wheelbase	3100 mm (122 in.)

Nissan Foria

Installation	Front-engined/rear-wheel drive
Front tires	R18
Rear tires	R18
Length	4350 mm (171.3 in.)
Width	1695 mm (66.7 in.)
Height	1370 mm (53.9 in.)
Wheelbase	2700 mm (106.3 in.)

Of all the Nissan concept cars launched recently, the Foria is certainly the most attractive. A dedicated 2+2 coupé with a front-engined, rear-wheel-drive configuration, it has a suitably long hood with the cabin set slightly rearward, allowing the driver to sit slap-bang between the wheels—the perfect place to feel the handling of the car.

The front end wraps around in plan like a Saab's might do; the grille has the headlamps incorporated, making the front graphically stronger. Above the grille an angled plane encircles the whole car and echoes the Lancia Fulvia as well as the Datsun Silvia of the 1960s. In fact the Foria as a whole could be seen as a modern interpretation of the latter car—and of course the pastel blue chosen for the show car was no accident. More modern, however, are the double side doors, the rear ones rear-hinged in the style of the Mazda RX-8 to improve rear-seat access.

This car achieves its visually compact look through the use of rounded profiles and short overhangs. The brushed-aluminum detailing around the windshield and side windows picks up details at the back of the fender and the wheels. The aluminum makes the Foria look light and spirited, precisely how a 2+2 coupé should be.

The interior too has a wonderful combination of materials, textures, and colors, all of which work well together. Quality hand-stitched saddle leather is used in combination with aluminum, creating a warm handmade feel balanced with sportiness. A traditional Japanese dimpled leather surface pattern is used on the steering-wheel grips, the back of the shift paddles, the gearshift knob, and other surfaces.

Elegant, Italianate, and impressive, the Foria is a gorgeous contemporary concept. Nissan owes it to car enthusiasts to put it into production.

Nissan GT-R Proto

There was a previous Nissan GT-R concept, which was featured in the very first edition of the *Car Design Yearbook*. The new version, suffixed Proto, is similar to the old in many ways but adds a series of minor styling changes such as new hood intakes and a blacked-out A-pillar. The new GT-R is said to be a strong indicator of the design of the replacement for the Skyline, a car with a near-fanatical following among performance car enthusiasts.

The design theory behind this macho beast is to make the car look powerful and well grounded—and it certainly succeeds in this regard. All the usual treatments are used, including large deep grille intakes at the front and vents at the back of the fenders: the Skyline's iconic quadruple circular tail lamps and four shiny exhausts bring up the rear.

More complex body sculpture is found at the base of the doors and there is a low two-tone skirting that encircles the whole car. This has the effect of drawing the eye downward and, coupled with the huge spoked wheels, makes the GT-R appear weighty and firmly planted on the road. Because the occupants are seated so low, the upper body is able to be quite small, with the roof gradually dropping rearward from the A-pillar. The GT-R will not win any design prizes—and most certainly not the award for subtlety—but the real test will come only once the dedicated Skyline enthusiasts have had the chance to pronounce on the final production version.

In 2003 Nissan announced that the production model planned for global sale would appear in 2007, so it is reasonable to assume that the showroom editions will stay close to the look, feel, and stance of this latest concept.

Nissan Note

The Nissan Note was originally shown as the Tone concept in September 2004 at the Paris Motor Show, and featured in *The Car Design Yearbook 4*. Sharing the same platform as the Nissan Micra and the Renault Clio, the Note has a wheelbase 170 mm (6.5 in.) longer than the Micra, giving it notably more cabin space. Its visual signature is of course completely different: this is a versatile compact minivan, in effect Nissan's reinterpretation of Renault's Modus.

At the front the plastic moulded grille shows off the new corporate style first used on this car. Viewed from the side, the Note has large headlamps that cut back into the fenders. The rear lamps, by contrast, are like boomerangs sitting high up on the C-pillars and roof, as previously seen on the Qashqai concept. Unlike some people-carrier designs, this is not a monovolume profile, as there is a distinct angle between the hood and the windshield. Nevertheless, the hood is quite short and the roof follows the windshield in a constant arch to the rear lamps. The side-window pillars are finished in black to make the Note look less upright.

Anyone who is looking for a practical five-seater family vehicle would do well to consider the Note. In the trunk there are reversible luggage boards that help keep the interior clean. Useful tables fold down from the backs of the front seats. This is a car for a young family that perhaps wants something more spirited than a dull sedan.

Built in the UK, this model will compete head on with the Opel Meriva, the Fiat Idea, the Ford Fusion, and Renault's own Modus. The Renault–Nissan alliance will naturally be hoping that the distinctive Nissan character will increase the two brands' combined market share rather than merely taking sales away from the Renault.

Engine	1.6 in-line 4 (1.4, and 1.5 diesel, also offered)
Power	81 kW (109 bhp) @ 6000 rpm
Torque	153 Nm (113 lb. ft.) @ 4400 rpm
Gearbox	5-speed manual
Installation	Front-engined/front-wheel drive
Front suspension	MacPherson strut
Rear suspension	Torsion beam
Brakes front/rear	Discs/drums
Length	4008 mm (157.8 in.)
Width	1690 mm (66.5 in.)
Height	1550 mm (61 in.)
Wheelbase	2600 mm (102.4 in.)

Nissan Pivo

As one of the most extreme concept cars shown at the Tokyo show, the egglike Pivo examines a possible future for urban electric vehicles.

The whole concept is based around a spherical cabin sitting on a trolley-like chassis, symmetrical at each end. The cabin can revolve 360 degrees, so there is never any need for the driver to look over his or her shoulder to reverse. The look of the cabin echoes an egg in an eggcup, perched on top of the chassis. This is made possible by storing all the control gear, including the lithium-ion battery, in the chassis and by using drive-by-wire technologies so that there need be no mechanical connections between cabin and chassis.

The Pivo seats three, with the driver centrally positioned. The doors, too, are wonderfully eccentric, powered electrically and sliding outward and back to make for easy access to the interior. The cabin design is friendly, with soft cream and taupe colors complementing the milky white exterior. On the chassis portion's flat surfaces in front of and behind the cabin, the Pivo features soft pads so that it can be used as seating when parked.

Inside, the Pivo has screens on its pillars that show what is on the other side, thus eliminating blind spots. Other technologies include an infrared commander that allows drivers to operate the navigation and audio system without taking their eyes off the road: this is done by simply pointing a finger or moving one's hand at the infrared commander. There is also a sophisticated telematics interface that displays information transmitted live from nearby locations: if the occupants want to know about that building up ahead, the dashboard screen will tell them.

The Pivo is a clever concept and certainly one of the most interesting proposals in this edition of *Car Design Yearbook*.

Engine	Lithium-ion electric power
Installation	Four-wheel drive
Length	2700 mm (106.3 in.)
Width	1600 mm (63 in.)
Height	1660 mm (65.4 in.)
Wheelbase	2000 mm (78.7 in.)

Nissan Sentra

Engine	2.0 in-line 4
Power	101 kW (135 bhp)
Torque	190 Nm (140 lb. ft.)
Gearbox	6-speed manual/CVT automatic
Installation	Front-engined/front-wheel drive
Front suspension	MacPherson strut
Rear suspension	Torsion beam
Brakes front/rear	Discs/drums
Front tires	205/60R15
Rear tires	205/60R15
Length	4567 mm (179.8 in.)
Width	1790 mm (70.5 in.)
Height	1512 mm (59.5 in.)
Wheelbase	2685 mm (105.7 in.)
Fuel consumption	7.1 l/100 km (33 US mpg)

The Sentra is Nissan's bread-and-butter model for the North American market: it sells in large numbers at a competitive price and has traditionally been cautious and conservative in its design. The 2007 model, shown at Detroit in January 2006, is noticeably stronger in its appearance and its engineering—one of the more tangible benefits of Nissan's worldwide alliance with Renault of France.

Taut surfaces and simple lines give a somewhat Ford-like initial impression, though the thrust-forward grille with its fine black mesh pattern is prominent in much the same way as that on the new Fiat Grande Punto. The headlamps are very different, however: the Nissan's are vertically stacked blocks, in contrast to the Fiat's smooth faired-in treatment.

The Nissan's profile is strongly wedge-shaped, with a rising beltline taken from the relatively low nose to the tall rear, itself reminiscent of the rather awkward design of the Toyota Prius. One consequence of the high rear—apart from a capacious trunk—is the impression of a lot of heavy mass and very deep flanks, particularly behind the C-pillar. This is not helped by the small wheels, which detract from the Sentra's on-road presence by not filling the wheel arches.

The interior is modern and neatly designed and finished in materials that are in line with the model's low sticker price. One notable feature is the dash-mounted gear shifter, an idea pioneered on the outgoing-generation Honda Civic. Seating is for five, with warm saddle leather being one of the upholstery options. Transmission options include CVT automatic and a six-speed manual. Buyers can also pay to upgrade their car with 16-inch wheels, a CD player, keyless entry, and Bluetooth telecoms.

The Sentra, available in 2006 as a 2007 model, is built at Nissan's plant in Aguascalientes, Mexico.

Nissan Sport Concept

Design	Nissan Design, Technical Center, Atsugi, Japan
Brakes front/rear	Discs/discs
Front tires	R20
Rear tires	R20
Length	4351 mm (171.3 in.)
Width	1806 mm (71.1 in.)
Height	1501 mm (59.1 in.)
Wheelbase	2601 mm (102.4 in.)

Continuing the theme established on previous concepts such as the Nissan Actic and the Azeal, the new Sport Concept is the latest in a series of sporty youth design studies aimed at generating a groundswell of support for the Nissan brand among young American buyers. Nissan's mission is to bring innovation, sportiness, and driving pleasure to the small-car sector, a category of vehicles that often lacks strong visual appeal—especially in the United States.

The Sport Concept, despite being launched at the 2005 New York show, is cast in the European mold of the hot hatchback, though in its presentation it is more extreme than any model that has yet made production. In fact, first impressions are in many respects similar to the wild special V6 edition of the Renault Mégane.

The exterior form of the Sport Concept is geometrical, young, and dynamic to the eye. There is a sense of energy emanating from this car, with its contrasting dark glass and pearlescent white bodywork heightening the feeling of drama.

The bulging angular bodywork, the large air intakes at the front, and the huge 20-inch wheels make the Sport Concept appear testosterone-fueled—a sure sign that Nissan sees its appeal closely focused on the young male market. Visible carbon-fiber panels at front and rear give a certain high-tech racing look but on a more practical level also provide a bonus in that their toughness will resist damage from stone chippings.

Inside the cabin, clear priority is given to the front-seat occupants. The deep figure-hugging leather seats at the front feature four-point harnesses and race-style wraparound head restraints, but the two seats molded into the rear to give a sporty feel for the rear passengers are placed directly ahead of the two powerful speakers mounted in the rear parcel shelf.

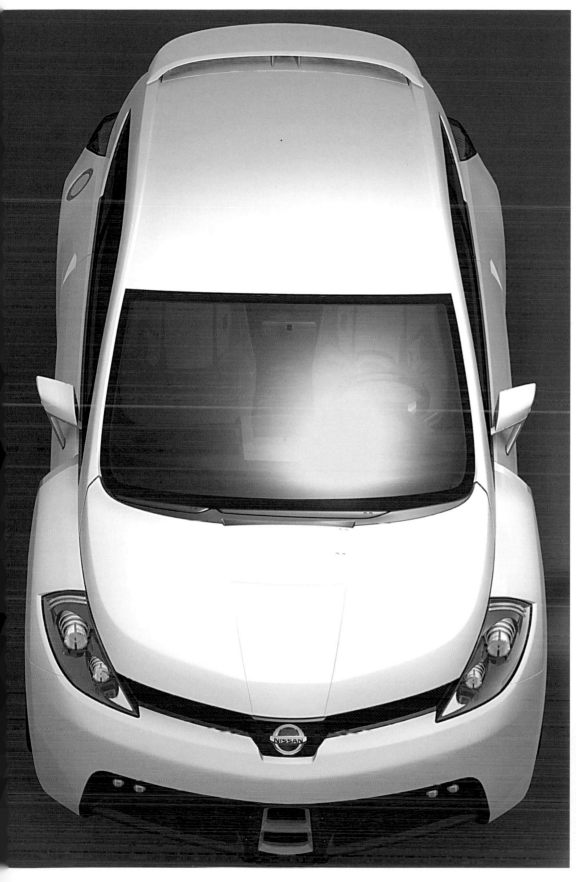

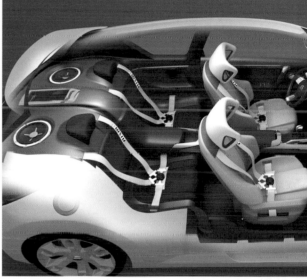

Nissan Terranaut

Design	Felipe Roo Clefas
Installation	Front-engined/four-wheel drive
Brakes front/rear	Discs/discs
Front tires	R19
Rear tires	R19
Length	4965 mm (195.5 in.)
Width	2100 mm (82.7 in.)
Height	2150 mm (84.6 in.)
Wheelbase	3075 mm (121.1 in.)

The Terranaut comes as the latest in a long line of Nissan concept vehicles exploring four-wheel-drive territory, the Dunehawk, Zaroot, and Qashqai being just three. Nissan appears to be set on a strategy to continue proposing different four-wheel-drive vehicle concepts until, eventually, one hits the bull's-eye and a completely new model can be added to the production lineup.

Conceived at Nissan's London Design Studio, the Terranaut is indeed something out of the ordinary. As its name suggests, it was designed to serve as a mobile research station for scientists, geologists, archaeologists, or other adventurers who travel to the most challenging corners of the planet. With this academic research angle it gains a useful extra dimension of interest over everyday SUVs—though the fundamentals of the format are still strictly those of a conventional large off-roader.

The exterior surfaces of the 5 meter (16 ft.) long body are taut and free of decoration: the front is imposing and a trifle severe, while the rear has more originality—especially in the strong shoulder line generated from the D-pillar. Noticeable despite the design's height are the glass dome, antennas, and raised camera pod on the roof.

A dedicated three-seater, the Terranaut features twin doors on the left side and a single door on the right, allowing space in the back for the scientific equipment. There is also a keyboard integrated into the third crew member's chair, while the domed glass roof allows light to flood in. Other innovations include the special tires developed by Goodyear, which claim to be puncture-proof and to work like conventional tires on normal roads but, by changing air pressure, transform themselves into chunky off-road tires.

Stripped of its attention-getting scientific mission equipment, this could indeed be the blueprint for a future production Nissan 4x4.

Nissan Urge

One of the aims of this dramatic concept car from Nissan is to connect with America's youth—the adrenalin-hungry generation brought up on a diet of PlayStation games, Internet, and instant excitement.

Like many lightweight sports cars, the Urge draws its inspiration from motorcycles, and has a terrific fun look to it. In its conception it could be seen as a Caterham Seven for the twenty-first century—the same close-to-the-road raw thrills, the same exposure to the elements, the same slender, lightweight construction.

The long hood and small windshield, which is little more than a wind deflector, push the front occupants rearward, back behind the center line of the car. The main body mass sweeps inboard at the front and rear, leaving add-on wheel arches the job of covering up the tires. The Urge actually has three seats, the rear passenger sitting centrally way out behind the roof in an exposed position that guarantees maximum exhilaration. The T-bar roof is another fun element, adding structural stiffness and doubling as a useful handhold when climbing in.

Front and rear overhangs are extremely short, lending the Urge an air of agility: at the rear the taillights are on stalks sticking out from the central fuselage—just like the indicators on a motorcycle. Yellow is used intensively in the interior and also to surround the long cut-outs in the doors that allow occupants a dizzying view of the road and permit onlookers to see right through the car. Steering is accomplished through a blue handlebar-like wheel.

The Urge has the look and feel of great fun, a car that takes motoring back to basics and creating, as its name suggests, the urge to get in and drive. And as befits a design aimed at techno-savvy youth, the Urge is not just about performance but is loaded with every conceivable modern electronic technology.

Design	Nissan Design America
Gearbox	6-speed manual
Installation	Front-engined/rear-wheel drive
Front suspension	MacPherson strut
Rear suspension	Torsion beam
Brakes front/rear	Discs/discs
Front tires	195/45R19
Rear tires	225/35R20
Length	3979 mm (156.7 in.)
Width	1824 mm (71.8 in.)
Height	1260 mm (49.6 in.)
Wheelbase	2650 mm (104.3 in.)
Curb weight	1087 kg (2400 lb.)

Nissan Versa

The Versa is a new venture for Nissan in North America and, though its format is familiar in Europe, it marks something of a departure from traditional US practice.

For a start, the Versa is an entry-level product sitting beneath the new Sentra in the Nissan range; secondly, it is initially only a hatchback, a body layout that has often struggled to succeed in the US. Thirdly, it is based on a current European platform, when many other producers in the US employ previous-generation platforms for their low-cost models.

The platform in question is a lengthened version of the B-segment architecture that carries the Nissan Micra, the Renault Clio, and many other Alliance models in Europe. The Versa is in fact a slightly altered version of the Japanese-marketed Tiida, itself closely related to the Nissan Note, also spawned from the Clio–Micra platform.

Yet despite this profusion of models, Nissan does not seem to be aiming for a common corporate identity on the front of its cars. With many different types of cars and trucks in the lineup, the designers tend to let each product speak for itself, allowing its individual personality to shine through, rather than worrying about instant identification of the brand.

In Nissan-speak, "Versa" is short for "versatile space," meaning interior functionality. By arching the roof and moving the A-pillar forward, the Versa offers large amounts of usable space. The design of the interior is very simple and slightly pedestrian, the downside of not wanting to put customers off.

The Versa comes initially in three-door and five-door hatchback versions; a sedan, which might be rather more in tune with American middle-of-the-road tastes, arrives later in 2007. With the US mindset having at last shifted toward some acceptance of fuel saving, cars like the Versa could be set to grow in commercial importance.

Engine	1.8 in-line 4
Power	89 kW (120 bhp) @ 6000 rpm
Torque	170 Nm (125 lb. ft.) @ 4800 rpm
Gearbox	4-speed automatic
Installation	Front-engined/front-wheel drive
Front suspension	MacPherson strut
Rear suspension	Torsion beam
Brakes front/rear	Discs/discs
Length	4468 mm (175.9 in.)
Width	1694 mm (66.7 in.)
Height	1534 mm (60.4 in.)
Wheelbase	2601 mm (102.4 in.)
Fuel consumption	6.2 l/100 km (38 US mpg)

Opel/Vauxhall Antara GTC

The Opel (Vauxhall in the UK) Antara GTC—for Gran Turismo Crossover—is an off-road sports coupé concept that previews the style of a wave of up-coming GM-group SUVs. These include the replacement for the Opel Frontera, a new GM Daewoo product to be marketed under the Chevrolet label in Europe, and at least one model for the US market.

This latest concept is closely related to the Daewoo–Chevrolet S3X shown at the Paris show in 2004. In its latest form it gains sportier, more dynamic crossover proportions, with an exterior with plenty of visual tension and aggression. The twin-tone body is adorned with many different shapes, curves, and features, all of which compete for attention and which in turn make the vehicle appear poised and ready for action. A darker-colored lower skirting is designed to resist stone chippings, yet the car does not have huge ground- or tire-to-body clearances, suggesting that the GTC is more of an on-road machine than one intended for serious off-road work.

At the front there are strong ridges on the top of the fenders, leading to the A-pillar along each side of the hood. Two converging surfaces run back from the headlamps and finish at the rear lamps. The frameless windows and B-pillar-free upper architecture are clean and uncluttered, as is the roof, with its two longitudinal glass panels. Lavish use of chrome—on the grille, in the vents in the hood, behind the wheel arches, and on the very large and chunky wheels—suggests an American flavor to the design, but in reality the Antara family will be a global product.

As presented, the Antara GTC concept uses dynamic design language in a bid to stir up excitement, but there is in fact little of true interest from a design perspective.

Design	Kurt Beyer
Engine	1.9 in-line 4 diesel
Power	158 kW (212 bhp)
Torque	400 Nm (295 lb. ft.) @ 1400 rpm
Length	4530 mm (178.3 in.)
Width	1970 mm (77.6 in.)
Height	1640 mm (64.6 in.)
0–100 km/h (62 mph)	8 sec
Top speed	210 km/h (130 mph)

Opel GT

Engine	2.0 in-line 4
Power	194 kW (260 bhp) @ 5300 rpm
Torque	350 Nm (258 lb. ft.) @ 2500 rpm
Gearbox	5-speed manual
Installation	Front-engined/rear-wheel drive
Brakes front/rear	Discs/discs
Length	4091 mm (161.1 in.)
Width	1813 mm (71.4 in.)
Height	1274 mm (50.2 in.)
Wheelbase	2415 mm (95.1 in.)
Curb weight	1320 kg (2910 lb.)
0–100 km/h (62 mph)	6 sec
Top speed	230 km/h (143 mph)

Rekindling the spirit of sports cars from days gone by has been a popular activity in the car industry in recent years. The Ford Mustang, the Chevrolet Camaro, and the Nissan Z are three such examples. In the case of the Opel GT, the 2006 model recalls a product of the same name but rather different in flavor—the classically curvaceous Opel coupé produced between 1968 and 1973, for which a big fan base still survives. However, as an open two-seater roadster the new car is completely different from the original 2+2 coupé and, unlike the Ford and Chevrolet examples, bears no resemblance to the original.

The new car is in fact drawn directly from the Pontiac Solstice two-seater launched by GM in North America in 2005. The classic front-engined, rear-wheel-drive layout is retained, giving the equally classic long hood and rearward seating position for the driver and passenger. The format is an exact parallel to that of the spectacularly successful Mazda MX-5, now in its third generation.

In terms of surface treatments, if not in mechanical layout, the GT's design is similar in many respects to the earlier Opel Speedster/Vauxhall VX220, itself based on the aluminum chassis concept of the Lotus Elise. Compared with the Speedster/VX, the GT is bulkier and its hood surfaces are higher, while at the rear the inset lamps are slimmer. Square exhaust tailpipes poke through the lower bumper, and the fairings trailing rearward from the head restraints are a distinctive difference compared with the MX-5.

Again reflecting its classic sports-car format, the Opel GT has an interior very similar to that of the Mazda, with a small steering wheel and twin paired instruments in front of the driver, and a restrained center stack in front of a stubby gear lever operating the five-speed transmission.

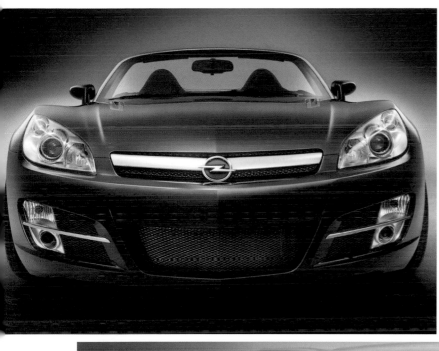

Peugeot 207

Engine	1.6 in-line 4 (1.4, and 1.4 and 1.6 diesel, also offered)
Power	82 kW (110 bhp) @ 5750 rpm
Torque	149 Nm (110 lb. ft.) @ 4000 rpm
Gearbox	5-speed manual
Installation	Front-engined/front-wheel drive
Front suspension	MacPherson strut
Rear suspension	Torsion beam
Brakes front/rear	Discs/discs
Length	4030 mm (158.7 in.)
Width	1720 mm (67.7 in.)
Height	1472 mm (58 in.)
Wheelbase	2540 mm (100 in.)
Track front/rear	1474/1469 mm (58/57.8 in.)
Curb weight	1263 kg (2784 lb.)

The new Peugeot 207 sits like a Russian nesting doll underneath the larger 307 and just above the highly successful 206, which, in the fullness of time, it will eventually replace. (The old 206 may be sidelined in Peugeot's fashion-conscious Western markets, but it is planned that it will live on, being produced at eight sites on three continents.) With the launch of the 207 the Peugeot range is now complete, with every model now sporting an 07 suffix.

Superficially, the 207 is very similar to both the 206—especially at the rear—and the recently facelifted 307, where the frontal likeness is strong. The dramatically swept-back headlamps are almost identical, and there is a similarly large gaping mouth grille—so large, in fact, that it incorporates a full-width bumper bar, blacked out so that it disappears visually. The hood opening is much shorter, with the whole bumper moulding taken high up to meet the hood and incorporate the Peugeot lion emblem, exaggerated in size and slightly inset.

The side view is distinctly sporty, with the rounded shoulder getting more pronounced as it travels rearward along the waistline. The rear screen angles forward quite sharply, lending a thrust-forward feel to the car's side profile. One consequence is that the rear lights and bumper appear to jut out somewhat, reinforcing the sporty appearance, but also making it more difficult to lean into the trunk to retrieve shopping bags.

Available as either a three-door or a five-door hatchback, the new 207 will be joined later by other body styles as the range evolves. As sporty compact hatches go, it has undoubted mass-market appeal—but, coming from a company that is frequently an innovator in small-car design, it still ranks as no more than a disappointingly cautious evolution.

Peugeot 20Cup

Design	Peugeot Style Center
Power	127 kW (170 bhp)
Torque	240 Nm (177 lb. ft.)
Gearbox	6-speed manual
Installation	Front-engined/front-wheel drive
Brakes front/rear	Discs/discs

Half car and half motorcycle, the 20Cup has been designed to show off the technical collaboration agreed on between PSA–Peugeot Citroën and BMW to produce new engines together. With its three wheels and two seats, the concept looks wildly dramatic and innovative.

As most of the weight is over the front wheels, the single rear wheel has to cope with all the lateral forces when cornering; accordingly, the tire has been made much wider than either wheel would have been in a conventional twin-tire configuration. Accordingly, the fat rear tire is given considerable emphasis in the design: it is entirely visible from the rear, and from the side the suspension arms are in full view.

The front face of the 20Cup has the more feline expression that we have become familiar with in Peugeots. The lionlike graphics along the side reinforce the idea of speed and agility, while there is a bright red band that runs along the center of the hood and through the cabin along a structural beam that separates driver from copilot. The body tapers behind the cabin to a smooth point in a motorcycle-style tail; underneath this are carried the rear lamps. In the interests of minimizing drag, there is no windshield or wind deflector; air escaping from the front wheel arch is directed away by a long body panel outside the rear wheel.

Peugeot is using a modified version of the 20Cup to help promote the brand's sporting credentials in the Le Mans endurance series events. This unusual machine might provide a glimpse of the future for Peugeot on the track, but its prime purpose is not as a serious design intention; rather, it is a promotional car produced by the Peugeot Style Center to highlight its own capacity for technical innovation.

Porsche Cayman S

Engine	3.4 flat 6
Power	220 kW (295 bhp)
Torque	340 Nm (250 lb. ft.) @ 4200–6000 rpm
Gearbox	6-speed manual
Installation	Mid-engined/rear-wheel drive
Front suspension	MacPherson strut
Rear suspension	MacPherson strut
Brakes front/rear	Discs/discs
Length	4341 mm (170.9 in.)
Width	1801 mm (70.9 in.)
Height	1305 mm (51.4 in.)
Wheelbase	2415 mm (95.1 in.)
Curb weight	1415 kg (3120 lb.)
0–100 km/h (62 mph)	5.4 sec
Top speed	275 km/h (171 mph)
Fuel consumption	15.3 l/100 km (15.4 mpg)

If you thought it was difficult to spot the difference between a 911 Carrera and a Boxster, Porsche-spotting is about to get trickier still. Positioned right between those two highly successful current Porsche models comes the new Cayman S.

Based largely on the Boxster, the Cayman S is powered by a larger 3.4-liter flat six-cylinder engine and is, in effect, a fixed-head coupé derivative of the Boxster. But it is much more than that, too, and the differences go much deeper.

The most distinctive difference of all, of course, is the solid domed roof that gives the Cayman S its own unique silhouette and proportion. How successful this altered profile is is still the subject of passionate debate among Porsche fans, but there can be no doubt about the useful practicality of the deep tailgate that opens to reveal a double-height luggage shelf.

Other differences take careful examination to discover. The Cayman S has 19-inch wheels, so it has a deeper air intake and taller fenders than the Boxster does, but otherwise the front end is very similar. Compared to the Boxster and the Carrera, the Cayman S has more muscular rear haunches, and the abbreviated D-shape of the rear quarter-window has a surprisingly big effect by making the car look more youthful and edgy than the Carrera.

The neat interior and taut surfaces trimmed in high-quality leather reflect current Porsche design, and a Sports Chrono package allows the driver to select different engine mappings and measure lap times on the racetrack. Timed on the Nürburgring near Cologne, the Cayman S was three seconds quicker when fitted with Sports Chrono than without.

The Cayman S is an extremely well-resolved Porsche that fits into a tiny but important niche in the lineup: that for a highly focused coupé that is more affordable than the 911 but just as rewarding to drive.

Renault Altica

Design	Patrick le Quément
Engine	2.0 in-line 4 diesel
Power	130 kW (174 bhp)
Torque	380 Nm (280 lb. ft.) @ 2000 rpm
Gearbox	6-speed manual
Installation	Front-engined/front-wheel drive
Brakes front/rear	Discs/discs
Front tires	245/35ZR21
Rear tires	245/35ZR21
Length	4270 mm (168.1 in.)
Width	1830 mm (72 in.)
Height	1360 mm (53.5 in.)
Wheelbase	2620 mm (103.1 in.)
Track front/rear	1540/1540 mm (60.6/60.6 in.)
Curb weight	1300 kg (2866 lb.)
0–100 km/h (62 mph)	7.5 sec
Fuel consumption	5.3 l/100 km (44.4 mpg)
CO_2 emissions	140 g/km

The Renault Altica is one of those designs that is hard to categorize. Hatchback, coupé, station wagon—it is all these. A "sports wagon" concept is how Renault prefers to describe it, and the talk in the design business is that it could provide cues for the next-generation Laguna in its wagon form.

Visually there is a lot going on for the eyes to take in, and it is not immediately easy to see through to the basic flowing long nose and extended rear of the Altica's form. The lower body is wide and the upper canopy inset a little, something that is necessary for the scissor-hinged door concept. A number of strong crisp lines delineate the car's shape: one, running along the side and dropping as it reaches the back of the door, helps to ground the car visually and emphasizes the rearward bias. Behind the front wheel, an aluminum panel depressed into the door adds the sporty feel of an air exit and presents an interesting feature when the doors are open. Highly distinctive is the mosaic overlay to the rear side windows, allowing a mix of privacy for the occupants and adequate visibility from the driver's seat.

Renault is a master at using two-tone paintwork to create modern-looking cars. This technique is used to powerful effect on the Altica, where the tailgate and lower sides are finished in a darker shade than the upper surfaces.

In the contemporary interior the front seats are set at the head of the load platform, from which twin rear seats can be hinged out; a compact pod, supported on four tubular arms, contains the steering wheel and the simple instrument panel. A patented synthetic jet mounted on the back of the roof controls the separation of airflow and reduces drag, improving fuel economy at higher speeds.

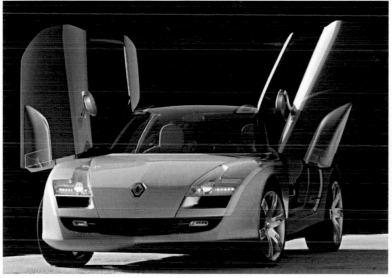

Renault Clio

Design	Patrick le Quément
Engine	1.6 in-line 4 (1.1 and 1.4, and 1.5 diesel, also offered)
Power	83 kW (111 bhp) @ 6000 rpm
Torque	151 Nm (111 lb. ft.) @ 4520 rpm
Gearbox	5-speed manual
Installation	Front-engined/front-wheel drive
Front suspension	MacPherson strut
Rear suspension	Torsion beam
Brakes front/rear	Discs/discs
Front tires	185/60R15
Rear tires	185/60R15
Length	3986 mm (156.9 in.)
Width	1707 mm (67.2 in.)
Height	1493 mm (58.8 in.)
Wheelbase	2575 mm (101.4 in.)
Curb weight	1150 kg (2535 lb.)
0–100 km/h (62 mph)	10.2 sec
Top speed	190 km/h (118 mph)
Fuel consumption	6.6 l/100 km (35.6 mpg)
CO_2 emissions	158 g/km

Renault's bestselling small hatchback has embarked on the third phase of its life slightly bigger than the previous model and reflecting a general trend in European car design in the B-sector.

Compared to the Clio II, the new car is very different from front to back, with a notably heavier and more substantial look. The headlamps now curve around their outer corners and there is a more three-dimensional shape to the front in general, with the smiling lower grille and the upper grille widening as it hits the headlamps.

The wheel arches have more flare and have a distinct feature line running around each one. Viewed from the side, there is a triangular-shaped surface starting behind the front wheel arch that runs through the door handles and rises up to the rear lamp. The upper B-pillar is now blacked out, in line with the current stylistic trend.

From the rear the Clio III looks very different and much bigger. A wraparound tail glass finishes with a striking V shape to the tailgate, but gone is the characteristic top-edge wrap of the old model. The tailgate now finishes lower for easier loading of the trunk. The rear lamps echo the shapes of the headlamps and serve to accentuate the haunches over the rear wheels.

Overall, however, this is a much more cautious design than the Mégane of 2003; uncharacteristically for Renault, the new Clio does not instantly proclaim itself as new, original, or innovative; nor is it immediately recognizable as a Renault.

The interior has a sophisticated two-tone color scheme that is warm and friendly—just like the shapes used for the dashboard and door panels. The control and instrument layout has the sophisticated feel of the larger Mégane and, just as with the Mégane, Renault has succeeded in scoring five stars (out of five) in the European New Car Assessment Programme (NCAP) crash test.

Renault Egeus

Design	Patrick le Quément
Engine	3.0 V6 diesel
Power	186 kW (250 bhp)
Torque	550 Nm (405 lb. ft.) @ 3000 rpm
Gearbox	7-speed automatic
Installation	Front-engined/all-wheel drive
Brakes front/rear	Discs/discs
Front tires	275–800/R560 PAX
Rear tires	275–800/R560 PAX
Length	4700 mm (185 in.)
Width	1920 mm (75.6 in.)
Height	1660 mm (65.4 in.)
Wheelbase	2900 mm (114.2 in.)
Track front/rear	1640/1640 mm (64.6/64.6 in.)
Curb weight	1950 kg (4299 lb.)

The Egeus is a thoroughly modern proposal from Renault for an elegant and luxurious coupé-flavored crossover—in some ways it represents an extension of the thinking behind the innovative but unsuccessful Avantime.

Patrick le Quément's team's design is curvaceous and smooth, with a striking frontal treatment that breaks up the body-colored panels by leaving strategic technical features, such as air intakes and headlamps, modeled in contrasting satin aluminum. The rounded front end looks both friendly and aerodynamic. The bold wheel arches are filled with huge 22-inch tires.

From the front fender a surface winds its way along the waistrail, eventually forming a large shoulder over the rear lamp. The side-window glass, complete with blacked-out pillars, runs rearward to the C-pillar, where it stops abruptly, dropping to meet the daylight opening line. The Egeus is a visual playground for challenging shapes: the lamps at front and rear resemble fingers, the rear screen is a trapezium wrapped at the corners, while, lower, triangular shapes are used in the design of the wheels, the exhaust tailpipes, and the sills.

The view from the rear is similar in some respects to the Initiale concept, the tailgate split into three planes by two vertical crease lines. The upper architecture is bubble-like, a look created by giving the windshield and rear screen lots of curvature and by making the glazed roof panel appear part of a continuous surface.

There are four individual seats inside what is a spacious interior, split centrally by a longitudinal spine. Instrumentation is kept to a minimum to ensure that the calming atmosphere is not interrupted. Each seat rotates outward for ease of access.

In the Egeus Renault has clearly demonstrated, yet again, its prowess in producing a design with innovative elements that all come together to deliver a refined but excitingly avant-garde concept.

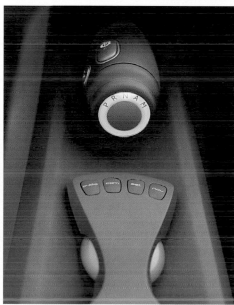

Rolls-Royce 101EX

Design	Ian Cameron
Engine	6.7 V12
Gearbox	6-speed automatic
Installation	Front-engined/all-wheel drive
Brakes front/rear	Discs/discs
Front tires	255/50R21
Rear tires	285/45R21
Length	5609 mm (220.8 in.)
Width	1987 mm (78.2 in.)
Height	1592 mm (62.7 in.)
Wheelbase	3320 mm (130.7 in.)

Following on from the 100EX convertible shown at Geneva two years previously, the 101EX is a gradual evolution and almost certainly a pre-study for the next generation Rolls-Royce coupé and convertible models. Based on the large Phantom limousine, the concept is 240 mm (9.4 in.) shorter as well as being lower. With all the exterior panels being new, the transformation from the original car is quite remarkable.

According to its designers, the 101EX should communicate effortless power—and with an enormous hood like that, few would be tempted to argue. The engine, this time a V12 rather than the 100EX's mammoth V16, is designed to give huge amounts of torque from revs as low as 1000, as befits the top luxury coupé from the world's most revered make.

The famous Rolls-Royce grille now has a touch of curvature to it and leans back slightly, with its surround gently blending into the large expanse of the polished aluminum hood. At the back of the hood is the windshield surround, also a massive aluminum structure and unusual in the way that it includes a somewhat ungainly A-pillar triangulation, again highlighted in bright aluminum.

The feature line running the length of the side of the car rises subtly over the rear wheels, emphasizing the power they transmit to the road. Compared with the 100EX, the rear corners are squared off a little more, the rear lamps are bigger, and the exhaust tailpipes are visible in the lower bumper trim.

The interior provides elegance and comfort, with a machined-aluminum dashboard sitting among the very best gray leather and rosewood and red oak veneers. A genuinely fantastic feature is the "starlight headliner," where fiber optics embedded in the leather roof lining give the impression of a star-filled night sky.

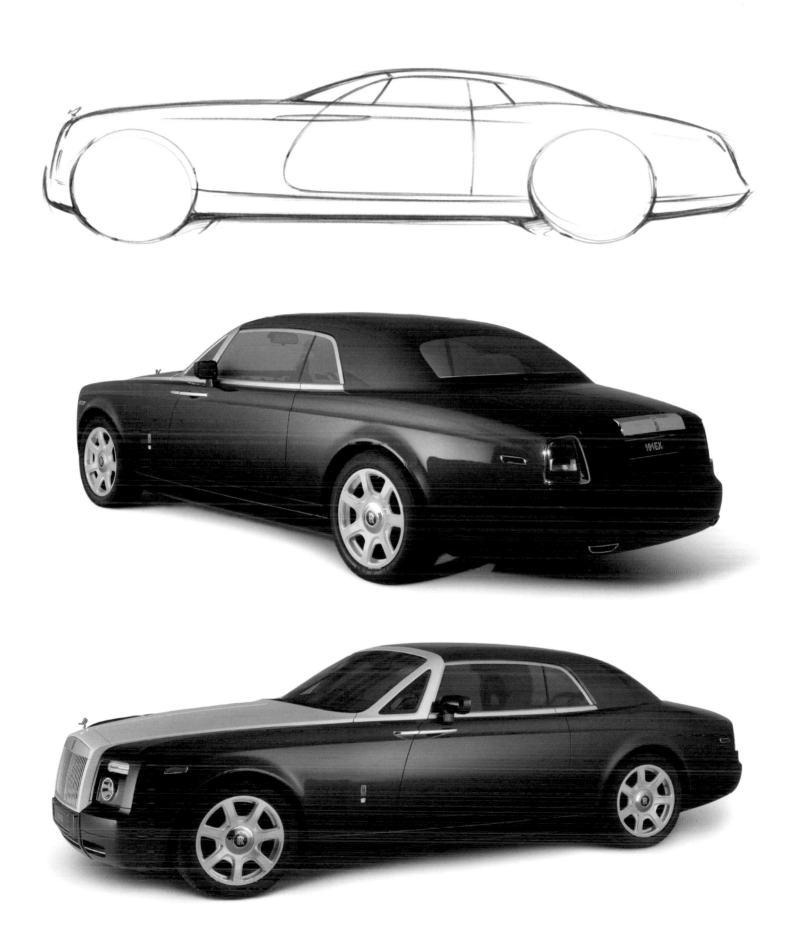

Concept

Saab Aero X

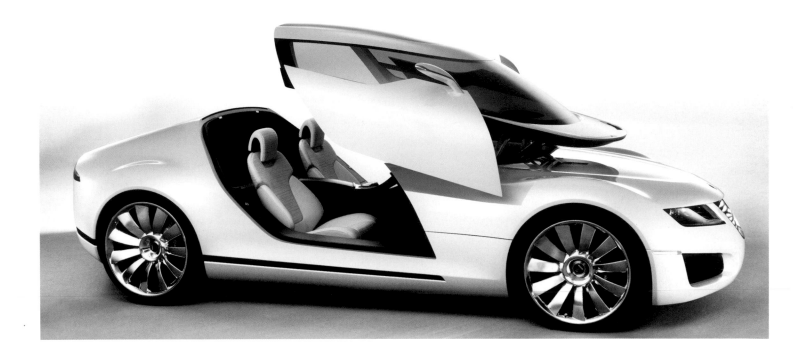

Design	Anthony Lo
Engine	2.8 V6 using bioethanol fuel
Power	298 kW (400 bhp) @ 5000 rpm
Torque	500 Nm (368 lb. ft.) @ 2000–5000 rpm
Gearbox	7-speed automatic
Installation	Front-engined/all-wheel drive
Front suspension	Double wishbone
Rear suspension	Multilink
Brakes front/rear	Discs/discs
Front tires	265/30R22
Rear tires	325/25R23
Length	4675 mm (184.1 in.)
Width	1918 mm (75.5 in.)
Height	1276 mm (50.2 in.)
Wheelbase	2795 mm (110 in.)
Track front/rear	1599/1579 mm (63/62.2 in.)
Curb weight	1500 kg (3307 lb.)
0–100 km/h (62 mph)	4.9 sec
Top speed	250 km/h (155 mph)

Launched at a preview to the Geneva show surrounded by 55 tonnes of specially imported Swedish ice, the Saab Aero X was one of the most highly regarded concepts at the show. Black and white in color, the evocative streamlined shape has echoes of the Chevrolet Corvette as well as the Maserati Birdcage concept designed by Pininfarina a year earlier.

Though a long, low, and lithe two-seater sports coupé, the Aero X has a great deal of curvature to its design, especially seen from above. The front of the hood, the windshield, and the roof all curve strongly in plan, like an aircraft. The wheel designs echo Saab's aircraft heritage, too. The body is muscular and has a balance of proportion with subtle detailing of which any car designer would be proud. The truncated rear, although not as fluid as the front, is itself designed simply to minimize aerodynamic drag.

But by far the most dramatic feature of the Aero X is its aircraft-style front-hinged cockpit that swings forward, complete with the doors. The windshield and side windows are a single glass molding—so with no A-pillar the Aero X has full 180-degree vision.

Like the exterior, the interior is clean and uncluttered, focusing instead on what is really needed in a driver-oriented sports car. The dashboard features a large display that can produce 3-D imagery on its clear acrylic surfaces.

This gorgeous concept stretches the Saab brand to a place it has never been before, showing the real scope of what is possible. Anthony Lo, who led the design team, believes the Aero X is a canvas on which to explore the potential signature cues for Saab's next-generation product portfolio—not just in visual style but also in engineering, where its powerful bioethanol engine is CO_2-neutral.

Scion t2B

Design	Alex Shen
Engine	2.4 in-line 4
Gearbox	4-speed automatic
Installation	Front-engined/front-wheel drive
Brakes front/rear	Discs/discs
Front tires	225/40R20
Rear tires	225/40R20
Length	4181 mm (164.6 in.)
Width	1791 mm (70.5 in.)
Height	1702 mm (67 in.)
Wheelbase	2700 mm (106.3 in.)

The all-new t2B from Toyota's "youth" brand Scion derives its name from "Tall Two-Box" and is a proposal for the future replacement of the xB. Compared to the current xB the new concept is even bolder than before, with a higher waistline and more masculine features.

The t2B clearly differentiates itself from the pack: it has a striking, solid appearance and is aimed at young people who want their first car to be distinctive and fun to drive. The t2B has an upright stance, giving lots of interior headroom; its panels feature little decoration—not even the door handles are visible. Narrow, deep-set headlamps and door mirrors indicate a car that has its arms open to new technology.

The body shape is asymmetric, created through the use of what Scion terms the *demado* design theme—Japanese for bay window. A sliding single door can be found on the right-hand side, whereas an easy-access, B-pillar-free two-door layout features on the left.

The interior design is very original: when the doors are closed, padded linings visually connect the doors to the seats, providing something of a lounge-like feel. The seats are made from multi-layered blue perforated leather, the perforations leaving a pattern as the different-colored underlayer is exposed.

There are two fixed sunroof panels that run nearly the entire length of the roof. The trilevel instrument panel provides access to movies, games, and music via downloads from the Internet. The upper layer of the instrument panel features an MP3 docking station, while the wide rear screen serves as a projection screen for movies, games, or screen savers. To accommodate large social gatherings, the screen can be viewed either from inside or from outside. Clearly, the designers at Scion are now seriously coming to grips with design for the new generation of young car owners.

Skoda Roomster

Design	Thomas Ingenlath
Engine	1.6 in-line 4 (1.2 and 1.4, and 1.4 and 1.9 diesel, also offered)
Power	78 kW (105 bhp)
Torque	155 Nm (114 lb. ft.) @ 3500 rpm
Gearbox	5-speed manual
Installation	Front-engined/front-wheel drive
Brakes front/rear	Discs/discs
Front tires	195/55R15
Rear tires	195/55R15
Length	4205 mm (165.6 in.)
Width	1684 mm (66.3 in.)
Height	1607 mm (63.3 in.)
Wheelbase	2617 mm (103 in.)
Track front/rear	1420/1484 mm (55.9/58.4 in.)
0–100 km/h (62 mph)	11.5 sec
Top speed	183 km/h (114 mph)

The eagerly awaited Skoda Roomster has finally arrived as a full production model. Three years after it was warmly applauded as a concept at the 2003 Frankfurt Motor Show, this innovative and highly practical take on the voguish miniwagon theme is set to enhance further the already enviable image of Skoda.

Overall, the showroom model has remained fairly true to the original concept, although the asymmetrical single rear door has gone in favor of a conventional lift-up hatchback tailgate, and there are many detailed tweaks. The effect of the wraparound windshield is still evident, as is the strong differentiation between the driver and rear passenger areas: the former is visually linked with the windshield, and the latter is graphically a separate entity with much deeper windows and with the door handle raised above the window opening line.

It is a pity that within such an exciting exterior the Roomster's interior lacks character and feels restrained. Skoda needed only to look at a Renault or a Mini interior for a very positive example of how it is possible to build more personality into interior design, even on a well-priced small car. Such a brand as Skoda, which has a strong quota of younger and more design-conscious buyers, is surely well placed to add a little excitement to the interior of a design that is already aimed at the more adventurous customer.

The Roomster is by far the most funky new model to come from Skoda and it has its own personality, much as the Renault Kangoo does. It marks a welcome break from the conservative formulae normally peddled by Skoda and Volkswagen; even if the interior is disappointing and the frontal design is a dreary corporate affair with a standard Skoda grille, nonetheless the rear and side views have plenty of character.

Spyker D12 Peking-to-Paris

Engine	6.0 W12 (Bentley)
Power	372 kW (500 bhp)
Gearbox	6-speed automatic
Installation	Front-engined/four-wheel drive
Brakes front/rear	Discs/discs
Front tires	R24
Rear tires	R24
Length	4950 mm (194.9 in.)
Width	2000 mm (78.7 in.)
Height	1680 mm (66.1 in.)
Curb weight	1895 kg (4178 lb.)
0–100 km/h (62 mph)	5 sec
Top speed	298 km/h (185 mph)

The Dutch company Spyker is little known outside specialist circles, but has ambitious plans to build 100 sports cars in 2006. The firm, which revives an illustrious classic name from the early part of the last century, has existed in its present revived form only since the first day of the new millennium: already, four models have been launched, all of them pitched firmly at the pinnacle of the luxury market. The D12 Peking-to-Paris is the firm's fifth model and is completely new, with Spyker defining it as a Super Sports Utility Vehicle.

An original Spyker was used in the grueling 1907 five-car race from Peking (Beijing) to Paris, which took three months; the Spyker finished second. The new car is designed to rekindle the spirit of the original race by offering big performance allied with much-needed comfort. The new car, says Spyker, comes in response to the wishes of an older generation of sports-car buyers who want comfort together with exotic looks—something that is difficult to find today.

The interior is certainly exotic and has an exquisite standard of workmanship in its leather, chrome, and milled-aluminum surfacing. Astonishing twin polished-metal pylons brace the roof from the transmission tunnel. There is nothing else quite as intense or as plush, even at these elevated price levels. The exterior, however, is unlikely to swing so many opinions: thanks to its raised ride height the impression is that of a coupé on stilts or an inflated Maserati Quattroporte. Yet the bold grille and curvaceous body are strangely attractive and mix design cues of the past with modern treatments.

Spyker has won races, featured in movies, and carried off several design prizes, and it is now finding itself a handy niche among the eccentric and extremely wealthy—so the company is obviously doing something right.

Spyker D12 Peking-to-Paris **Concept** 247

Subaru B5-TPH

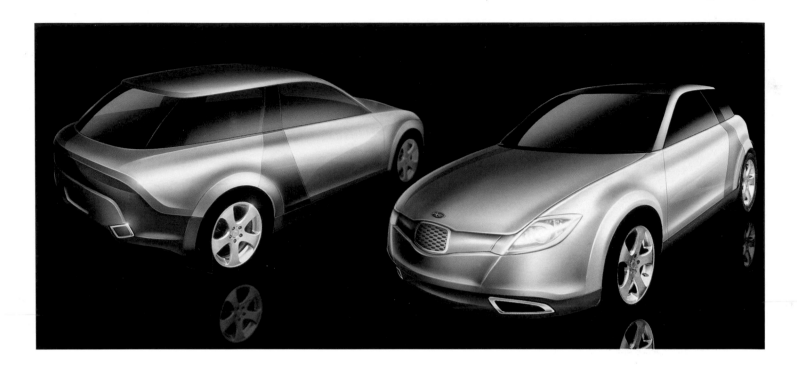

Although famed for its rally-dominating all-wheel-drive technology, Subaru has never quite managed to bring to market the right aesthetic designs to attract the larger volumes of sales that the brand could perhaps command.

At the 2005 Tokyo Motor Show Subaru showed one way of combining high power with an environmentally conscious hybrid powertrain. The TPH in the coupé/sports-wagon crossover concept stands for "Turbo Parallel Hybrid"; the engine compartment comes packed with an electric motor sandwiched between the 2-liter turbocharged flat four and the automatic transmission. The electric motor is powered by a new type of manganese lithium-ion battery that charges quickly and operates not only in city driving but also when cruising.

The B5-TPH has deliberately challenging design elements all over its coupé package. At the front the rather simplistic-looking grille is not as suggestive of the powerful car beneath as one would perhaps expect, though incorporating the headlamps and grille into a single flowing bar across the front of the car is a nice modern touch. The lower air intakes echo the headlamp design and, unusually, the B-pillar is picked out in a contrasting color and drawn rearward at its base to create a more coupé-like effect. The front door is deliberately set at an angle, clearly signaled by the way its body-color finish cuts into the dark sill panel.

It may have a potentially interesting powertrain, an element of crossover practicality, and an unusual design, but the B5-TPH still manages to emerge short on memorability. Worse, some of its intentionally novel design features simply fail to work effectively. Lacking the impact a decent sports car should rightfully have, the TPH is not as successful a design concept as the recent B9 Scrambler.

Suzuki Grand Vitara

Engine	2.0 in-line 4 (1.6, and 1.9 diesel, also offered)
Power	103 kW (138 bhp) @ 6000 rpm
Torque	183 Nm (135 lb. ft.) @ 4000 rpm
Gearbox	5-speed manual
Installation	Front-engined/four-wheel drive
Front suspension	MacPherson strut
Rear suspension	Multilink
Brakes front/rear	Discs/discs
Front tires	225/65R17
Rear tires	225/65R17
Length	4470 mm (176 in.)
Width	1810 mm (71.3 in.)
Height	1695 mm (66.7 in.)
Wheelbase	2640 mm (103.9 in.)
Track front/rear	1540/1570 mm (60.6/61.8 in.)
Curb weight	1505 kg (3318 lb.)
0–100 km/h (62 mph)	12.5 sec
Top speed	175 km/h (109 mph)
Fuel consumption	9.1 l/100 km (25.8 mpg)
CO$_2$ emissions	220 g/km

Launched at the Frankfurt Motor Show in 2005, the new Grand Vitara continues from where its predecessor left off in staking Suzuki's claim to a piece of the action in the compact SUV segment—a market dominated by such models as the Toyota RAV4 and the Honda CR-V. As such, it is predominantly aimed at leisure activities rather than serious off-roading, placing affordability and everyday practicality higher up the priority list than ultimate rock-climbing ability.

The outgoing Vitara had come to look seriously dated, with its body style majoring in rounded corners and soft, ill-defined surfaces. Perfectly on cue, the new Vitara is much crisper and much more contemporary, and it looks larger and more substantial, too.

Sharp feature lines, rectangular headlamps with clear lenses, and a body with taut surfaces all add up to a much more modern package. Findings from Suzuki's research into its own customer base were a strong influence on the design of the new model: owners called for better off-road and on-road performance as well as enhanced practicality in terms of passenger and luggage space. These, along with the high "command" driving position, were seen as important attributes in a vehicle the main role of which would be everyday transport.

The Vitara's principal engine is a 2-liter gas: in some markets a V6 gas and a 1.9-liter turbo diesel are offered. Each of these engines is mounted north–south in the body, which is now of unitary construction rather than the previous body-on-frame structure. The driveline now incorporates full-time four-wheel drive—a useful advance on the earlier switchable 4WD arrangement.

Inside, the interior is not only roomier and better equipped and finished, but also more stylish than before. The treatment is sober, technical, and tough-looking, with a mix of black and satin aluminum in a styling theme incorporating circular highlights.

Suzuki Ionis

The Suzuki Ionis is a forward-looking four-seater compact minivan with bold sculptural forms and graphically strong features. One-box in profile, it is unusually radical for such a small vehicle.

At the front is what is perhaps the Ionis's most unfortunate feature—its sad-looking, down-mouthed fish-faced grille; above this, the profile sweeps steeply upward to meet the bold Suzuki logo, which sits on a full-width polished-metal band that forms the base of the windshield. This band runs up along the cant rails above the windows before finally turning downward to form the D-pillar. The headlamps and taillamps are very futuristic-looking in their semitransparent light-blue finish and with their dramatic scythe-like shaping.

At the rear, the large concentric semicircles cut into the bumper area echo the style of the grille at the front and, again like the front, point upward toward the Suzuki logo. Yet overall, the rear is something of a mess of free-form surfaces and geometric designs that seem to bear little relationship to one another.

The fuel cell is located beneath the floor, allowing more space in the full-length cabin. To help give more versatility the seats can be rearranged and moved in all directions, although the highly stylized leather chairs framed in polished metal do not look inviting. Other advanced technologies include an entertainment system with which passengers can download music via wireless Internet access and watch satellite TV.

The Ionis is in many respects a reasonably well-resolved design. Suzuki maintains that it is designed to convey the image of water, and in some of its organic forms it recalls Gaudí's organic architecture in Barcelona. Sadly, with so many ideas fighting for space on the much smaller canvas of a minicar, the technique is less effective.

Suzuki LC

The Suzuki LC is a modern-day re-creation of the 1955 Suzulight, which was Suzuki's first-ever car. Japanese carmakers appear prone to regular and often productive bouts of retro fever; occasionally the results are very attractive indeed. The Nissan Figaro and S-Cargo van, for instance, were charming evocations of bygone styles.

The Suzuki LC is a cutesy concept whose task is to remind the world that Suzuki has been making cars for fifty years. The closest European equivalent to the Suzulight would have been the Goggomobil or one of a number of grown-up bubble cars.

Being a dedicated two-seater despite its three-box shape, the LC has enough room only for a small storage shelf behind the seats. And despite the air vents on the rear flanks that hint at a fifties-style rear engine, the modern-day powerplant is a 660 cc unit up front.

There are quite a number of design features that together can be combined to make any car look 1950s—these include chrome-rimmed circular headlamps, an upright windshield edged with chrome and with rounded corners, non-tinted glass, fender-mounted rearview mirrors, and white-walled tires. The exterior design of the LC has blunt front and rear ends, a domed roof, and very little exterior ornamentation.

Inside, the trim is very simple and, some might say, modern minimalist. The white steering wheel echoes the white-walled tires, and there are gearshift paddles on the steering wheel disguised as an old-style chrome horn rim. The classic-style speedometer is grossly exaggerated in size, in the style of the Mini—though it is wrapped around the steering column rather than centrally placed.

When one considers how successful the new Mini has been, this cute, fun-loving car does not seem so ridiculous. Who knows—Suzuki might even find a ready clientele for its nostalgic charms.

Suzuki MPW

The Suzuki MPW, or "Mom's Personal Wagon" to be precise, is a study that looks at how women use their car when driving with young children. As such, it is to be welcomed: too many car designs ignore the needs of families by aiming themselves at the business executive market.

In its proportions the MPW is that short and tall shape familiar from previous generations of Japanese and Korean microcars. Yet Suzuki has succeeded in avoiding the slab-sided design language commonly found on such practical cars: instead, there are curves and sculptural surfaces. The overall look is deliberately cheerful, the aim being to make children that little bit happier when climbing aboard. The design mounts its headlamps slightly higher than normal so as not to make the upper cabin look too tall. Yet, apart from the changed proportions, there is little other innovation on the exterior to set it apart from many other compact hatches.

Inside, a whole host of useful features serves to make life aboard more family-friendly. Examples are the numerous storage spaces, the easily foldable seats allowing parents to reach around the cabin, a useful step in front of the rear seat, and the calming and stylish brown and beige overall color scheme.

The dashboard is somewhat toylike, especially the central gear lever. As with the Suzuki LC concept there are strong hints of the 1950s, with the cream switch panel and the central speedometer. The concentric vent design echoes the graphic on the rear lamps and is carried across to the floor pedals.

The MPW may well provide a preview of the next-generation Wagon R+ for Europe: it will be interesting to see how many of the family-friendly features in this concept Suzuki can carry over into production.

Suzuki PX

The PX is an imposing, original, and somewhat intimidating design that proves under its shiny metallic skin to be a family-friendly six-seater minivan. The vehicle, says Suzuki, is tailored around the needs of middle-aged Japanese men who do not have a typical everyday routine; curiously, it takes its thematic inspiration from the legendary American Airstream caravan. It could perhaps be described as the retro-future. There is growing interest in this type of concept, much of it triggered by Volkswagen's Microbus study presented several years ago. Two years ago, Mitsubishi showed its Se-ro concept; this year it is the turn of Suzuki to join the trend.

In terms of its proportions the PX is a monovolume design with a shortish hood and a high waistline. The roof is domed and echoes the domed surfaces of the hood. The exterior combines linear features with circular, especially evident along the sides where the three door lines, a key characteristic of the Airstream, sit alongside the bold bolted wheel arches.

The rear is original in its execution, too: the large tailgate glass is curved in two planes to give a bubble effect, while the triangular taillight clusters occupy the corners on either side.

As with most people-carriers, the interior is where much of the design innovation is found: in the PX the color scheme is ice-cool and mixes white leather with blue electroluminescent lighting. There are three rows of limousine-style seats, and enough space for individual comfort. The interior gives a nod to various design themes: Art-Deco for much of the geometric chrome, plus modern electronics for the digital screens and early Corvettes for the twin-cowl dashboard.

The PX is practical, original, and appealing, and could develop a definite following if the trend for retro—highlighted in Detroit, too—begins to take hold.

Engine	2.0 in-line 4
Installation	Front-engined/front-wheel drive
Brakes front/rear	Discs/discs
Length	4420 mm (174 in.)
Wheelbase	2998 mm (118 in.)

Tata Cliffrider

It is interesting that Tata, India's largest vehicle-builder and second-biggest carmaker, chose the Geneva show at which to present its Cliffrider design study. As an evolution of the Crossover concept launched a year earlier, also at Geneva, the Cliffrider is first and foremost a pickup in its configuration, using very much the same design language as the Crossover.

The shape is described by Tata as that of a high-slung sedan: there are four side doors to the arched cabin, and where the trunk would normally be is now the pickup cargo deck. Side rails, running from the roof to the rear lights, triangulate the gap left between the top of the C-pillar and the rear corner. A high beltline, taut panel surfaces, and the futuristic-looking slotted headlamps trailing rearward along the front fenders all add up to a unique Tata look and feel.

The interior design is extremely modern, with soft colors, simple shapes, and twin glass panels at either side of the central roof spine giving generous light levels. Behind the rear seats, easily accessed thanks to the rear-hinged doors, is a partition that can be removed so as to link the pickup bed and the passenger area for carrying very long loads. Seats, doors, and dashboard are all graceful and simple in their design, though the extensive use of white on the display car would limit real-life practicality. Still, if Tata does eventually release a production version of the Cliffrider it would be wise to try to maintain this strong contemporary identity, as something that would set it apart from its slower-moving competitors.

Although it is only a concept at this stage, the Cliffrider's mix of design, affordability, and ruggedness could gain a good European following and could be helpful in Tata's plans for expanding beyond India.

Engine	V6
Installation	Front-engined/four-wheel drive
Brakes front/rear	Discs/discs
Length	5080 mm (200 in.)
Width	1900 mm (74.8 in.)
Height	1800 mm (70.9 in.)
Wheelbase	3150 mm (124 in.)
Curb weight	2000 kg (4409 lb.)

Toyota Camry

Engine	3.5 V6 (2.4 in-line 4 and gas–electric hybrid also offered)
Power	200 kW (268 bhp) @ 6200 rpm
Torque	337 Nm (248 lb. ft.) @ 4700 rpm
Gearbox	6-speed automatic
Installation	Front-engined/front-wheel drive
Front suspension	MacPherson strut
Rear suspension	Dual-link MacPherson strut
Brakes front/rear	Discs/discs
Front tires	215/60R16
Rear tires	215/60R16
Length	4806 mm (189.2 in.)
Width	1821 mm (71.7 in.)
Height	1460 mm (57.5 in.)
Wheelbase	2776 mm (109.3 in.)
Track front/rear	1575/1565 mm (62/61.6 in.)
Curb weight	1560 kg (3440 lb.)
Fuel consumption	8.7 l/100 km (27 US mpg)

In recent years the Toyota Camry has taken on a role as America's car for Mr Average. With monotonous regularity it has finished each year as America's bestselling passenger car—to the extent that it has become something of a byword for cautious, middle-of-the-road design that upsets no one.

So Toyota had to play a careful balancing act when crafting the 2007 redesign of this, its big earner in North America. On the one hand, Toyota wanted to move the design on, in order to attract younger and less conservative buyers; on the other hand, with upward of 400,000 units a year needing to find buyers, the stakes were very high and the styling could not afford to offend.

Toyota's chosen path was to enhance the new Camry's appeal by making it appear slightly more sporty. This the designers have done by sweeping the headlamps back, making them slightly less dominating than before, and making the whole frontal design smoother and more streamlined. At the rear the smaller tapering lamps are the main difference, allowing the simpler surfaces of the body to stand out. From the side view, two parallel crease lines at top and bottom visually lengthen the car; the fast C-pillar is a strong element, imparting a sense of forward movement to the car. The stance on the road is much improved.

The interior is of high quality, as befits a car influenced by Lexus. The controls, switches, and instrumentation are clear, simple, and attractive, and the long cabin can seat five with plenty of legroom: the top XLE model even has rear seats that can recline by six degrees to enhance comfort. Three powertrain choices are offered, all with front-wheel drive: a 2.4-liter four cylinder, a V6 of 3.5 liters and, unusually, a hybrid setup promising 40 US mpg (5.9 l/100 km).

Toyota Endo

The Endo is a playful design experiment for a very small four-seater city car. It comes with compact proportions, though the height of 1.7 meters (5 ft. 6 in.) gives it a decent feeling of interior space. As with the Smart car, the wheels are pushed right to the corners of the vehicle, making it look highly maneuverable for city driving and sporty at the same time.

There is a distinct visual split between the upper and the lower architecture. The lower body uses free-form design language that plays with light and shadow along the side of the car. By contrast, the upper body is finished in white, is oval in shape, and uses constant curves and surfaces. This twin-tone color and styling is very effective at making an exciting statement with what could otherwise have been a potentially dull city car. The Endo is designed for maximum effectiveness in cities, and it can use parking spaces too small even for a Smart thanks to its doors and tailgate having double-link hinges so they do not swing out so far when open.

Inside, ingenuity and technology abound. The two main seats can be complemented by twin jump-seats that fold out of the trunk walls: this makes the vehicle a four-seater when needed—something that would be a huge advantage over a Smart. There is a large screen that spans the whole width of the dashboard, which gives a wealth of information and customization possibilities. The door interior panels have reflective surfaces, so by changing the background color of the dashboard screen the interior mood can be changed to suit the driver's wishes.

The much-trumpeted "Vibrant Clarity" ethos of Toyota's European design center in Nice is aimed at creating fresh, visually exciting models, and the Endo can be seen as one of the best examples of this philosophy in practice.

Design	Laurent Bouzige
Length	3000 mm (118.1 in.)
Width	1690 mm (66.5 in.)
Height	1520 mm (59.8 in.)

Toyota Estima Hybrid

The 2005 Tokyo Motor Show played host to a large and stylish minivan from Toyota that previews the third generation of the company's principal big multiseater, known as Previa in Europe and Estima in Asia. The show car, fitted with a gas/electric drivetrain, was billed as the Estima Hybrid concept, though it is thought to reflect the exact style of the production model to be released later in 2006.

Visually, the Estima is a long, sweeping mass that appears to glide through the air, with its pointed front end and swept-back hood and windshield offering little resistance to the airflow. Headlamps integrated with the grille create a striking graphic shape, and one that echoes the pointed theme of the front end. There is a sense of dynamism even when at rest: the headlamps sweep dramatically rearward from the nose, while toward the rear the developing body-side feature line becomes more pronounced over the rear wheels. The body pillars are black, to make the colored body mass appear more grounded and linear. The darkened windows running around the entire car give the impression of a strong two-layered sandwich, and are picked up by the lower body trim finished in a similar color.

The interior is high-tech, with multiple digital screens, yet at the same time restful, with cool, calm colors. The long instrument canopy over the dashboard emulates the length and aerodynamics of the exterior, though the rectangular center stack seems to jar with the sleek upper dash.

The show concept comes with a variation on Toyota's latest hybrid driveline: a 2.4-liter gas engine, allied with an electric motor, powers the front wheels, while a second motor on the rear axle provides four-wheel-drive capability. Hybrid, as well as gas and diesel, will be offered on production versions.

Length	4820 mm (189.8 in.)
Width	1800 mm (70.9 in.)
Height	1760 mm (69.3 in.)

Toyota F3R

Concerned that minivans in the US are bought by an aging sector of the population, the F3R concept is a proposal by Toyota's studio in California for a large multiseater that will help to make this type of vehicle more attractive to younger purchasers.

The F3R is a large people-carrier able to accommodate eight. But that is as far as the resemblance to conventional minivans goes. Those eight people sit in an interior that can range between anything from a living room on wheels to a rolling nightclub; the seats can be in rows or arranged, sofa-fashion, around the sides. There are two passenger doors on each side, and these open like a set of veranda doors onto this flexible social space.

The body is more extreme still. A large, thrusting hood emerges from an even bigger passenger compartment, which looks as if it is extruded rearward; the roof is almost completely flat, accentuating the wedge look produced by the slightly rising waistline. This long window graphic itself highlights the length and space within the cabin. At the rear corner there is a hint of Renault with the neatly wrapped tail glass: it is a well-resolved and very attractive style, especially from the rear.

The front end has a surprisingly strong American-retro look to it, with a large grille that is deep in the center, old-car style, but which extends outward to take in the swept-back lights. Again, it is a bold treatment that integrates well with the wide, sporty low-rider look produced by the large 22-inch wheels set tight in their arches.

Toyota is sure to be carefully monitoring the reaction to this concept. Many doubted whether it was possible to produce a large multiseater with attitude and serious funky appeal. Toyota has just supplied the answer.

Design	Ian Cartabiano and Alan Schneider
Engine	Hybrid synergy drive
Front tires	R22
Rear tires	R22
Length	5080 mm (200 in.)
Width	2055 mm (80.9 in.)
Height	1850 mm (72.8 in.)
Wheelbase	3150 mm (124 in.)

Toyota Fine-X

The name Fine-X places this latest Toyota study as the most recent in a long line of concept cars dating back many years. As such, it represents a snapshot of Toyota's 2005 vision of what a car of the near future should embody.

The overarching principle behind every aspect of the Fine-X's design is that of environmental conservation and sustainability. Naturally, the drive system is a zero-emissions fuel-cell hybrid arrangement, located for maximum space efficiency under the passenger compartment floor. In a bid to make the car carbon-neutral, Toyota has opted to use as many plant-based materials as possible for the interior and exterior components: the aim is to ensure that there will be no net addition to the CO_2 burden on the environment, though Toyota does not claim to have achieved this yet with the Fine-X.

In engineering terms there is real innovation in the Fine-X chassis: electric motors on each wheel give truly independent drive, while thanks to drive-by-wire electrical architecture all four wheels steer independently too, giving large steering angles and much-enhanced maneuverability. This even extends to on-the-spot rotation, although the tight wheel arches do not appear to allow such dramatic wheel articulation.

The most obvious convenience features are the large gullwing doors, but the Fine-X also provides "welcome" seats that pivot to the side to allow easy entrance. The design is only slightly bigger than the new Yaris, yet the interior space is that of a much larger car. This seemingly impossible packaging is achieved by placing the wheels right at the corners and having a steep screen at the front so that the occupants can be positioned further forward. The digital dashboard shows just how little space is needed for display packaging, and the steering control looks more like something you might find on a futuristic bicycle.

Engine	Hydrogen fuel-cell hybrid
Length	3860 mm (152 in.)
Width	1750 mm (68.9 in.)
Height	1550 mm (61 in.)

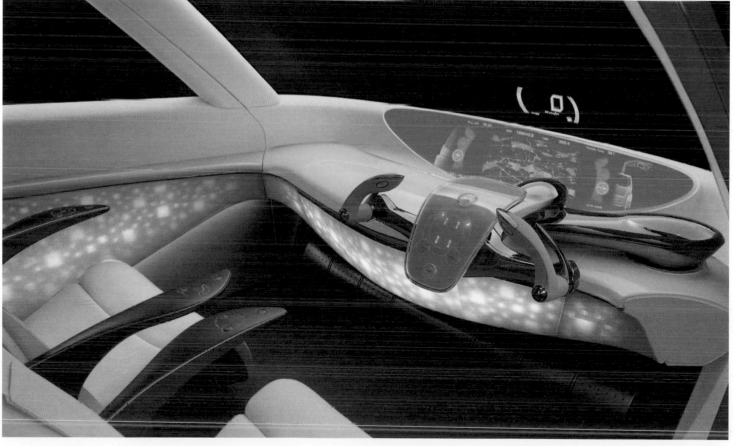

Toyota Hilux

Engine	2.5 in-line 4 diesel
Power	75 kW (100 bhp) @ 3600 rpm
Torque	260 Nm (192 lb. ft.) @ 1600–2400 rpm
Gearbox	5-speed manual
Installation	Front-engined/four-wheel drive
Front suspension	Double wishbone
Rear suspension	Leaf spring
Brakes front/rear	Discs/drums
Length	5255 mm (206.9 in.)
Width	1760 mm (69.3 in.)
Height	1680 mm (66.1 in.)
Wheelbase	3085 mm (121.5 in.)
Track front/rear	1510/1510 mm (59.4/59.4 in.)
Curb weight	1555 kg (3428 lb.)
0–100 km/h (62 mph)	16.8 sec
Top speed	150 km/h (93 mph)

Unlikely as it may sound, the Hilux is Toyota's second-bestselling model of all time, after the Corolla. More than twelve million examples of the versatile and rugged pickup family have been sold since the vehicle was first launched in Japan back in 1967.

Such figures as these demonstrate how large and important the global pickup market is; they show, too, how successful Toyota has been in retaining its lead in the market for a vehicle that combines the durability of a utility workhorse with the comfortable accommodation and easy driving manner of a passenger car.

Now in its sixth edition, the Hilux looks more American than ever: it revels in a heavy chrome bar at either side of the big Toyota logo on the grille, and it boasts modern headlamps, tauter door surfaces, and a larger, rugged-looking front bumper. Each generation has succeeded in being more luxurious than the last, yet that vital load bay and off-road ability have remained uncompromised. It is easy to picture Toyota designers having actively to restrain themselves from making the Hilux look too fashionable, as this could undermine its reputation for utility and toughness.

Three different versions are offered: a single cab, an "extra" cab (seating four), and a double cab (seating six). The new car is built on a completely new ladder-frame chassis and is stiffer than the previous model, giving better road handling and refinement. All three versions are longer, wider, and taller than before, resulting in more interior space and greater load-bay capacity.

The interior follows the tried-and-tested format of a slightly sporty design with easily found switches and controls. The Hilux has a massive following in the practical trades and construction worlds and among people with active lifestyles who want to chuck bikes or surfboards in the back with ease.

Toyota i-Swing

Where else but the Tokyo Motor Show would you find a concept as groundbreaking as the i-Swing? The i-Swing is the latest in a line of single-seat personal vehicles from Toyota, following the Pod from 2001, the PM of 2003 and, most recently, the i-Unit displayed at the Frankfurt show in 2005.

At low, walking-type speeds, the gyroscopically stabilized i-Swing stands upright on two wheels. But when drivers want to go faster they adopt a skiing position, take hold of the joystick, and shift their weight when cornering: under these conditions the i-Swing sits lower, stretches its polyurethane body out, and rides on three wheels.

The body appears to fit snugly around the user, for the i-Swing is really designed as an extension of the person. Toyota claims that the i-Swing communicates with the driver using artificial intelligence, enabling it to learn the habits and preferences of its owner and store relevant data about him or her. Different i-Swings can even communicate with one another.

The front door and rear surface contain embedded LED panels that can be customized to display a video, or an image to suit the driver's mood. This idea was first seen on the Toyota Pod. The chassis structure of the vehicle allows it to tilt through corners and even lean back and do wheelies. Electric power to the wheels ensures maximum maneuverability, and the gyro sensor maintains stability during changes of direction.

Nevertheless, with less occupant protection than a motorbike, the i-Swing would need specially designated zones for its use and would be far too dangerous to be used in the thick of city traffic. Wildly futuristic though this personal transportation device might appear, with the right safe environment and with decent range, speed, and price, the i-Swing could have global appeal.

Length	985/1275 mm (38.8/50.2 in.)
	(using two wheels/three wheels)
Width	800 mm (31.5 in.)
Height	1800/1710 mm (70.9/67.3 in.)
	(using two wheels/three wheels)

Toyota i-Unit

For as long as wheeled transport has existed, designers have been fascinated by microcars. Be it the Smart, the Fiat 500, or the BMW Isetta, compact, cute cars have always attracted a big following. Today especially, with so many people traveling alone in their cars, the same urge exists for exploring new concepts offering environmentally friendly personal transportation.

This is not the first time that Toyota has toyed with futuristic personal transportation. The Toyota PM, a concept presented at the Tokyo Motor Show in 2003, embodied similar thinking, with the driver seated right at the front of the cockpit and the wheels exposed. However, the PM was 650 mm (2 ft.) longer than this latest concept, which makes the i-Unit a very different prospect.

Unusually, its design was inspired by a leaf. This can be seen clearly in the leaf-shaped exoskeletal cell that wraps around the driver. At the top of this structure there is a clear visor to protect the driver's face—but that is the sum total of the protection he or she gets. The concept operates first in an upright mode, where the driver is seated, and then when more speed is required the i-Unit begins to recline, making the wheelbase longer and the center of gravity lower to enhance stability.

The i-Unit's components are made from decomposable and recyclable materials to reduce the machine's impact on the environment. According to Toyota, the i-Unit is designed to balance freedom of movement, harmony with society, and harmony with the Earth's natural environment. Transport like the i-Unit would require radical changes in our urban traffic management for adequate safety—yet the combination of widespread pedestrianization and i-Unit style personal transportation could lead to a much-improved city-center environment if there were the political will to implement such a policy shift.

Engine	Electric, with lithium-ion battery
Installation	Rear-wheel drive; wheel motors
Length	1100–1800 mm (43.3–70.9 in.)
Width	1040 mm (40.9 in.)
Height	1800–1250 mm (70.9–49.2 in.)
Wheelbase	540–1300 mm (21.3–51.2 in.)
Track front/rear	850/830 mm (33.5/32.7 in.)
Curb weight	180 kg (397 lb.)
CO_2 emissions	0 g/km

Toyota RAV4

Engine	2.2 in-line 4 diesel (2.0 and 2.2 gas also offered)
Power	130 kW (174 bhp) @ 3600 rpm
Torque	400 Nm (295 lb. ft.) @ 2000–2600 rpm
Gearbox	6-speed manual
Installation	Front-engined/four-wheel drive
Front suspension	MacPherson strut
Rear suspension	Double wishbone
Brakes front/rear	Discs/discs
Front tires	235/55R18
Rear tires	235/55R18
Length	4395 mm (173 in.)
Width	1815 mm (71.5 in.)
Height	1685 mm (66.3 in.)
Wheelbase	2560 mm (100.8 in.)
Track front/rear	1560/1560 mm (61.4/61.4 in.)
Curb weight	1595 kg (3516 lb.)
0–100 km/h (62 mph)	9.3 sec
Top speed	200 km/h (124 mph)
Fuel consumption	7.2 l/100 km (32.7 mpg)
CO_2 emissions	190 g/km

The designation RAV4—for Recreational Active Vehicle with four-wheel drive—is a very special one for Toyota. The original RAV4, launched in 1994, was an unexpected and massive hit, its funky looks and fun-to-drive personality leading to the emergence of a whole new market segment for compact, stylish, and sporty urban SUVs. Now, every carmaker feels the need to be represented in this sector.

Two generations later, the RAV has matured into a very different animal. The third-generation model is 145 mm (6 in.) longer and 80 mm (3 in.) wider than the current car, itself much bigger than the first. Clearly, this is useful in providing extra legroom and shoulder space. The new car naturally has a cleaner and more contemporary look, too: the headlamps and taillamps cut back into the body more, the doors have more space uninterrupted by detail, and there are sharper lines and more shape at the rear. Yet the wheel arch trim added to some models looks like an afterthought, detracting from the sculpted feel; it would look much cleaner if it were pressed into the fender panels themselves.

More fundamentally, however, the RAV4's styling has become quite soft and rounded—perhaps in order to draw more female customers. In so doing, Toyota has lost the strong, tough personality of the first two generations and gone for a more conservative touch that could just as well be a station wagon or a people-carrier.

Despite Toyota's professed pursuit of its corporate "Vibrant Clarity" design ethos, the new RAV4 is a disappointment in that it is precisely clarity that the design lacks. Too many details fight for attention, especially at the front. At best, this is a non-objectionable design that will certainly sell well for Toyota— but it will never be as memorable as the characterful original from 1994.

Toyota Urban Cruiser

The Toyota Urban Cruiser is a one-shot design study created by Toyota's European design center ED2, and it is certainly quite different from what one has come to expect from the habitually conservative Japanese brand.

A mini-SUV to fill the gap left by the RAV4's jump in size, status, and price, the Urban Cruiser is designed to reflect the "Vibrant Clarity" philosophy that currently underpins Toyota's styling work. The exterior uses quite bold features to communicate the car's values to the onlooker, and it has little in the way of decoration or complex surfaces. The message is clear that the Urban Cruiser is a thoroughly modern design; the trouble is that it just is not attractive. An ugly front is formed by the wide rectangular mesh grille and the silver surround, topped by a strangely organic-looking triangular hood. The whole effect is not helped by the froglike green color.

The side view is the best, with the various design elements working in proportion with each other; it also helps that the strange front and gloomy rear are out of sight. Certain details are troubling, too: the rims of the wheel arches do not form a consistent arc, yet neither are they distinctly squared off to look like a design feature. Instead they look like a blunder.

The interior design was done by Yi Yeong Jae, who claims to have brought inspiration from fashion and modern furniture. This is more successful and fits the Vibrant Clarity theme well. The extensive use of light gray for the dashboard and seats risks looking unsophisticated, but the use of form and bright colors is interesting.

The Urban Cruiser is not the most successful of concepts: the design has the unusual distinction of looking simplistic, ordinary, and ugly, all at the same time. Toyota's designers have achieved much more fully resolved products that are selling well and are in the showrooms right now.

Design	Elvio D'Aprile

Toyota Yaris

Design	Toyota ED2 Studio, France
Engine	1.4 in-line 4 diesel (1.0 and 1.3 gas also offered)
Power	66 kW (89 bhp) @ 3600 rpm
Torque	190 Nm (140 lb. ft.) @ 1800–3000 rpm
Gearbox	5-speed manual
Installation	Front-engined/front-wheel drive
Brakes front/rear	Discs/discs
Front tires	185/60R15
Rear tires	185/60R15
Length	3750 mm (147.6 in.)
Width	1695 mm (66.7 in.)
Height	1530 mm (60.2 in.)
Wheelbase	2460 mm (96.9 in.)
Track front/rear	1475/1460 mm (58.1/57.5 in.)
Curb weight	1055 kg (2326 lb.)
0–100 km/h (62 mph)	10.7 sec
Top speed	175 km/h (109 mph)
Fuel consumption	4.5 l/100 km (52.3 mpg)
CO_2 emissions	119 g/km

With a plethora of awards to its name, the French-built Yaris is Toyota's top-selling B-segment car, with more than 1.2 million buyers in Europe since its launch in 1999.

With the original renowned for its quality, safety, versatility, and space efficiency, Toyota has resorted to making the second-generation Yaris bigger in order to offer an across-the-board improvement over the previous model. A further consideration is the arrival of Toyota's smaller and cheaper Aygo, giving the new Yaris the freedom to move slightly upmarket.

So, with its overall length, width, and height all subtly stretched, the new car follows the lead of such competitors as the new Clio and Punto by offering more space in a more sophisticated overall package.

Designed entirely at Toyota's studios in France, the new car has gained a more solid, more planted feel. Strongly sculpted forms at the front include bigger headlamps that are set back into the bumper and that provide a radius running back into the door mirror. Longitudinal creases in the hood lead into the grille, V-shaped at the base, to provide a link with the outgoing model.

A crease line now runs through the doors, and the upper B-pillars have been blackened to lengthen the car visually; the waistline rises through the rear door to give the car a dynamic poise, as dictated by Toyota's "Vibrant Clarity" design philosophy. Inside, the distinctive single instrument panel in the center is retained.

The Yaris may have grown up a little, but the generation change has left it just as charming as it was before—with the benefit of more space and a more substantial, more mature presence. All in all, the new Yaris rates as a highly professional evolution that builds on the appeal of the original but successfully addresses its few shortcomings.

Volkswagen Concept A

Design	Exterior: Marc Lichte
	Interior: Thomasc Bachorski
Engine	1.4 in-line 4, turbo+ supercharged, natural gas
Power	112 kW (150 bhp)
Torque	220 Nm (162 lb. ft.)
Gearbox	6-speed manual
Installation	Front-engined/all-wheel drive
Brakes front/rear	Discs/discs
Front tires	295/35R20
Rear tires	295/35R20
Length	4350 mm (171.3 in.)
Width	1850 mm (72.8 in.)
Height	1550 mm (61 in.)
Wheelbase	2600 mm (102.4 in.)
Fuel consumption	5.0 kg natural gas/100 km

With crossover being the most popular buzzword at the moment, Volkswagen is planning to capitalize on the halo of its Touareg luxury SUV by developing a smaller SUV of Golf size. But if the Concept A is anything to go by, this will be no ordinary RAV4 rival: instead, it will have much more of a sports-car look and avoid the me-too stigma of being just another off-road machine.

The Concept A is a sports coupé first and foremost; its crossover credentials stem from its raised suspension, to give more tire clearance. It looks great fun and, thanks to its coupé-like sloping rear roof, it cannot possibly be confused with run-of-the-mill SUVs.

Equally importantly, the Concept A is also very different from any other Volkswagen. It is less conservative and has much more energy: a new frontal treatment with an aluminum H-structure separating the grille area and the adjacent headlamps looks dynamic and technical and conveys agility. VW goes so far as to claim that the aluminum grille was modeled on the face of a cheetah.

The overall proportion is that of a classic coupé, with a long hood, rising waistline, sloping rear screen and truncated rear end—but there are also four doors. However, the raised body and large wheel arches give it an added dimension, making it a design of car that no other manufacturer yet has. For added appeal, the roof rolls back along the sloping top to a fully open position. At the rear the tailgate splits horizontally and swings upward to give access to the compact trunk.

The interior's four seats are trimmed in black and pale gray nubuck leather, with visible stitching. The dashboard is less successful but, overall, this is a fantastic concept that can soon be expected to appear as a series production car.

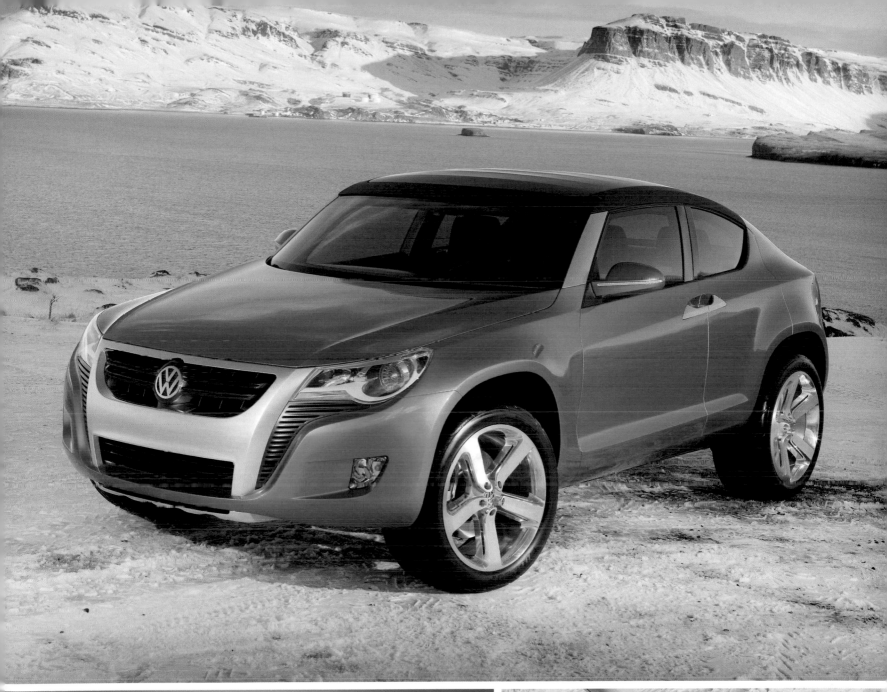

Volkswagen EcoRacer

The Volkswagen EcoRacer is a high-performance mid-engined sports car designed also to achieve astonishing fuel economy—just 3.4 liters per 100 km, nearly 70 miles per gallon. This is achieved by combining an advanced 1.5-liter diesel engine with a lightweight body structure that gives an overall weight of just 850 kg. The extremely low weight comes from the extensive use of expensive special carbon-fiber composite panels.

Today when we think of economical vehicles, we tend to think of small electric cars styled according to the dictates of the wind tunnel. The EcoRacer dispels this myth: the canary-yellow bodywork has tight proportions and is as dynamic as any other sports car: the big open grille at the front does nothing to signify the Volkswagen brand, perhaps deliberately so as the EcoRacer has such a different temperament from VW's current range of somewhat conservative models.

Inside, everything is tailored around the driver. The black leather bucket seats nestle within the carbon-fiber cockpit, void of unnecessary trim that would only add weight. The switches are designed purely for function and as a result the whole interior looks more like the inside of a one-shot circuit car than anything destined for production.

A fingerprint recognition system allows the owner of the EcoRacer to program the car if required, so that less experienced drivers can be authorized to drive only at reduced power. When getting in and out the doors work via keyless remote access, swinging open electromechanically in combination with the pop-up roof wing panels.

The T-bar roof and the rear hatch can be completely removed for open-top motoring, and for real wind-in-the-face speedster sensation the full-height windshield can be swapped for a low racing-style deflector offering little or no protection.

Dynamic in its performance and style, yet no less dramatic in its economy, this next-generation gem has a name that says it all.

Engine	1.5 in-line 4 turbo-diesel
Power	100 kW (134 bhp) @ 4000 rpm
Torque	250 Nm (184 lb. ft.) @ 1900–3750 rpm
Installation	Mid-engined/rear-wheel drive
Front suspension	Double wishbone
Rear suspension	Multilink
Brakes front/rear	Discs/discs
Front tires	175/55R17
Rear tires	225/45R17
Length	3770 mm (148.4 in.)
Width	1740 mm (68.5 in.)
Height	1210 mm (47.6 in.)
Wheelbase	2480 mm (97.6 in.)
Curb weight	850 kg (1874 lb.)
0–100 km/h (62 mph)	6.3 sec
Top speed	230 km/h (143 mph)
Fuel consumption	3.4 l/100 km (69.2 mpg)

Volkswagen Eos

Design	Marc Lichte
Engine	3.2 V6 (2.0 in-line 4, and 2.0 diesel, also offered)
Power	184 kW (247 bhp)
Torque	330 Nm (243 lb. ft.) @ 2750 rpm
Gearbox	6-speed manual
Installation	Front-engined/front-wheel drive
Brakes front/rear	Discs/discs
Front tires	235/45R17
Rear tires	235/45R17
Length	4410 mm (173.6 in.)
Width	1790 mm (70.5 in.)
Height	1440 mm (56.7 in.)
Track front/rear	1550/1550 mm (61/61 in.)
0–100 km/h (62 mph)	7.3 sec
Top speed	248 km/h (154mph)

Looking remarkably similar to the Volkswagen Concept C that was first shown at the Geneva Motor Show in 2004, the Eos, named after the Greek goddess of sunrise, is Volkswagen's re-entry into the premium convertible market after the disappearance of the classic Golf convertible. This positions it above the Beetle convertible but below the offerings of corporate partner Audi.

The main visual differences from the concept are the black grille, larger door mirrors, and different wheels; in other respects the car remains faithful to the original. Notable on the Eos is the world's first five-section folding glass roof in a four-seater car—something that gives a glimpse of future developments in roof technology but will be available in the showrooms when the Eos goes on sale in mid-2006.

The profile of the Eos shows a stylish, poised wedge shape with very little exterior ornament. Taut surfaces and simple straight feature lines dominate the exterior, creating a lithe, contemporary look that avoids any racy feel. Along the side, particularly, there is a single curve that strikes through the door and the rear body panel to give a sense of dynamism to the vehicle. The rear lamps echo those of more upmarket Volkswagens, with the feature lights superimposed on a large red trapezoidal base shape. This apart, the rear is very plain, and the eye is drawn out to the lamps to accentuate the effect of the vehicle's stability. Up front, the large headlamps echo the shape of the rear lights, and are slightly covered by the hood—making them look as if they are peering out from underneath.

The interior design is simple, almost sterile, conveying little impression other than that of German functionality. This lack of interior design flair is disappointing in a convertible, which should be all about enjoying life.

Volkswagen GX3

Design	VW California Design Center
Engine	1.6 in-line 4
Power	93 kW (125 bhp) @ 6500 rpm
Torque	152 Nm (112 lb. ft.) @ 3000 rpm
Gearbox	6-speed manual
Installation	Rear-engined/rear-wheel drive
Front suspension	Double wishbone
Rear suspension	Mono swing-arm
Brakes front/rear	Discs/discs
Front tires	215/45R17
Rear tires	315/30R18
Length	3753 mm (147.8 in.)
Width	1850 mm (72.8 in.)
Height	1210 mm (47.6 in.)
Wheelbase	2700 mm (106.3 in.)
Track front	1630 mm (64.2 in.)
Curb weight	570 kg (1257 lb.)
0–100 km/h (62 mph)	5.7 sec
Top speed	200 km/h (124 mph)
Fuel consumption	5.2 l/100 km (45.2 mpg)

Half sports car, half motorbike, the Volkswagen GX3 concept is the latest of many attempts to combine the raw thrills of two wheels with the security and (to a lesser extent) the comfort offered by four-wheeled solutions. Put together by a team of young designers and engineers based at Volkswagen's California studio, the GX3 is all about affordable exhilaration in a two-seater package.

From a design standpoint the GX3 takes inspiration from GP motorbikes and F1 racing cars. The engine and occupants are enclosed by a tight tubular body with a large air intake at the front and open at the rear, where the engine is partially exposed; fully exposed at the rear is the swinging-arm suspension that takes the chain drive to the single rear wheel and its wide, low-profile tire. Above the wheel sit the exhausts, which exit through the rear point of the fuselage, while the rear bodywork also supports the twin rollover hoops, which, though important for safety, look heavy and visually raise the center of gravity of the vehicle. Cleverly, the rear lights are integrated into the edges of these hoops.

The front wheels and suspension are exposed, too, and only the legal minimum of guarding protects the tires. The two headlamps are well back on the hood top, close to the cockpit. Inside, the GX3 is very basic indeed. Driver and passenger sit side by side, with not even a windshield to protect them. Each is secured by a five-point racing harness; there is a pair of motorcycle-style instruments set into the bulkhead, and VW's famous GTi golfball-design gear knob. And that is about all.

The GX3 is highly unconventional for a Volkswagen—yet at the concept's Los Angeles unveiling VW boss Wolfgang Bernhard talked of building it if customer reaction proved positive enough.

Volvo C30

Design	Simon Lamarre
Engine	2.4 in-line 5
Power	194 kW (260 bhp) @ 5500 rpm
Torque	364 Nm (268 lb. ft.) @ 2100–5000 rpm
Gearbox	6-speed manual
Installation	Front-engined/front-wheel drive
Brakes front/rear	Discs/discs
Front tires	225/35R19
Rear tires	225/35R19
Length	4253 mm (167.4 in.)
Width	1783 mm (70.2 in.)
Height	1447 mm (57 in.)
Wheelbase	2640 mm (103.9 in.)
0–100 km/h (62 mph)	6 sec
Top speed	250 km/h (155 mph)

When launching the C30 concept at the 2006 Detroit show, Volvo officials made it very clear that this design was the blueprint for a full showroom-ready model due to be revealed at the Paris show and enter volume production in 2007.

Volvo has been toying with the idea of producing a smaller car for some years, and the C30 is the result. The design steers clear of the blocky, heavy shapes of competitors in the C segment and instead touches on Volvo's heritage for its inspiration. At the rear the forward-leaning blackened glass tailgate harks back to the 480ES and the earlier P1800ES sports wagon. This alone would make the C30 distinctive, but it gains further identity through its typically Volvo strong shoulder profile that runs the length of the car and broadens toward the rear as the cabin tapers. This recalls earlier Volvo concepts and gives rise to highly unusual L-shaped rear lights that do not just follow the profile of the exaggerated rear haunches but are stacked up on the C-pillars too.

In side profile the design is sporty and muscular, with a considerable degree of wedge from front to rear. The front has a certain softness about it, first seen on Volvo's Safety Concept Car of 2001, but the C30's lamps are much more in keeping with the rest of the Volvo lineup. Because Volvo wanted to present this as a sporty model, the C30 was shown with 19-inch wheels and copper-brown trim that runs around the lower edge of the car.

The C30 is intended to appeal to young professional customers who might otherwise have chosen an Audi A3. It needed to be a visually entertaining car both inside and out that would fit with the target customer's lifestyle—and it looks as if Volvo has judged it well.

Volvo C70

Design	Fedde Talsma
Engine	2.5 in-line 5 (2.4 diesel also offered)
Power	164 kW (220 bhp)
Torque	320 Nm (236 lb. ft.)
Gearbox	6-speed manual
Installation	Front-engined/front-wheel drive
Front suspension	MacPherson strut
Rear suspension	Multilink
Brakes front/rear	Discs/discs
Front tires	235/40R18
Rear tires	235/40R18
Length	4580 mm (180.3 in.)
Width	1820 mm (71.7 in.)
Height	1410 mm (55.5 in.)
Wheelbase	2640 mm (103.9 in.)
Track front/rear	1550/1560 mm (61/61.4 in.)

Volvo's second-generation C70 convertible was born from a collaboration between Volvo and Pininfarina. Under the joint venture, Pininfarina brings development and convertible-manufacturing skills to the partnership but Volvo keeps ownership of the design.

The new car joins the growing ranks of convertibles with a folding hardtop roof—so a single C70 can do the job of both the coupé and the soft-top versions in the outgoing C70 range. The new metal roof clearly gives better security and refinement than the old soft-top, and its two-piece structure means that the vehicle is able to retain elegant proportions in either open or closed configuration.

Slightly shorter and lower than its predecessor, the new C70 is developed from the modern S40 platform, which also supports the Ford Focus and the Mazda3. In terms of design technique it uses headlamps that are set back to yield a strong shoulder line running from front to back, a feature now shared on all new Volvos. While many other designers are moving toward razor-edge styling, Volvo succeeds in combining crisp lines with rounded forms. For example, the headlamps and grille have rounded corners, making the C70 look friendly and fun to drive. At the rear the lines are fresh and horizontally emphasized, echoing the sportiness of the BMW 3 Series convertible, perhaps.

The interior will comfortably seat four, though it is much darker and more technical-looking than the old C70. In line with Volvo's mission as a safety innovator, the C70 launches a novel type of side-impact airbag that can provide useful head protection even when the roof is stowed. Altogether sportier and fresher in feel than the old C70, the new car is definitely aiming to add a younger group of buyers to the more mature clientele that until now has been drawn to Volvo's convertibles.

Volvo S80

The 2006 Volvo S80 may be a completely new car and full of important engineering innovation, but in terms of aesthetic design it comes across as merely an evolution of the old car—a model that, it should be remembered, completely changed the corporate look of Volvo when it was launched in 1999.

It is the same length as the outgoing model, but both taller and wider. Several factors combine to make it smoother, sleeker, and sportier in its stance: the windshield has a greater rake, the hood has lost its unsightly hump at the front, and the headlamps have a more focused look. Along the side the door surfaces no longer flow inboard above the rubbing strip: instead, they now remain full with a small crease running through the panels. The rear door is extended in length and the rear quarter-light now forms part of the door rather than being attached to the body. The side of the rear lamps now angles forward, in the manner of a Ford or Mercedes.

Moving to the interior, the two-tone wave dashboard is a masterly design, and all the switches and instrumentation are easily accessible. There is a recurring theme of slim panels throughout: the overall effect is sophisticated and elegant.

Numerous safety features are engineered in to prevent collisions: intelligent cruise control, a blind-spot information system, active headlamps, and more. But should an unavoidable accident occur, the S80 is equipped with the very best in airbags, including dual-chamber side airbags, as well as anti-whiplash head restraints.

The new S80 comes across as a handsome and highly competent executive car with no obvious visual flaws. What it all adds up to is an intelligent evolution—a more cautious design step than the major leap made by its predecessor, but a significant improvement nonetheless.

Engine	4.4 V8 (2.5 in-line 5 and 3.2 in-line 6, and 2.4 in-line 5 diesel, also offered)
Installation	Front-engined/all-wheel drive
Front suspension	MacPherson strut
Rear suspension	Multilink
Brakes front/rear	Discs/discs
Length	4850 mm (190.9 in.)
Width	1860 mm (73.2 in.)
Height	1488 mm (58.6 in.)
Wheelbase	2836 mm (111.7 in.)
Track front/rear	1588/1585 mm (62.5/62.4 in.)

Profiles of Key Designers

Donato Coco

Luc Donckerwolke

Henrik Fisker

Donato Coco

Ascending to one of the highest pinnacles of success in the car business, Donato Coco was appointed as Ferrari's new chief designer in November 2005. His move filled the void left by Frank Stephenson, who earlier that year had moved to head the Fiat, Lancia and Light Commercial Vehicles styling center. Coco is based in Maranello, Italy, where he works alongside the GT team led by deputy general manager Amedeo Felisa.

Coco moved from Citroën in France, where he was chief designer for small cars. He secured his position there in an unusual way—by winning a design competition. While at Citroën he oversaw the development of almost the entire lineup: the C1, C2 and C3 hatchbacks, the Xsara Picasso compact minivan, and the novel, multifunctional Pluriel.

Donato Coco, now fifty-two, was born in Rignano Garganico, in Italy's southern Apulia region; he emigrated to France with his family at the age of five. In his studies he focused principally on artistic subjects, studying

architecture at Besançon in France and then completing an MA in vehicle design at the Royal College of Art in London. For six years before settling into the car industry he worked in a variety of jobs, including as a children's book illustrator, a photographic illustrator, and a designer of sports accessories.

Coco got his crucial break with Citroën in 1983 when he won a national design competition organized by the French car company. Since then he has remained in the automotive field, leading the design of several of Citroën's small and medium cars, from the restyle of the AX to the most recent C1, where he was faced with the challenge of differentiating, at minimum cost, the Citroën design from those of Peugeot and Toyota. Through his work on the Saxo, Xsara, C2, C3, and Pluriel, Coco has played a major part in shaping the visual identity of the French brand.

The cars that Coco designed for Citroën all have their own individual personalities. The smallest, the C1, is a cutesy but thoroughly modern hatchback with looks that are designed

Top
The cutesy Citroën C1 celebrates a love for affordable modern design.

Opposite
The Xsara Picasso is a successful people-carrier and Citroën's answer to the Renault Scenic.

to cheer; the larger C2 hatch has a more angular, sporty design and comes with a distinctive angled base to the rear side windows that sets it apart from the competition. The Xsara Picasso has been popular, its long, sweeping monovolume design providing practical family transport. The C3 hatchback has perhaps been Coco's least successful product, the tall body and strong arched shape not finding immediate favor with its target market.

Ironically, perhaps, Coco's most distinctive work so far is a derivative of the C3—the Pluriel. This is a low-priced car, but one with multiple identities: it can be a sedan, a cabriolet, a spider,

or even a pickup. It is a car that puts function before convention—a mindset that might become useful when designing a Ferrari.

Shaping the look of the most famous and most exotic car make in the world is a dream job to which almost any self-respecting designer would aspire. Crucially, it will involve not just managing Ferrari's own in-house studio but also stimulating and directing the creativity of Ferrari's highly respected design partners, notably Pininfarina, whose relationship with Ferrari is as old as the company itself.

Donato Coco's move to Ferrari comes at a time when Ferrari is enjoying strong sales and

has just renewed its entire model range. Ferrari design has come in for some criticism in much of the enthusiast media in recent years: it will be Coco's enormous responsibility to guide Ferrari into a new era of forward-looking design, while at the same time maintaining the trust and appreciation of the traditionalists who treasure the prancing-horse heritage above all else.

Opposite top
The edgy Citroën C2 is a visually strong design for a typically young target customer.

Opposite bottom
The Citroën C3 with its arched roof harks back to the 2CV to make it unmistakable as a Citroën.

Above
The Pluriel is a car in the creation of which the designers had an unusually free hand.

Luc Donckerwolke

Luc Donckerwolke is a Belgian citizen but was born in Lima, Peru, in 1965. The son of a diplomat, he attended various schools in South America and Africa before going on to study industrial engineering in Brussels and then transportation design in Vevey, Switzerland. There is no doubting that Donckerwolke likes to travel around; he speaks Italian, French, Spanish, English, German, Flemish, and Swahili!

In 1990 Donckerwolke's career began as a designer at Peugeot in France. Two years later he moved to Audi Design in Ingolstadt, Germany. From 1994 to 1996 he worked at the Skoda Design Center Mlada Boleslav in the Czech Republic. In 1996 he returned to Audi and was responsible for concept development at Audi Design for a year each in Munich and Ingolstadt.

Since 1998, the year that it was acquired by Audi, Luc Donckerwolke has been working for Lamborghini in Sant'Agata, Italy. He was appointed head of design there in March 2003. With SEAT design now falling under the control of the Audi Brand Group, Donckerwolke assumed the position of SEAT design director in September 2005, replacing Walter De'Silva who retained his position as the Audi Brand Group's director of design. This movement between Lamborghini and SEAT design areas also emphasizes the continued synergies and the high level of collaboration between the brands of the Audi Brand Group, the "sporty" branch of the Volkswagen Group, which has included SEAT since 2002, together with Audi and Lamborghini.

Donckerwolke also took over the running of the Spanish company's Design Center. De'Silva commented at the time that "the appointment of Luc is another step in reinforcing SEAT's commitment to design, which is one of the brand's key values for its new positioning." With the recent Lamborghini designs being so well received, it will be extremely interesting to see how Donckerwolke visually positions SEAT, a brand with tremendous potential for Mediterranean flair.

Luc Donckerwolke is still relatively young in terms of experience but he has so far managed

Above
The compact Lamborghini Gallardo with its racy, taut design.

Opposite top
The Lamborghini Murciélago is the first of a new series of Lamborghinis sporting a new design language.

Opposite bottom
The Audi R8 Le Mans from 2003 with its distinctive color scheme and graphics.

to clock up a number of cars to which he can put his name. These include the Audi A4 Avant, widely regarded as an excellent-looking wagon; and the Audi R8 Le Mans, which, although a racing car, was made distinctive by its silver, black, and red color scheme rather than by stylistic treatments, as these after all were mostly determined in the wind tunnel.

Donckerwolke also turned his hand to the Skoda Octavia and Fabia, both cars that were designed with more personality but maintain a different market position than the conservative Volkswagen models. Aesthetically, at least, Skoda has moved gradually upmarket. But

it is his radical rethinking of the Lamborghini brand that has made Luc Donckerwolke a much more highly regarded figure in the industry, and saw him awarded the Red Dot Award in 2003 for the Lamborghini Gallardo and Murciélago. The design language now used by Lamborghini seems a well-established look, distinctive and modern. It also very clearly differentiates Lamborghini from the likes of Ferrari, which uses flowing forms.

It is early yet to see how the SEAT brand evolves under the Belgian's leadership, but radical shifts are possible and indeed likely considering SEAT's outspoken commitment to design.

Above
The Audi A4 Avant of 2001 was highly regarded and achieved strong sales.

Opposite top
Skoda Fabia, a simple, inoffensive car for the mass market.

Opposite bottom
The Skoda Octavia is slowly helping to push the perception of Skoda upmarket.

Henrik Fisker

After graduating from California's Art Center College of Design in 1989, Danish-born Henrik Fisker began his career in Germany with BMW, working in the advanced design studio at BMW Technik GmbH.

One of the most notable exterior designs he worked on while at BMW was the Z07 concept sports car, showcased in Tokyo in 1997. This was the forerunner of the Z8 roadster, also a Fisker design, which would be launched in 1999. The Z8 is already a latter-day classic; a modern–retro design with a barreled fuselage-style body. In January 2001 Fisker began a brief stint as president and CEO of BMW's California-based industrial design subsidiary, DesignworksUSA, before moving to the Ford group.

One of Fisker's first appointments at Ford was as creative director of its London-based Ingeni creativity center, an innovative unit designed to research design and culture trends for all of Ford's brands. To the regret of many—though perhaps not Ford's accountants—this center was closed early in 2004 as Ford's financial troubles began to put a strain on the group's eagerness to invest in idealistic creative processes.

Fisker was also acting director of design at Aston Martin during this period—and this is when he created what are probably his best-known works, the Aston Martin DB9 and the V8 Vantage. At the same time he was a director of Ford's Global Advanced Design Studio in Irvine, California. Other models for which he was

Opposite top
Aston Martin's DB9, a Fisker design, is highly regarded and sales are strong.

Above
The V8 Vantage, lower in cost than traditional Aston Martins, is pitched as an alternative to the Porsche 911. It has the potential to generate a quantum leap in Aston's production.

Left
The Latigo CS from Fisker Coachbuild, based on a BMW 6 Series coupé, made its debut in 2005.

responsible include the Lincoln Zephyr concept car and the Shelby GR1. This showcased at the 2005 Detroit Auto Show and featured a barreled body similar to that of the BMW Z8.

However, restless in the face of all these responsibilities and opportunities, Fisker suddenly switched to something diametrically different. In January 2005 he partnered up with Bernhard Koehler, who had been director of operations at Ford's Global Advanced Design Studio in California, and with whom Fisker had already worked at BMW, Ingeni, and Aston Martin. The new company was to be called Fisker Coachbuild, and its mission was to produce highly individual cars for wealthy clients. To date, Fisker Coachbuild has produced two cars, the Latigo CS and the Tramonto. Both are based on

German chassis and have been given restyled bodies to distinguish them as Fisker models.

Fisker Coachbuild is aiming to satisfy the needs of customers who want exotic high-performance cars with a guarantee of exclusivity; in this mission, as his company name suggests, Fisker is taking car design techniques back sixty years to the golden age when the Italian coachbuilders held sway among the rich and influential of the time. When asked where he finds his inspiration, Fisker has commented that he simply starts sketching and the ideas then follow—sometimes a whole car can begin with just a detail.

Fisker is interested in looking back to see what made people fall in love with coachbuilt cars in their prewar heyday. His aim is to under-

stand what makes a person choose one particular car over another, and to identify the human behavior and desires that translate themselves into purchasing decisions; anyone who isolates this secret will be in line for surefire success in the showrooms. Perhaps there is an element of this in the BMW Z8 and the Shelby GR1 that Fisker created: both are very emotional cars.

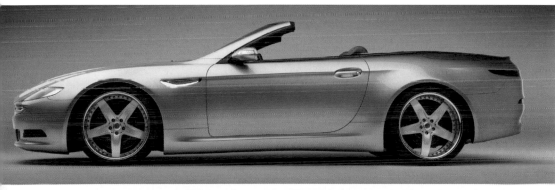

Opposite

The Lincoln Zephyr concept of 2005: the production version is now on sale.

Left top

The BMW Z8 of 1999 became a modern-day classic as soon as it was launched. It featured in the Bond film *The World is Not Enough*.

Left second from top

BMW's Z07 concept from 1997 was the forerunner of the Z8.

Left second from bottom

The Fisker Coachbuild Tramonto of 2005 is based on the Mercedes-Benz SL55 AMG.

Left

The all-aluminum Ford Shelby GR1 was a one-shot concept.

Profiles of Key Designers   **309**

Technical Glossary

Where the New Models were Launched

Major International Motor Shows 2006–2007

Makes and their Parent Companies

Technical Glossary

Specification tables

The following list explains the terminology used in the specification tables that accompany the model descriptions. The amount of data available for any given model depends on its status as a concept or production car. More information is usually available for models currently in or nearing production.

engine   Engine size is quoted in liters, and refers to the swept volume of the cylinders per crankshaft rotation; 6.0, for example, means a 6-liter (or 6000-cc) engine. "In-line" or "V" followed by a number refers to the engine's number of cylinders. An in-line 4 engine has four cylinders in a single row, while a V8 engine has eight cylinders arranged in a V-formation. A flat-four engine has four cylinders lying in a horizontal plane, two opposing each other. In-line engines of more than six cylinders are rare today because they take up too much packaging space—an in-line 12, for instance, would require a very long hood. Only Volkswagen makes a W12, an engine with its twelve cylinders arranged in a W-formation. The configuration of cylinders is usually chosen on cost grounds: the higher the car's retail price, the more cylinders product planners can include.

power   Engine power is given in both metric kilowatts (kW) and imperial brake horsepower (bhp). Both are calculated at optimum engine crankshaft speed, given in revolutions per minute (rpm) by manufacturers as a "net" measurement—in other words, an engine's output after power has been sapped by other equipment and the exhaust system—and measured by a "brake" applied to the driveshaft.

torque   Simply the motion of twisting or turning, in car terms torque means pulling power, generated by twisting force from the engine crankshaft. It is given in newton meters (Nm) and pounds feet (lb. ft.). The higher the torque, the more force the engine can apply to the driven wheels.

gearbox   The mechanical means by which power is transmitted from the engine to the driven wheels. There is a wide variety of manual (with a clutch) and automatic (clutchless) versions. There have been recent trends for clutchless manual systems, called "semiautomatic" or "automated manual," and automatics with an option to change gear manually, sometimes called "Tiptronic," "Steptronic," or "Easytronic." "CVT" (continuously variable transmission) refers to an automatic with a single "speed": the system uses rubber or steel belts to take engine power to the driven wheels, with drive pulleys that expand and contract to vary the gearing. A "sequential manual" is a manual gearbox with preset gear ratios that are ordered sequentially.

suspension   All suspension systems cushion the car against road or terrain conditions to maximize comfort, safety and roadholding. Heavy and off-road vehicles use "rigid axles" at the rear or front and rear; these are suspended using robust, leaf-type springs and steel "wishbones" with "trailing arms." "Semirigid axles" are often found at the back on front-wheel-drive cars, in conjunction with a "torsion-beam" trailing-arm axle. "Independent" suspension means each wheel can move up and down on its own, often with the help of "trailing arms" or "semi-trailing arms." A "MacPherson strut," named after its inventor, a Ford engineer called Earl MacPherson, is a suspension upright, fixed to the car's structure above the top of the tire. It carries the wheel hub at the bottom and incorporates a hydraulic damper. It activates a coil spring and, when fitted at the front, turns with the wheel.

brakes   Almost all modern cars feature disc brakes all round. A few low-powered models still feature drum brakes at the back for cost reasons. "ABS" (antilock braking system) is increasingly fitted to all cars: it regulates brake application to prevent the brakes locking in an emergency or slippery conditions. "BA" (brake assist) is a system that does this electrohydraulically, while "EBD" (electronic brake-force distribution) is a pressure regulator that, in braking, spreads the car's weight more evenly so that the brakes do not lock. "ESP" (electronic stability program) is Mercedes-Benz's electronically controlled system that helps keep the car pointing in the right direction at high speeds; sensors detect wayward roadholding and apply the brakes indirectly to correct it. "Dynamic stability" is a similar system. "Brake-by-wire" is a totally electronic braking system that sends signals from brake pedal to brakes with no mechanical actuation whatsoever. "TCS" (traction-control system) is a feature that holds acceleration slip within acceptable levels to prevent wheelspin and therefore improves adhesion to the road. 'VSC' (vehicle stability control) is the computer-controlled application of antilock braking to all four wheels individually to prevent dangerous skidding during cornering.

tires   The size and type of wheels and tires are given in the internationally accepted formula. Representative examples include: 315/70R17, 235/50VR18, 225/50WR17, 235/40Z18, and

225/40ZR18. In all cases the number before the slash is the tire width in millimeters. The number after the slash is the height-to-width ratio of the tire section as a percentage. The letter R denotes radial construction. Letters preceding R are a guide to the tire's speed rating, denoting the maximum safe operating speed. H tires can be used at speeds up to 210 km/h (130 mph), V up to 240 km/h (150 mph), W up to 270 km/h (170 mph), and Y up to 300 km/h (190 mph). Finally, the last number is the diameter of the wheel in inches. A "PAX" is a wheel-and-tire in one unit, developed by Michelin (for example, 19/245 PAX means a 19 in. wheel with a 245 mm tire width). The rubber tire element is clipped to the steel wheel part, rather than held on by pressure. The height of the tire walls is reduced, which can free up space for better internal packaging, or for bigger wheels for concept car looks. It can also run flat for 200 km at 80 km/h, eliminating the need for a spare.

wheelbase	The exact distance between the center of the front wheel and center of the rear wheel.
track front/rear	The exact distance between the center of the front or rear tires, measured across the car on the ground.
curb weight	The amount a car weighs with a tank of fuel, all oils and coolants topped up, and all standard equipment but no occupants.
CO_2 emissions	Carbon dioxide emissions, which are a direct result of fuel consumption. CO_2 contributes to the atmospheric "greenhouse effect." Less than 100 g/km is a very low emission, 150 g/km is good, 300 g/km is bad. 'PZEV' (partial zero emission vehicle) refers to a low-level emission standard that was created to allow flexibility on ZEV standards in California.

Other terms

A-, B-, C-, D-pillars	Vertical roof support posts that form part of a car's bodywork. The A-pillar sits between windshield and front door, the B-pillar between front and rear doors, the C-pillar between rear doors and rear window, hatchback, or wagon rear-side windows, and the D-pillar (on a wagon) between rear side windows and tailgate. Confusingly, however, some designs refer to the central pillar between front and rear doors as a B-pillar where it faces the front door and a C-pillar where it faces the rear one.
all-wheel drive	A system delivering the appropriate amount of engine torque to each wheel via a propshaft and differentials, to ensure that tire slippage on the road surface is individually controlled. This system is ideal for high-performance road cars, such as Audis, where it is called "quattro."
beltline	*See* daylight opening line.
cant rail	The structural beam that runs along the tops of the doors.
coefficient of drag	Also known as the Cd, this is shorthand for the complex scientific equation that proves how aerodynamic a car is. The Citroën C-Airdream, for example, has a Cd of 0.28, but the Citroën SM of thirty years ago measured just 0.24, so little has changed in this respect. "Drag" means the resistance of a body to airflow, and low drag means better penetration, less friction, and therefore more efficiency, although sometimes poor dynamic stability.
daylight opening line (DOL)	The line where the door glass meets the door panel, sometimes referred to as beltline or waistline.
diffuser	A custom-designed airflow conduit, often incorporated under the rear floor on high-performance and competition cars, which controls and evenly distributes fast moving airflow out from beneath the speeding car. This ducting arrangement slows the flow of rushing air behind the car, lowering its pressure and so increasing aerodynamic downforce. The result is improved roadholding.

drive-by-wire technology	Increasingly featured on new cars, these systems do away with mechanical elements and replace them by wires transmitting electronic signals to activate such functions as brakes and steering.
drivetrain	The assembly of "organs" that gives a car motive power: engine, gearbox, driveshaft, wheels, brakes, suspension, and steering. This grouping is also loosely known these days as a "chassis," and can be transplanted into several different models to save on development costs.
fairing	A sculpted body surface blending different parts of a vehicle together to achieve a streamlined effect.
fastback	This refers to the profile of a hatchback that has a rear screen at a shallow angle, so that the tailgate forms a constant surface from the rear of the roof to the very tail end of the car.
fast windshield	A windshield angled acutely to reduce wind resistance and accentuate a sporty look.
feature line	A styling detail usually added to a design to differentiate it from its rivals, and generally not related to such functional areas as door apertures.
four-wheel drive	This refers to a system delivering a car's power to its four wheels. In a typical "off-road"-type four-wheel-drive vehicle, the differentials can be locked so that all four wheels move in a forward direction even if the tires are losing grip with the road surface. This makes four-wheel drive useful when traveling across uneven terrain.
glasshouse/greenhouse	The car-design industry's informal term for the glazed area of the passenger compartment that usually sits above the car's waist level.
head-up display	A technology by which useful data are projected upward onto the inside of the windshield so that information can be displayed in the driver's line of vision.
HVAC	Initials standing for Heating, Ventilation, and Air-Conditioning system.
instrument panel	The trim panel that sits in front of the driver and front passenger.
Kamm tail	Sharply cutoff tail that gives the aerodynamic advantages of a much longer, tapering rear end, developed in racing in the 1960s.
monospace/ monovolume/"one-box"	A "box" is one of the major volumetric components of a car's architecture. In a traditional sedan, there are three boxes: one for the engine, one for the passengers, and one for the luggage. A hatchback, missing a trunk, is a 'two-box' car, while a large MPV such as the Renault Espace is a "one-box" design, also known as a "monospace" or "monovolume."
MPV	Short for "multipurpose vehicle," this term is applied to tall, spacious cars that can carry at least five passengers, and often as many as nine, or versatile combinations of people and cargo. The 1983 Chrysler Voyager and 1984 Renault Espace were the first. The 1977 Matra Rancho was the very first "mini-MPV," but the 1991 Mitsubishi Space Runner was the first in the modern idiom.
packaging space	Any three-dimensional zone in a vehicle that is occupied by component parts or used during operation of the vehicle.
platform	Also known as the "floorpan": the invisible, but elemental and expensive, basic structure of a modern car. It is the task of contemporary car designers to achieve maximum aesthetic diversity from a single platform.
powertrain	The engine, gearbox, and transmission "package" of a car.
regenerative braking	When braking in a hybrid electric vehicle, the electric motor that is used to propel the car reverses its action and turns into a generator, converting kinetic energy into electrical power, which is then stored in the car's batteries.

rotary engine	The rotary engine is very different from a conventional piston engine, being, essentially, a triangular-sectioned shaft that rotates within an elongated chamber to create the compression and combustion cycle. It was developed by Felix Wankel in the 1950s.
shift paddles	A term used for steering-column-mounted levers that, when pulled, send electronic signals to the gearbox requesting a gear change. They were first used in Formula One motor racing.
spaceframe	A structural frame that supports a car's mechanical systems and cosmetic panels.
splitter	Sometimes found at the front of high-performance cars near ground level, this is a system of undercar ducting that splits the airflow sucked under the car as it moves forward, so the appropriate volume of cooling air is distributed to both radiator and brakes.
subcompact	You need to rewind fifty-six years for the origins: in 1950, Nash launched its Rambler, a two-door model smaller than other mainstream American sedans. The company coined the term "compact" for it although, by European standards, it was still a large car. Nash's descendant American Motors then invented the "subcompact" class in 1970 with the AMC Gremlin, a model with a conventional hood and a sharply truncated hatchback tail; this was quickly followed by the similar Ford Pinto and Chevrolet Vega. In the international car industry today, "subcompact" is used as another term for "A-segment," the smallest range of cars, intended mostly for city driving.
SUV	Short for "sport utility vehicle," a four wheel-drive car designed for leisure off-road driving but not necessarily agricultural or industrial use. Therefore a Land Rover Defender is not an SUV, while a Land Rover Freelander is. The line between the two is sometimes difficult to draw, and identifying a pioneer is tricky: SUVs as we know them today were defined by Jeep in 1986 with the Wrangler, Suzuki in 1988 with the Vitara, and Daihatsu in 1989 with the Sportrak. There is also a trend toward more sporty trucks, which has led to the more specific term "SUT," or "sport utility truck."
swage line	A groove or moulding employed on a flat surface to stiffen it against warping or vibration. In cars, swage lines add "creases" to bodywork surfaces, enabling designers to bring visual, essentially two-dimensional interest to body panels that might otherwise look slab-sided or barrel-like.
Targa	Porsche had been very successful in the Targa Florio road races in Sicily, so, in celebration, in 1965 the company applied the name "Targa" (the Italian for shield) to a new 911 model that featured a novel detachable roof panel. It is now standard terminology for the system, although a Porsche-registered trademark.
telematics	Any individual communication to a car from an outside base station, for example, satellite navigation signals, automatic emergency calls, roadside assistance, traffic information, and dynamic route guidance.
transaxle	Engineering shorthand for "transmission axle": this is the clutch and gearbox unit that is connected to the driveshafts to transfer power to the driven wheels. All front-wheel-drive and rear- or mid-engined, rear-wheel-drive cars have some type of transaxle.
tumblehome	The angle of the door glass when viewing a car from the front. The more upright the glass, the less tumblehome.
venturi tunnel	A venturi is an air-management system under a car designed to increase air speed by forcing it through tapered channels. High air speed creates a low-pressure area between the bottom of the car and the road, which in turn creates a suction effect holding the car to the road. Pressure is then equalized in the diffuser at the rear of the car.
waistline	*See* daylight opening line.

Where the New Models were Launched

New York International Auto Show
April 9–18, 2005

Concept
Nissan Sport Concept
Scion t2B Concept

Production
Hyundai Accent
Hyundai
 Azera/Grandeur
Jeep Commander
Mercedes-Benz
 R-Class

Frankfurt International Motor Show
September 15–25, 2005

Concept
Citroën
 C-SportLounge
Daihatsu
 D-Compact 4x4
Daihatsu HVS
EDAG Roadster
Fisker Coachbuild
 Latigo CS
Ford Iosis
Jeep Patriot
Karmann SUC
Maybach Exelero
Mazda Sassou
Mini Concept
 Frankfurt
Mitsubishi Concept
 Sportback
Opel/Vauxhall
 Antara GTC
Peugeot 20Cup
Renault Egeus
Toyota Endo
Toyota i-Unit

Production
Audi Q7
Dacia Logan
Fiat Grande Punto
Ford Galaxy
Jaguar XK
Kia Magentis
Mercedes-Benz
 S-Class
Nissan Note
Porsche Cayman S
Renault Clio
Suzuki Grand Vitara
Toyota Hilux
Toyota RAV4
Toyota Yaris
Volkswagen Eos
Volvo C70

Tokyo Motor Show
October 22 – November 6, 2005

Concept
Audi Shooting Brake
Chrysler Akino
Daihatsu Costa
Daihatsu UFE-III
Honda FCX
Honda Sports4
Honda WOW
Hyundai Neos-3
Italdesign
 Ferrari GG50
Mercedes-Benz
 F600 Hygenius
Mitsubishi Concept-X
Mitsubishi Concept D:5
Nissan Amenio
Nissan Foria
Nissan GT-R Proto
Nissan Pivo
Subaru B5-TPH

Suzuki Ionis
Suzuki LC
Suzuki MPW
Suzuki PX
Toyota Estima Hybrid
Toyota Fine-X
Toyota i-Swing
Volkswagen EcoRacer

Production
Bugatti Veyron 16.4
Mitsubishi i
Mitsubishi Outlander

Bologna Motor Show
December 3–11, 2005

Concept
Citroën C-AirPlay
Oltre Fiat

Greater LA Auto Show
January 6–15, 2006

Concept
Volkswagen GX3

Production
Chevrolet Aveo
Chevrolet Suburban
Mazda CX-7

North American International Auto Show (NAIAS)
January 14–22, 2006

Concept
Aston Martin Rapide
Audi Roadjet
Chevrolet Camaro
Chrysler Imperial
Dodge Challenger
Ford F-250
 Super Chief
Ford Reflex
Hyundai HCD9 Talus
Infiniti Coupé
Kia Soul
Lamborghini Miura
Lincoln MKS
Lincoln MKX
Mazda Kabura
Mitsubishi CT MIEV
Nissan Urge
Toyota F3R
Volvo C30

Production
Acura RDX
Buick Enclave
Cadillac Escalade
Chevrolet Tahoe
Chrysler Aspen
Ford Edge
Hyundai Santa Fe
Jeep Compass
Jeep Wrangler
Lexus LS460
Mercedes-Benz
 GL-Class
Nissan Sentra
Nissan Versa
Toyota Camry

Geneva International Motor Show
March 2–12, 2006

Concept
Bertone Suagnà
Dacia Logan Steppe
Dodge Hornet
Hyundai HED-2
 Genus
Inovo Lirica
Kia c'eed
Lotus APX
Mitsubishi EZ MIEV
Nissan Terranaut
Renault Altica
Rolls-Royce 101EX
Saab Aero X
Spyker D12
 Peking-to-Paris
Tata Cliffrider
Toyota Urban Cruiser
Volkswagen
 Concept A

Production
Alfa Romeo Spider
Chevrolet Captiva
Chevrolet Epica
Ferrari 599 GTB
 Fiorano
Fiat Sedici
Ford S-Max
Lotus Europa S
Opel GT
Peugeot 207
Skoda Roomster
Volvo S80

Major International Motor Shows 2006–2007

Paris Motor Show
(Mondial de l'automobile)
September 30 – October 15, 2006
Paris Expo, Paris, France
www.mondialauto.tm.fr

Prague Auto Show
October 9–22, 2006
Prague Exhibition Grounds, Prague, Czech
Republic
www.incheba.cz

Tokyo Motor Show
October 27 – November 11, 2006
Nippon Center, Makuhari, Chiba, Tokyo, Japan
www.tokyo-motorshow.com

Riyadh Motor Show
November 22–26, 2006
Riyadh Exhibition Center, Riyadh, Saudi Arabia
www.recexpo.com

Greater LA Auto Show
December 1–10, 2006
Los Angeles Convention Center, Los Angeles, CA
www.laautoshow.com

Motor Show di Bologna
(Salone Internazionale dell'Automobile)
December 7–17, 2006
BolognaFiere, Bologna, Italy
www.motorshow.it

North American International Auto Show
(NAIAS)
January 13–21, 2007
Cobo Exhibition Center, Detroit, MI
www.naias.com

Canadian International Auto Show
February 16–27, 2007
Metro Toronto Convention Center and SkyDome,
Toronto, Canada
www.autoshow.ca

New York International Auto Show
April 6–15, 2007
Jacob Javits Convention Center, New York, NY
www.autoshowny.com

Melbourne International Motor Show
March 1–12, 2007
Melbourne Exhibition Center, Melbourne,
Australia
www.motorshow.com.au

Geneva International Motor Show
March 8–18, 2007
Palexpo, Geneva, Switzerland
www.salon-auto.ch

Frankfurt International Motor Show
September 13–23, 2007
Trade Fairgrounds, Frankfurt am Main, Germany
www.iaa.de

Makes and their Parent Companies

Hundreds of separate carmaking companies have consolidated over the past decade or so into thirteen groups: BMW, DaimlerChrysler, Fiat, Ford, General Motors, Honda, Hyundai, MG Rover, Peugeot, Proton, Renault, Toyota, and Volkswagen. These account for at least nine of every ten cars produced globally today. The remaining independent makes either produce specialist models, offer niche design and engineering services, or tend to be at risk because of their lack of economies of scale. The global overcapacity in the industry means that manufacturers are having to offer increased choice to the consumer to differentiate their brands and maintain market share. Not all parent companies fully own the carmakers listed as under their control. Subaru, for example, operates within the General Motors alliance but is only 21% owned by the US giant.

BMW
BMW
Mini
Riley*
Rolls-Royce
Triumph*

DaimlerChrysler
Chrysler
De Soto*
Dodge
Hudson*
Imperial*
Jeep
Maybach
Mercedes-Benz
Nash*
Plymouth*
Smart

Fiat Auto
Abarth*
Alfa Romeo
Autobianchi*
Ferrari
Fiat
Innocenti*
Lancia
Maserati

Ford
Aston Martin
Daimler*
Ford
Jaguar
Lagonda*
Land Rover/
    Range Rover
Lincoln
Mazda
Mercury
Th!nk
Volvo

General Motors
Buick
Cadillac
Chevrolet
Corvette
Daewoo
GM
GMC
Holden
Hummer
Isuzu
Oldsmobile*
Opel
Pontiac
Saab
Saturn
Subaru
Suzuki
Vauxhall

Honda
Acura
Honda

Hyundai
Asia Motors
Hyundai
Kia

MG Rover
Austin*
MG*
Morris*
Rover*
Wolseley*

Proton
Lotus
Proton

PSA–Peugeot Citroën
Citroën
Hillman*
Humber*
Panhard*
Peugeot
Simca*
Singer*
Sunbeam*
Talbot*

Renault–Nissan Alliance
Alpine*
Dacia
Datsun*
Infiniti
Nissan
Renault
Renault Sport
Samsung

Toyota
Daihatsu
Lexus
Scion
Toyota
Will*

Volkswagen Group
Audi
Auto Union*
Bentley
Bugatti
Cosworth
DKW*
Horch*
Lamborghini
NSU*
SEAT
Skoda
Volkswagen
Wanderer*

Independent makes
Austin-Healey*
AviChina
Beijing
Bertone
Bristol
Byd
Caterham
Chery
Dongfeng
Donkervoort
EDAG
Elfin
ETUD
Farboud
Fenomenon
Fioravanti
Fisker Coachbuild
Heuliez
Hindustan
Inovo
Invicta
Irmscher
Italdesign
Izh
Jensen
Joss
Koenigsegg

Lada
Mahindra
Marcos
Maruti
Mitsubishi
Mitsuoka
Morgan
Pagani
Panoz
Paykan
Perodua
Pininfarina
Porsche
Rinspeed
Sivax
Spyker
SsangYong
Stola
Tata
Tramontana
TVR
Venturi
Volga
Westfield
Wiesmann
Zagato
ZAZ
ZIL

* Dormant makes

Acknowledgements

I would like to thank everyone at Merrell Publishers closely involved in the creation of the *Car Design Yearbook* series, all of whom have helped make it a continued success—in particular Rosie Fairhead, Kirsty Seymour-Ure, Anthea Snow, John Grain, Nicola Bailey, and Paul Shinn.

Thanks are also due to Alistair Layzell for his publicity campaign, Tony Lewin for his editorial expertise, and the manufacturers' press offices for providing information, including the photographs. And finally, very special thanks go to my wife, Hannah, and to Scooby-Doo, the family dog.

Stephen Newbury
Henley-on-Thames, Oxfordshire
2006

Picture Credits

MERRELL

First published 2006 by Merrell Publishers Limited

Head office
81 Southwark Street
London SE1 0HX

New York office
49 West 24th Street, 8th Floor
New York, NY 10010

merrellpublishers.com

Publisher Hugh Merrell
Editorial Director Julian Honer
US Director Joan Brookbank
Sales and Marketing Manager Kim Cope
Sales and Marketing Executive Amina Arab
Sales and Marketing Assistant Abigail Coombs
Associate Manager, US Sales and Marketing
    Elizabeth Choi
Co-editions Manager Anne Le Moigne
Managing Editor Anthea Snow
Project Editors Claire Chandler,
    Rosanna Fairhead
Editor Helen Miles
Art Director Nicola Bailey
Designer Paul Shinn
Production Manager Michelle Draycott
Production Controller Sadie Butler

A catalog record for this book is available from
the Library of Congress

ISBN-13: 978 1 8589 4319 0
ISBN-10: 1 8589 4319 1

Consultant editor: Tony Lewin
Copy-edited by Kirsty Seymour-Ure
Proof-read by Barbara Roby
Americanized by Chuck Brandstater
Designed by John Grain
Design concept by Kate Ward

Printed and bound in Singapore

Frontispiece: Mercedes-Benz S-Class
Pages 4–5: Porsche Cayman S
Pages 8–9: Ford Edge
Pages 20–21: Toyota Endo
Pages 34–35: Mercedes-Benz S-Class
Pages 296–97: Citroën Pluriel
Pages 310–11: Nissan Urge